WHAT THE SUFFRAGISTS DID NEXT

WHAT THE SUFFRAGISTS DID NEXT

HOW THE FIGHT FOR WOMEN'S RIGHTS WENT ON

MAVIS CURTIS

AMBERLEY

For my family, past, present and future

First published 2017

Amberley Publishing
The Hill, Stroud
Gloucestershire, GL5 4EP

www.amberley-books.com

British Library Cataloguing in Publication Data.
A catalogue record for this book is available from the British Library.

ISBN 978 1 4456 6154 4 (hardback)
ISBN 978 1 4456 6155 1 (ebook)

Typesetting and Origination by Amberley Publishing.
Printed in the UK.

Let us now praise famous women and the mothers who have borne us; for these are our spiritual mothers and all that we have today we have from their hands.

Maude Royden, on the occasion of the granting of the franchise to women in 1918

Contents

Abbreviations

ARP	Air Raid Precautions
ATS	Auxiliary Territorial Service
CMC	Children's Minimum Council
FGM	Female Genital Mutilation
ILP	Independent Labour Party
LCRS	Liverpool Central Relief Society
LMH	Lady Margaret Hall
NFWI	National Federation of Women's Institutes
NUWSS	National Union of Women's Suffrage Societies
ODNB	Oxford Dictionary of National Biography
OFWI	Oxford Federation of Women's Institutes
OWSSWS	Oxford Women Students' Society for Women's Suffrage
PSF	People's Suffrage Federation
SCR	Senior Common Room (the staff room for academic university staff)
SSFA	Soldiers' and Sailors' Families Association
SWH	Scottish Women's Hospital
UDC	Union of Democratic Control
VAD	Voluntary Aid Detachment
WAAF	Women's Auxiliary Air Force
WCG	Women's Co-operative Guild
WRAF	Women's Royal Air Force
WR(E)NS	Women's Royal Naval Service
WVS	Women's Voluntary Services
WILPF	Women's International League for Peace and Freedom

Preface

When I started to write this book I intended it to be about what feminists achieved after they had obtained the vote in 1918, seeing the first time women could vote in a general election as being the beginning of a process of emancipation. The more I read, the more I realised that the battle for women's rights had started a good seventy years before, and that getting the vote was just one event in a continuous fight to redress the balance between men and women in our society.

Much has been written about the suffrage movement but few people differentiate between the suffragettes – Emmeline Pankhurst's Women's Political and Social Union (WPSU) and the suffragists – the National Union of Women's Suffrage Societies (NUWSS). The suffragists had been active since the 1850s and had a substantial network of branches throughout the country. Their constitution provided the foundation for other women's movements that came after them: the Women's Institute and the Townswomen's Guild. The NUWSS under the leadership of Millicent Fawcett had a regular income monitored by a treasurer, and a journal: *The Common Cause*. The suffragettes had no monitoring of money – it came in and went out equally rapidly – though they eventually had a journal, *The Suffragette*. They had no structure, and decisions were made by a small coterie of people, mainly friends of the Pankhursts – mother and daughters. They did, however, have enormous energy and they were impatient with all the lobbying and the discussion. Their motto was 'Deeds, not words', and they lived up to their motto, with escalating violence against property, which provoked the authorities to use violence against them.

On the outbreak of war in 1914, the NUWSS, under the leadership of Millicent Fawcett, decided to support the war effort. The WSPU stopped their violent demonstrations and encouraged men to enlist. Millicent Fawcett's decision to support the war effort split the NUWSS, with some members believing the most important work women could do was to support the international peace movement. This difference of opinion became very bitter, and the two sides were never reconciled.

Whether pacifists or supporters of the war effort, for a while, they put to one side their work for the suffrage and in 1917, when the vote had been given to some women, though by no means all, the WSPU felt their work was done and they dissolved the organisation, so this book is not about them. The suffragists, on the other hand, carried on, because while their immediate goal was the franchise, there were other things they wanted for women, some of which they achieved, some of which they did not.

This book tells the story of eight suffragists whose lives were caught up in the dramatic events they lived through. Their early lives are laid out here so we can see how their childhoods, so different from ours today, affected their outlook on life and led them to the work they did, to right the injustices they saw in society and to make women's lives better. Their achievements formed the bedrock on which the second wave of feminism, from the 1970s onwards, could build.

A note about some of the language: I have used the language that was current at the time, so 'madness', 'lunacy' and 'insanity' are common descriptions of mental ill health. Writing 'The Ellen Terry Home for Blind and Defective Children' made me shudder! Similarly, the assumption of white superiority and imperialist references to 'the coloured races' made me cringe. But it seemed to me to be more true to the spirit of the times, more historically accurate. And indeed it demonstrates in a small way how hard people have worked in the last hundred years to restore people of colour to their rightful place in society (even though there is a long way still to go) and to give the public an understanding of disability.

1

Looking Back

On 23 February 1912, the National Union of Women's Suffrage Societies (NUWSS) – the suffragists – organised a meeting at the Royal Albert Hall. Millicent Fawcett, their revered leader, was in the chair and the main speaker was Lord Lytton. They were expecting trouble so, as people entered the hall, a leaflet was handed out:

> The order of this Meeting can be preserved by
> ABSOLUTE QUIET on the part of the MAIN BODY
> of the AUDIENCE.
> If anyone interrupts, do not turn round.
> TAKE NO NOTICE.

Who were they expecting to make trouble? Not only the usual assortment of people they might have met at an outdoor meeting, intent on having a laugh at the women's expense and honing their heckling skills. They were also expecting trouble from the Women's Social and Political Union, the WSPU, the suffragettes, led by the Pankhurst mother and daughters, who grabbed the headlines then, and still do today. The suffragettes, they thought, might seek to break up the meeting, but the NUWSS tactic for dealing with trouble was successful and the meeting was concluded without interruption.

A month later, when the Oxford branch of the NUWSS advertised a meeting in the town hall on 19 March 1912 the organisers had taken all possible precautions against any disruption. It was an important meeting. On 28 March Parliament would be discussing the Conciliation Bill, which, they thought, would give at least some women the vote.

Parliament had discussed the Bill in February, and there seemed no doubt about the outcome. So the platform was crowded with the great and the good of Oxford, forty-seven people in all.

To be on the safe side, and to make sure nobody was pelted with eggs or rudely interrupted, all the tickets for the meeting had been sold beforehand so entry was tightly controlled. Questions to the speakers had been written and handed in before the meeting. A guard had been put on the banners, which had on previous occasions been purloined by mischievous students, and the town hall stage was decorated with banks of flowers.

The meeting was significant for two reasons: firstly, the timing, and secondly, the speakers on the platform. In the autumn of the previous year, 1911, the Liberal government under Prime Minister Asquith had been preparing the Conciliation Bill to widen the franchise to include more of the male population. Asquith had met with representatives not only of Liberal women supporters, mainly from Millicent Fawcett's NUWSS, but also from the Pankhursts' WSPU, and he appeared to agree to include amendments extending the franchise to women. However, Asquith had then been approached by the Anti-Suffrage League who told him that the inclusion of women's suffrage in the Bill would be a big mistake. At the same time, Mrs Pankhurst and two colleagues had invaded Downing Street, hurling stones at the windows of No. 10 while other women smashed plate-glass windows of shops, post offices and government buildings throughout the capital. As a result, 150 women had been arrested and sent to Holloway Prison. The offices of the WSPU had been raided by the police and Christabel Pankhurst had fled to Paris to maintain the leadership of the movement, safe from arrest.

On 28 March there was a lively debate in Parliament, unheard by any of the women in the suffrage movement, since all women had been excluded from Parliament because of previous public demonstrations. There was no one there to boo Mr Harold Baker, the Liberal Member of Parliament for Accrington, who spoke against the motion. 'I think the breaking of windows has let in a good deal of fresh air on this subject,' he joked. 'It goes to show that those who claim to have more power to persuade women are exactly those who are least fitted to exercise political power.' Viscount Helmsley was of the opinion that the violence practised by the WSPU 'lends a great deal of colour to the argument that the mental equilibrium of the female sex is not as stable as the mental equilibrium of the male sex'.

The women fighting for the suffrage to be extended to them were unlucky that day. Thirteen Labour Party MPs, who would have voted for them, were unavoidably detained in their constituencies because of a coal strike. The Irish contingent of MPs, who had previously shown support for an extended franchise, voted against the Bill because they thought if they voted for the amendment that would influence government attitudes to Irish Home Rule. Votes for women had been pushed to one side, yet again.

The meeting arranged in Oxford on 19 March was meant to demonstrate that in that city at least, there was consensus among right-thinking people – the intelligentsia and the political elite – that the time had come to give women the vote, however the politicians at Westminster might vote. It obviously failed in its purpose. Nevertheless, the three listed speakers demonstrated by their very presence the progress that had been made towards rights for women in the previous hundred years. The main speaker was Viscount Haldane of Cloan MP, the Secretary of State for War, who was followed by Manchester's first woman city councillor, Miss Margaret Ashton, elected to the post four years previously. In the chair was Miss Jane E. Harrison LLD, a woman with a doctorate in law, albeit an honorary one. The movement for women's rights had, therefore, by this time acquired representation in Parliament, the possibility of pursuing academic study, and the ability to take part in the political process at the level of town and city councils and as members of the Poor Law boards and education committees.

The women on the platform and in the body of the hall were, of course, middle-class women. But this stands in sharp contrast to the world of the middle-class woman as experienced by Caroline Norton in the early part of the nineteenth century and described by Florence Nightingale in mid-century Britain. The only respectable career for most middle-class women was marriage. As Jane Austen pointed out in *Pride and Prejudice,* marriage was 'the only honourable provision for well-educated young women of small fortune, and however uncertain of giving happiness, must be their pleasantest preservative from want'. Marriage, however, gave her no rights. Indeed, it took away any she might have had as a single woman, including the right to see her children in the event of divorce or separation.

Access Rights to Children of a Marriage

At the beginning of the century when a woman married, any money or goods she brought with her into the marriage, any money she might earn or goods she might acquire during the marriage, any children she might bear, all belonged to her husband. Because a woman had a husband, who represented her in every aspect of her life, she had no rights in law. This was challenged in 1839 by Caroline Norton, who wanted to see her children, whom her estranged husband had the care of.

Though Caroline had no money, she had influential friends, and a reputation as a writer. She used both to good effect. She wrote pamphlets about her situation and lobbied Parliament and, eventually, obtained limited access to her children. So a happy ending of sorts and a tentative step in the right direction for married women.

The Expansion of the Feminist Movement

When Caroline Norton was working to change the law in the 1830s, though she had the support of friends locally, she appears to have been battling almost entirely on her own in the political field. The 1840s, however, saw huge changes in the social fabric of society. The Industrial Revolution, which saw the growth of industrial cities in the North of England, also created the need for faster communications. With the Penny Post, established in 1840, a letter could be posted in Liverpool and delivered in London the following day, carried on the rail network, now spreading the length and breadth of the country. The Post Office was the internet of its day. This meant, as with social media of today, ideas could spread quickly both between friends and among the huge Victorian families, with their multiplicity of cousins. So from the 1840s onwards, people could easily and quickly establish links to like-minded people.

It is surprising how interconnected many of the early feminists were. Renowned for her work establishing nursing as a profession, and presenting medical data in pie charts, Florence Nightingale, the first woman member of the Royal Statistical Society, was the cousin of Barbara Bodichon, *née* Leigh Hunt, and had contact with Anne Jemima Clough's brother, all of them involved in opening up education for women.

Mrs Bodichon was a member of the Langham Place group, whose aim was to increase work opportunities for women. Their journal, *The English Woman's Journal,* became the focus of a women's employment bureau, but they also addressed other issues such as opening Marylebone baths to women, and supported Augusta Webb when she was dismissed from the South Kensington School of Art for whistling. They formed the Society for Women Artists, where presumably artists could whistle to their heart's content.

Education

The census of 1851 established that there were many more women than men in the country and, therefore, a considerable number of single women needed to be able to support themselves. There were few opportunities for middle-class women to earn a respectable living: being a governess or a seamstress were the respectable careers open to most women.

As anyone who has read *Jane Eyre* would know, being a governess was not an easy job. Not that all employers, or even a few, had mad wives hidden in the attic. A governess's position in the household was precarious; she held a difficult and lonely position somewhere between the domestic staff and her employers. By and large, governesses were badly educated themselves and had little knowledge to impart to their charges, who often despised them. Education, therefore, was seen as a very important factor in improving women's lives.

Barbara Bodichon's friend Emily Davies, a friend of Elizabeth Garrett Anderson and her sister Millicent Fawcett, was intent on opening up higher education for girls and to this end organised exams for girls to be taken at the age of sixteen, called 'Junior Locals' by the Cambridge University Examination Board, so girls could be ranked like boys. She followed this in 1887 with an exam at eighteen called 'Highers' to show what they had learned. This was so useful it was taken up for boys, and when the results were compared it was found that while girls were poor at arithmetic (because they had not been taught it) they compared very favourably with the boys in reading, writing and mastering the facts of history and geography.

The Schools Enquiry Commission, set up by the government in 1864 to inspect educational establishments, had not thought to include girls' schools. Miss Davies suggested they should, which they duly did and found, to no one's surprise, that standards of teaching were appalling.

Miss Davies, Barbara Bodichon and some of their associates then put money into a scheme that would provide university-level education for young women, which eventually became Girton College, two miles distant from the fleshpots of Cambridge, so sufficiently far away to reassure parents of their daughters' safety.

Meanwhile, Anne Jemima Clough, whose brother had been Florence Nightingale's assistant, was living in Liverpool and was a friend of Josephine Butler, wife of the principal of Liverpool College. Together they set up a series of lectures for ladies. They employed lecturers to travel between various towns, each man giving the same lecture. The first man to undertake this exploration into unknown territory in 1867 was James Stuart. He spent his summer vacation that year touring Liverpool, Manchester, Leeds, Sheffield, Rotherham and Crewe, delivering an eight-week course on astronomy. Miss Clough and Mrs Butler were very worried that not enough people would turn up to the lecture. They need not have worried. The lecture rooms were crowded with, in all, 550 students; the circulating libraries had to order new consignments of books and the editions of several scientific works were sold out. Mr Stuart had arranged for a question-and-answer session at the end of his lecture, but this was thought improper. He therefore arranged for questions to be printed and said he would read and correct any answers that came in to him. He expected about thirty. He got 300 and had a hard time correcting and commenting on them all before the next lecture. He certainly earned his £200 fee.

These lectures formed the basis of the University Extension Scheme, which soon began to admit men. The idea was taken up in 1869 by Henry Sidgwick, a Professor of Philosophy at Cambridge, who hired a house as a hostel for female students and asked Miss Clough to run it. This was the start of Newnham College.

One place where many young women met and were educated was Queen's College, set up in London by Frederick Denison Maurice, Professor of English Literature and History at King's College London. He had started a series of evening lectures for governesses entitled, like James Stuart's astronomy course, 'Lectures for Ladies', which were so popular he and his supporters decided to extend the idea down the age range to accommodate girls from the age of thirteen. In 1848 this had become Queen's College, with a royal charter in 1853 from Queen Victoria, who believed in a sound Christian education for girls, though opposed to 'this mad wicked folly of Women's Rights'.

Queen's College became an important meeting ground for like-minded women. Through its portals passed Sophia Jex-Blake, who was to go on to open up medical education for women, as well as Florence Buss and Dorothea Beale. Florence Buss went on to develop her mother's school into the North London Collegiate School, while Dorothea Beale became head of Cheltenham Ladies' College. She founded St Hilda's College in Oxford, originally meant for ex-Cheltenham girls, but as this proved financially unviable, it was opened to anyone with the requisite standard of education, making a third college alongside Lady Margaret Hall and Somerville Hall, for women. Cheltenham Ladies' College became an important school, turning out well-educated young women who went on to become heads of schools throughout the country.

The first time votes for women was discussed in any systematic way was in 1868 when all the women mentioned in the previous paragraphs – Miss Buss, Miss Beale, Miss Clough, Mrs Bodichon, Elizabeth Garrett Anderson, Miss Davies and others – met in what became known as the Kensington Society. It was very short-lived, closing in 1871 when its leader, Charlotte Manning, was appointed Principal of Girton College.

Medicine

There was one important aspect of women's education that was more difficult to crack: medicine. There were fewer women interested in medicine as a discipline, and the training led to a lucrative career, where men felt that competition from women would diminish their own career prospects. There was also the feeling that it was unseemly for women to be seeing and treating men's bodies, a taboo that was not dispelled until the First World War.

In brief, the first two women to have their names added to the medical register in Britain were Elizabeth Blackwell and Elizabeth Garrett, while Sophia Jex-Blake opened up the profession to women. There is no room here to describe the battles that ensued between Edinburgh University and Sophia Jex-Blake, but it is spelled out in graphic detail by Ray Strachey in *The Cause*. Suffice to say that, having failed to persuade Edinburgh to allow women to study medicine, Sophia and her supporters decided to turn to Parliament and to use politicians sympathetic to their cause to bring two Bills before Parliament, the first conferring on universities the power to admit women and the second to allow women's qualifications gained abroad to be recognised. The first Bill was drafted and introduced immediately by Russell Gurney and a group of cross-party members.

Sophia Jex-Blake was an impatient woman. While waiting for something to happen, she decided to start her own school of medicine for women. She had only a few hundred pounds and very few medical men who would support her. Dr Blackwell and Dr Garrett (now married and known as Dr Garrett Anderson) were doubtful if this was the right time, but she went ahead anyway.

In 1875 the Russell Gurney Bill was passed and finally Sophia could see how her school could join the medical establishment. Edinburgh University, having suffered at the hands of Sophia, was reluctant to admit women, but King's in London and Queen's College of Physicians in Ireland saw no problem and agreed to examine and grant medical degrees to women. Sophia herself took her own degree at Berne University in 1877 and in the same year went on to Dublin to be examined there. The Royal Free Hospital agreed to admit students from her medical school, and following the Enabling Act, passed in 1876, London University agreed to admit not only women medical students but women into any course being run by it.

Politics of the Women's Movement

Mary Wollstonecraft was the first to put the eighteenth-century ideas of freedom and equality into a feminist perspective with the *Vindication of the Rights of Women*, published in 1792. Unfortunately her way of life – affairs, and the birth of her first daughter Fanny outside marriage – alienated many people, and her ideas did not receive the following they deserved until many years after her death.

Women were involved in politics, despite not having the vote. The Chartist movement, formed in the 1830s, wanted universal suffrage for men over the age of twenty-one and initially also asked for votes for women, although this was quickly abandoned. The movement also wanted a secret ballot, no property qualification for Members of Parliament, payment for MPs, and constituencies of equal size. It was at its height between 1838 and 1858 but fizzled out without achieving any of its aims, although a further Reform Act in 1867 gave more urban men the vote, secret voting was brought in during 1872, and MPs began to receive payment in 1911. Women had also been active in the Anti-Corn Law League, campaigning for a repeal of the Corn Laws that taxed imported grain between 1815 and 1848, so keeping the price artificially high.

The British and Foreign Anti-Slavery Society was another forum where women could gain political experience, though not directly. They could not, for instance, take part in debates or influence the proceedings of the organisation, but they could, and did, raise money and support the men. In 1839, the society organised a convention in London to which a contingent of Americans was invited, led by their charismatic leader, William Lloyd Garrison. English abolitionists were agog to hear what he had to say but Mr Garrison was delayed and of the seven members who did turn up, four of them were women. The British organisers of the convention were astonished and appalled. The idea that the women should take part in the convention was 'subversive of the principles and traditions of the country, and contrary to the Word of God', said the organisers, and the women could not be admitted. The organisers spent the first day debating this distressing situation, and in the end settled for allowing the women into the body of the hall, albeit behind a curtain. The following day the American women seated themselves in the observers' gallery. Then Mr Garrison arrived. The convention rushed to welcome him, but when asked to speak all he said was, 'I prefer to join the ladies.' He then took himself up into the gallery, refusing to take an active part in the proceedings.

On returning home the American women grouped together and in 1848 organised a Woman's Rights Convention in Seneca Falls, the first in the world, demanding full civic, religious and domestic liberties. The more radical elements of British society were of the same mind, Disraeli among them.

Another man who supported the women's cause was John Stuart Mill. When he was twenty-four he met Harriet Taylor, already married and the mother of three children. The two were intellectually and philosophically very close, and after the death of her husband they married. Everything Mill wrote was discussed with her but it was not until three years after her death that he produced his highly important *The Subjugation of Women* in 1861. In it he argued not just for women's suffrage or equal laws but for the removal of the subjection and submission of women to men, an idea he maintained he had learned from Harriet.

John Stuart Mill was instrumental in organising and teaching the suffragists about the political process. He encouraged them to have Bills drafted and to present petitions to eminent politicians. He, Henry Fawcett and Russell Gurney were the women's links to Parliament, and they presented several Bills putting forward women's right to vote, all to no avail.

While much was happening in London, there was also a great deal going on in the new industrial heartland of Britain, the North, in particular Manchester and Liverpool. A woman called Lydia Becker had heard Barbara Bodichon's paper 'Reasons for the Enfranchisement of Women', which she had presented in 1866 at the National Association for the Advancement of Social Sciences. Miss Becker returned to Manchester and the following year convened the Manchester Women's Suffrage Society. No sooner was the society up and running than a curious anomaly in the voting system occurred. A woman who earned her living and was bringing up her children on the proceeds of a small china shop, Mrs Lily Maxwell, was by a quirk of fate accidentally put on the list of voters in a parliamentary by-election so, accompanied by Miss Becker, she went to the polling station and cast her vote.

This gave Miss Becker the idea to send members of her committee out to canvas house-to-house to collect the names of female householders. There were 5,346 names of women who requested that they should be allowed to vote. Counsel for the women was Dr Richard Pankhurst, future husband of Emmeline Pankhurst, *née* Goulden. Unsurprisingly, the women lost their case.

Women had very little experience of speaking in public, it being thought unbecoming for a woman to speak for herself, but they felt they must raise public awareness of the injustice of women's situation and that it must be done by women themselves. In July 1869, a meeting was arranged in London, at the Architectural Society, at which women would be speakers. There were also several men who supported the cause, among them John Stuart

Mill; Charles Kingsley, the author of *The Water-Babies*; and Professor Henry Fawcett, who married Millicent Garrett.

The idea of women standing up in public and expressing their own opinions was so revolutionary and shocking that the matter was raised in the House of Commons, where one member mentioned that 'two ladies, wives of Members of the House, recently disgraced themselves by speaking in public'.

Lydia Becker raised awareness of women's suffrage in the North by organising speaking tours across the north of England. It was, however, hard work because of the mockery and verbal abuse that was meted out to them. Miss Becker lobbied for and obtained the right for women to vote in municipal elections and, in 1870, campaigned for and managed to establish the right for women to sit on school boards. She herself was on the Manchester school board until her death in 1890. She also lobbied for and obtained the vote for women to the House of Keys, the Isle of Man's Parliament, so making the Isle of Man the first place in the British Empire to allow women the vote. She and a friend, Jessie Boucherett, founded the *Women's Suffrage Journal*, which functioned for twenty years, closing on the death of Miss Becker. It was in 1874 on one of the speaking tours organised by Miss Becker that the fifteen-year-old Emmeline Goulden (after her marriage, Mrs Pankhurst) first had an opportunity to speak.

In the 1890s the 'mill girls' of the northern textile towns became involved in the drive for women's suffrage. Because they had an income independent of their menfolk, they had never been encumbered by the trappings of middle-class Victorian society and they could easily find employment in the mills because they were cheaper to employ than men. The last quarter of the nineteenth century saw an increase in the number of trade unions, of which women in the industrialised north were prominent members. As the end of the century approached, the trade unions were considering introducing a political levy, with a view to supporting the Independent Labour Party (ILP), newly formed in 1893. But what use to women was a political levy if they did not have a vote? They became seriously interested in the question of votes for women. A petition containing the names of 67,000 textile workers was sent to Parliament. Their aim was not only to encourage factory workers to take an interest but to encourage the new Labour Party to adopt the idea. But, like the Chartists before them, the Labour Party thought votes for women would damage their political agenda and they dragged their feet on the issue.

At this point Mrs Pankhurst, who had been an enthusiastic adherent of the Labour Party, decided they were too pusillanimous and formed her own Women's Social and Political Union (WSPU). She found the democratic processes of the established political parties too slow, too indecisive. Private bills drafted by supporters of the movement and taken to Parliament by men sympathetic to the cause were regularly talked out by members of Parliament such as Henry Labouchere, violently anti-suffrage, homophobic (he drafted the Bill which criminalised any sexual activity between men) and an anti-Semite.

The WSPU was based in Manchester and, having neither money nor contacts, was unable to work in the same way as the NUWSS. But on the eve of the 1903 election, when Viscount Grey, a Liberal, came to Manchester to speak, they seized their chance. Annie Kenny and Christabel Pankhurst went to hear him speak and during the question time that followed the set speech, they asked whether Viscount Grey would be prepared to support votes for women. He ignored the question so Annie jumped on a chair and asked again, unfurling the banner 'Votes for Women'. Both young women were hustled out of the room and pushed down the stairs into the street. They held a protest meeting on the spot and were promptly arrested for causing an obstruction. That was the beginning of the campaign of civil disobedience by the suffragettes, which ceased only with the onset of the First World War.

The suffragists of the NUWSS distanced themselves from the WSPU because they thought violence was counterproductive. They could not, however, ignore them. The WSPU began its violent demonstrations in 1906, which drove the NUWSS into more public action. In 1907 the first of the big demonstrations organised by the NUWSS took place in London. It became known as the Mud March because of the rain that poured all day. Organised by Philippa Strachey on behalf of the NUWSS, and led by Millicent Fawcett, the procession left Hyde Park with banners flying and proceeded to Exeter Hall. It was the first demonstration of its kind and in spite of the weather was a great success, with its mix of academics, middle-class women and textile workers. It demonstrated to the crowds who turned out to watch that most women who asked for the vote were not freaks of nature, nor were they violent. They were ordinary women from across the social spectrum who had an extraordinary sense of purpose.

By 1913, matters seemed to be coming to a head. The WSPU had escalated their use of violence and were now setting fire to empty buildings and pouring bleach on golf courses. When arrested, they were going on hunger strike so they had to be released. In exasperation, the government enacted what became known as the Cat and Mouse Act, which meant that the likes of Emmeline Pankhurst, when released from prison after a hunger strike that threatened her health, could then be rearrested when her health had improved. The summer of that year saw the death of protester Emily Wilding Davison under the hooves of the king's horse at the Derby, and the NUWSS organised a huge pilgrimage starting from eight different points of the country and gathering in London on 26 July. It was a triumph of organisation and spectacle as the thousands of women paraded through the streets of London carrying their banners.

Public opinion was beginning to shift in favour of women's suffrage, affected by the public speaking and the peaceful demonstrations of the suffragists and by the cruel treatment of the suffragettes, the force feeding and the physical violence meted out to them by the police. The Cat and Mouse Act made martyrs out of the suffragettes, who were admired for their courage while being severely criticised for their violence against property.

The declaration of war by Germany in August 1914 changed everything. The Pankhursts did a complete *volte face* and supported the government, even going so far as to encourage young men to join the armed forces. Millicent Fawcett supported the war effort and felt the movement should use its networks and structure, which by this time were countrywide, to provide aid to the government. There were others who felt that war was against everything the Women's Movement stood for, and wanted to pursue the path of peace by negotiation with the enemy. In 1915, the matter came to a head but was not resolved. Long-established workers for the NUWSS, women such as Maude Royden, resigned from the NUWSS, along with half the executive committee.

By 1916 the country had begun to think ahead to the reconstruction that would be needed when the war ended. The NUWSS had, by this time, managed to reconstruct itself after the resignation of so many of its leading members and it resumed its activities, encouraging societies all over the country to send deputations to their MPs, and NUWSS officers interviewed Cabinet ministers. Opinion within the country was overwhelmingly supportive of the right for women to have the vote. An all-party conference was set up to look at the whole question of the franchise but, being within Parliament, it contained no women! Its proceedings were behind closed doors and no outside evidence was admitted. However, following the fall of the Asquith government and the access to power of Lloyd George in January 1917, the committee duly made its conclusions known. They recommended that some form of women's suffrage should be conferred, that householders and wives of householders should be given the vote, and that the age at which women could vote should be thirty or thirty-five.

On the whole the suffragists, though disappointed, thought it was a reasonable starting point. They would have a foot in the door. The age limit was ridiculous but was intended to deal with the anxiety often expressed that there were many more women in the country than men, which could give women more say in the running of the country than men. The NUWSS endorsed the findings of the committee but said they could only support the measure if the lower age limit was agreed to. They also wanted reassurance that votes for women would be included in the Bill from the start, and not added on as an amendment, as had happened in 1912. Given their disappointments in the past, the NUWSS felt the need to show the support they had in the country and organised a demonstration of women war workers. Representative women from seventy different trades – lamplighters, policewomen, engine-cleaners, postwomen, actresses, nurses, lace-makers, headmistresses – were all there.

When the time came for the debate on the Representation of the People Bill, women crowded the ladies' gallery from where they could see only the tops of the heads of the men debating their future. The debate went their way, and at the second reading 385 men voted for the Bill while only 55 voted against it. Between then and the final reading, the suffragists obtained a further concession from the government. They asked that the franchise for local government elections, which allowed only householders or unmarried or widowed women with property to vote, be extended to match the conditions for the national franchise. A final hurdle still existed – the House of Lords. The Bill went before the Lords in January 1917 and 134 peers voted for it, with only 71 against and

31 abstentions. The Bill received the royal assent on 6 February, and after fifty years of campaigning and disappointments, votes for some women had been achieved. Having achieved something of what they wanted, the Women's Political and Social Union was wound up and suffragettes took no further part in the politics of the day.

The following year, much to the surprise of the suffragists, without any fuss, a law was passed to allow women aged twenty-one and over to stand for election as Members of Parliament. Sixteen women came forward, including Christabel Pankhurst. They were all defeated except for Countess Markovicz who, in spite of her name, was Irish. She chose to take her seat in the Irish Dáil and refused to take the oath at Westminster.

Having gained what they had worked so hard for, there then arose a heated discussion within the NUWSS on how they should proceed. Some drifted away from the movement but others reformed into another organisation that would continue to fight for equal rights for women, the National Union of Societies for Equal Citizenship (NUSEC). Millicent Fawcett resigned and her place was taken by Eleanor Rathbone.

2

Margaret Llewelyn Davies (1861–1944) and the Women's Co-operative Guild

Margaret Llewelyn Davies bridges the gap between the suffragists who had worked since the mid-1870s for the vote and the younger generation who carried on the struggle for female emancipation. Three years older than suffragist leader Millicent Fawcett, Margaret was fifty-three years old in 1918 when women over thirty got the vote. Much of her working life was, therefore, behind her but she is included here because her influence carried on long past her own death.

By 1918, she had paraded before Parliament with placards and was an active member of the NUWSS. Her great achievement was that she facilitated and moulded the opinions of working-class women through the Women's Co-operative Guild and gave them a voice that they used to press, among other things, for universal suffrage. She and her colleagues in the Guild recognised that one of their first tasks must be to establish the legitimacy of women's voices in the discussion about women's place in society.

Margaret wrote no autobiography and no biography of her exists. She is an elusive character whose name crops up as chairing this meeting, attending that, without any coherent assembly of the facts. This was not because of a lack of confidence on her part. She was supremely confident and a persuasive speaker, and writer, but she saw no need to write about herself and no one else thought to do it for her.

Leonard Woolf, husband of the famous Virginia, knew Margaret's brothers at Cambridge, though they were much older than he, and has this to say about the family:

> (The brothers) belonged to a remarkable family. Their father had four sons and one daughter, all of them extremely intelligent, finely built, beautiful – they all had great personal charm, immense energy. Though they were almost fanatical in their integrity and high principles, they were, unlike so many exceptionally serious and good people, amusing and interesting, companionable and lovable. They were friends of the Stephen family (Virginia Woolf's family) and Virginia often saw Margaret Llewelyn Davies, the daughter. She was secretary of the Women's Co-operative Guild. To the vast majority of my readers the last sentence will convey little or nothing and it would have conveyed even less in 1912. Yet Margaret was one of the most eminent women I have known and created something of great value – and at the time unique – in the Guild.

He goes on to say that her name does not appear in *Who's Who*, 'which is the kind of fact that made – and makes – feminism the belief or policy of all sensible men'. He would be pleased to know that her name *does* appear in the Oxford Dictionary of National Biography (ODNB) though it contradicts his score of family members. There were seven children of the Reverend Davies, a Christian Socialist, one of a band of churchmen who concerned themselves not only with the spiritual life of their flock but also with their physical wellbeing and the state of the society they were living in.

Margaret was the youngest child, having six, not four, older brothers. She was born in Marylebone, where her father was vicar, and lived there till 1899 when her father moved from this poor city parish to the rural delights of Kirby Lonsdale, situated in the Lune valley in East Lancashire. Margaret and her friend and coworker Lilian Harris, daughter of a Bradford banker, ran the office of the Women's Co-operative Guild (WCG).

What the ODNB also tells us is that Margaret was the niece of the redoubtable Emily Davies, tireless worker for women's higher education and co-founder of Girton College. It goes without saying that Margaret was educated at Girton, and before that Queen's College.

She became secretary of the WCG in 1889. It had by then been in existence six years. It had been started very modestly indeed by the 'Women's Corner' in the *Co-operative News*, which itself was the organ that brought together the early Co-operative Movement's various branches. The 'Corner' was the brainchild of Mrs Alice Acland, whose husband was an Oxford academic. Mr Acland lectured on the Oxford University Extension scheme, bringing knowledge and learning to the culture-starved working men of the north of England.

The Aclands were staunch supporters of the Co-operative Movement and were familiar with the work of the Rochdale Pioneers, the first co-operative movement in England. The Rochdale co-operative movement was only one of several co-operative schemes, many of which failed, but Rochdale survived because of their seven principles, which became the template for future co-operatives. Their principles were:

Open and voluntary membership
Democratic member control
Members would set policies and make decisions
Members must buy into the organisation, in however small a way
Each area would be autonomous and independent
Each co-operative must provide education and training to members and the public
Co-operatives should co-operate with other co-ops.
They should show concern for their communities.

The co-operative societies aimed to give their members wholesome, unadulterated food at a reasonable price. None of them were available to the poorest of the poor, because they all required some form of subscription and some people were not keen to have bread unadulterated with chalk, since it was less white, more expensive and your hunger pangs were not kept at bay for as long.

Looking for ways to involve the women in the Co-operative Movement, Mrs Acland thought it would be a good idea, if Samuel Bamford, the editor, agreed to assemble a series of topics that might interest the wives of co-operative members. Following that modest beginning in February 1883, she suggested that women might like to collect together with their sewing or knitting to listen to someone reading some co-operative tract, which they could then discuss.

The movement was slow to get off the ground, but by May 1883 at the Co-operative Congress, held that year in Edinburgh, some fifty women, wives of the men who were attending the congress, met to discuss the way forward. By the end of their meeting, they had appointed Mrs Acland as the President of the Women's League for the Spread of Co-operation, which in 1884 was renamed the Women's Co-operative Guild. They also agreed a subscription of 6*d* a year, appointed local secretaries in areas where there were already the beginnings of a movement, and established an outline organisational structure. Their aims were:

> To spread a knowledge of the advantages of co-operation
> To stimulate among those who knew its advantages a greater interest in the principles of co-operation
> To keep alive in themselves, their neighbours and especially in the rising generation, a more earnest appreciation of the value of co-operation to themselves, their children and the nation;
> To improve the conditions of women all over the country.

The women at the conference went home with the aim of setting up branches in their home towns. Hebden Bridge was the first to set up a branch that by 1884, had sixty members. There was one more branch in the north of England. As one might expect it was Rochdale. There were three in London – Woolwich, Norwood and Chelsea – with one, Coventry, situated in the Midlands.

The last quarter of the nineteenth century saw a huge increase in the number of co-operatives and also the diversification of activities. The Co-operative Wholesale Society (CWS) was formed in 1863 and the movement spread from retailing to banking and insurance. The spread of co-operatives went hand-in-hand with the spread of the Women's Co-operative Guild, helped by donations from the Co-operative Union, which in 1886 provided a grant of £10 to cover expenses. This had risen to £200 by the end of the century.

Margaret Llewelyn Davies joined her local branch of the WCG, the Marylebone branch, in 1883 and progressed swiftly through the ranks until, by 1889, she was appointed General Secretary of the Guild. She had realised the potential of the organisation to bring about social change. Under her guidance, in the thirty-two years she was General Secretary, the Guild emphasised their fourth aim: 'to improve the conditions of women all over the country'.

The Guild adopted her unique blend of socialism and feminism, which stayed with the organisation and its individual members until the end of the twentieth century. She lays out her beliefs in the concluding pages of *Life As We Have Known It*, subtitled *The Voices of Working-Class Women*, a collection of short autobiographies in letter form from six Guild members. Published by the Hogarth Press, the Woolfs' very own publishing firm, the introductory letter by Virginia Woolf must have ensured good sales.

Margaret Llewelyn Davies writes:

People are apt to think of Co-operation as a thrift movement ... How little is it realised by economists and others that Co-operation is the beginning of a great revolution! The Movement shows in practice that there is nothing visionary or impossible in the aspirations of those who desire to see the Community in control, instead of the Capitalists. Under the Co-operative system, no individuals can make fortunes ... No profits are made; the surplus, inseparable from trading, is shared among the purchasers, according to the amount each spends. Capital becomes the tool of labour, and not its master.

She goes on to explain the structure of the Co-operative Movement and that of the Guild then turns her attention to the educational aspects of the Guild:

It is usual to regard education as quite apart from practice. But the characteristic of the Guild education is that it is bound up with appropriate action... The study of Co-operation leads Guild women not only to buy consistently at the Store, but also to press forward enlightened policies affecting the whole Movement.'

She describes the progress that has been made in involving women not just in the Guild but in the management and educational committees of their various co-operative societies and expresses satisfaction that 'Guildswomen, starting from buying bread and butter on revolutionary principles, have reached an international outlook' through their involvement with the International Co-operative Women's Guild, which by 1931 when this article was written, had been in existence for ten years.

Leonard Woolf attributes the vitality and inspiration of the Guild mainly to Margaret. What had driven her to action was the realisation of the grimness of life for most working-class women and also, as Woolf puts it, their strength and great potential not merely as human beings but as political animals. She was a born leader with immense energy and enthusiasm. She had a deep contralto voice, a spontaneous laugh and a beautiful face, even, as Woolf puts it, when she 'had grown fat and almost an old woman'. But as well as all these attributes, she had what he describes as 'a kind of virginal purity of mind and motive' that enabled her to reach out to these working women and inspire them with the same enthusiasm to fight against ignorance, poverty and injustice. In spite of being a rich woman – she left more than £23,000 in her will – she never patronised the many women with whom she came into contact and, as a consequence, they loved her dearly and thought of her as their friend.

When she took over as General Secretary, she seized the Guild by the scruff of its neck and gave it a sense of purpose. One of the first things she did was to write and send out a 'Winter Circular', in which she urged members not to allow the meetings to develop into a 'mothers' meeting' where the discussion focused on sewing and baking. They should remember that their aim was to spread the idea of co-operation, which they could do by educating themselves and others. She urged them to draw up a definite programme for meetings and to organise lectures. At the first annual meeting after she assumed leadership of the organisation, she even invited men.

In 1892 she issued a clarion call to Guild members. 'Members have not yet half realised all they may get and give by means of the Guild,' she wrote.

> Self-governed, free from outside patronage, with money at its back, it ought to become a very powerful instrument for bringing all kinds of help to women in their different capacities... There is a good deal yet in the lives of women that is not exactly rose-coloured and changes are not likely to occur without determined action on the part of women themselves.

By then she had got to grips with the structure of the Guild and had realised that it had a role to play in regulating the working conditions of co-operative employees. In the annual report of that year, she defined the duty of the Guild as:

> To secure satisfactory conditions for employees
> To see that trades union regulations were carried out as regards wages and hours
> Propaganda for the Co-operative movement needed to be organised.
> Members should be trained in the business side of store life with a view to taking a more direct share in the management of societies,
> Municipal questions needed to be studied.
> Sick benefit clubs should be provided for members.
> Institutions for young people should be promoted.

It is difficult to separate what the Guild lobbied for and Margaret Llewelyn Davies' ideas of what was important. She and the Guild during her General Secretaryship were as one. She seems to have acted as a conduit between well-meaning middle-class women who wanted to improve the lives of the poor, and working-class women who were suffering under the sometimes appalling conditions of the time.

G. D. H. Cole, a historian of the Co-operative Movement, considered that 'from the moment she assumed control of the Women's Co-operative Guild it began to become a really powerful progressive force'. She regularly topped the poll in votes cast for membership of the central committee, quite a way ahead of others on the ballot paper. Not only did she write pamphlets setting out the problems and send them out for discussion by the members, she was a frequent visitor to local branches and her presence was welcomed wherever she went. One member said Miss Llewelyn Davies was very good at explaining things in a straightforward and down-to-earth way. It was this skill which enabled the Guild, made up of many women who had little or no education, to discuss complex issues in a meaningful way.

The conclusions the branches came to were conveyed to the organisation as a whole through the annual meeting where each delegate was given a five-minute slot to speak. The agenda was, however, carefully controlled and directed by the Central Committee. Their campaigns were ahead of their time, and still resonate today.

A Living Wage

They wanted a minimum wage – a 'living wage' for employees of the Co-op. In 1908 the Co-operative Congress drew up a scale of wages for women co-operative workers. It was implemented four years later.

Since 1902, in the country as a whole, there had been demands for an old-age pension for those too old to work and threatened by the workhouse, and by 1908 Lloyd George's government had set up a scheme providing an old-age pension for the over-seventies, though the pension would be dependent on income. The Guild vigorously supported the idea of an old-age pension and suggested it should be provided from the age of sixty-five, not seventy, and that the means test should be abandoned, providing the pension for everyone.

Lloyd George proposed to increase taxes by large amounts to pay for this measure, which was opposed, naturally enough, by the House of Lords that at this time had a veto on Acts passed by the House of Commons. This tussle led to delays in implementing the law and was followed in 1909 by a law restricting the powers of the House of Lords so the Lords' role was more advisory than previously.

Divorce

The Guild also supported the idea of a change in the divorce law, bringing the law for women into line with that for men. Under divorce law in Victorian England a man could divorce his wife for adultery, but she could not divorce him on these grounds. All that was available to her, if he were violent or unfaithful, was separation. There was at this time only one divorce per 450 marriages, not surprising considering the expense and the social opprobrium it entailed. The Guild was by no means the only body lobbying for a change in the law, and in 1909 a royal commission was set up to consider the matter, to which Margaret Llewelyn Davies gave evidence. She came well prepared. She had asked for views from the branches by sending out a questionnaire. When the matter came up for discussion at the annual congress, delegates did not want to discuss the matter. They wanted to vote. Only five voted against. Armed with the information from the questionnaires – and 131 letters from members, recounting their experiences of violence, marital rape, forced miscarriage and abortion – she could present a very persuasive case for easier and cheaper divorce. 'We want to get rid of the idea that a man owns his wife just as he does a piece of furniture,' said one letter.

Margaret argued the value system that stigmatised divorce took the subordination of women for granted.

> If divorce is considered a sin, and the patient endurance of degradation and compulsory suffering a virtue, a most serious moral confusion is created. It means that women's self-respect and happiness are sacrificed, and adultery on the part of the man is condoned.
>
> We housewives were well aware that some women were bullied by their husbands. How could it be otherwise when the balance of power in a marriage was so heavily weighted against them?

The work Margaret Llewelyn Davies and the Guild were doing to liberalise the divorce laws alienated Roman Catholic members of the Co-operative Movement to such an extent that the Guild was threatened with withdrawal of its grant from the wider Co-operative Movement. Miss Llewelyn Davies steadfastly refused to change her, or the Guild's, position and from then on the Guild was financially independent of the Co-op. This was helped by the fact that neither she nor Lilian Harris were paid for their administrative work but the income of the Guild decreased substantially for a time, so limiting its expansion.

The 1914–18 war changed attitudes in society to catch up with those of the Guild, and in 1923 the Matrimonial Causes Act evened up the law, giving women the right to divorce their husbands on the grounds of adultery. Society had to wait until 1937, however, for the grounds for divorce to be broadened. It was through the unlikely agency of A. P. Herbert, novelist, humourist, lawyer and Member of Parliament, who drafted a private member's bill to widen divorce to include desertion and incurable mental illness. From then on, Mr Rochester's mad wife in the attic was no longer a plot device available to would-be novelists.

Jury Service
The Guild wanted jury service to be available to women because of a woman's greater understanding of women who came to court. They had to wait until 1921 for this to be put into practice.

Universal Suffrage

Forward-thinking as the Guild was, thanks to the general secretary, while they could affect what went on in the Co-operative Movement by using their buying power within the stores to control wages and prices of goods, as Leonard Woolf pointed out, they were not well known in society as a whole, or at least among the decision-making elites that ran the country. What the Guild needed was political clout, which some members felt they might get if they had the vote – so it was natural that they should turn their attention to the suffrage movement.

These women were not prepared to throw rocks through windows, as the suffragettes did. They were respectable wives and mothers who knew the value of money, who were practical, careful, determined and, above all, patient. Some Guild members were apprehensive and distrustful of the drive for women's suffrage, which they saw as an intrusion into men's territory. The way for many Guild women into politics was through involvement in local committees such as the Poor Law, school boards and parish vestries. These rights were being steadily eroded, however. In 1899 the London Government Act abolished parish vestries and instituted Borough Councils, from which women were barred. Similarly, the 1902 Education Act replaced school boards, where women could be represented, by local authority boards to which women could not be elected, only co-opted. This drove women, even those who had had misgivings about women's suffrage, to reconsider the matter. Sarah Reddish, a trade unionist and Guild activist who had worked in a cotton mill from the age of eleven, put forward a resolution at the Guild Congress of 1904 that enfranchisement for women should be on the same terms as men.

The Guild's first task in relation to women's suffrage was to tackle opposition in the ranks of the male members of the Co-operative Society. In 1906 the Co-operative Congress refused to accept a motion concerning women's suffrage on the grounds that it was 'political'. Guild members then spent the next two years leafleting the various Co-operative Societies and conducting a postal vote of husbands of Guild members. This showed an overwhelming support for women's suffrage and at the 1908 Co-operative Congress, the resolution calling for a government bill to enfranchise women was passed, with only one dissenting voice.

The Guild members also wanted to form links with the suffrage movement, so established a separate suffrage fund and started to collaborate in joint actions with them. In 1906 they lobbied alongside the North of England Weavers' Association, the Women's Liberal Federation and the ILP, demanding universal suffrage, with the vote being allotted on a personal basis rather than on the basis of owning property. This put them at odds with the NUWSS, so in 1910 Margaret Llewelyn Davies was instrumental in setting up the People's Suffrage Federation (PSF), through which the Guild's energies were channelled. It united the socialist and the feminist causes, its slogan being: 'One man, one vote; one woman, one vote.' It pressed for suffrage for every adult on a short residential qualification. The PSF said, 'The present franchise law favours property and penalises labour.' They intended to change that.

By 1911, sixty-eight branches had affiliated and they were joined by many of the women's trade unions, leading socialist women such as Margaret Bondfield, the trade union activist Mary Macarthur and left-leaning academics such as Bertrand Russell and Sidney and Beatrice Webb. When the NUWSS drew much nearer to the Labour Party in 1912, this enabled the Guild to join the mainstream of suffrage agitation.

A Co-operative Settlement

One project dear to the heart of Margaret Llewelyn Davies was the possibility of bringing the benefits of the co-operative system to those who were too poor to participate. She knew about the work of the first University Settlement, Toynbee Hall, in the East End, which linked the men graduates of Oxford with the poor. She would have been familiar with the Blackfriars Settlement, which was supported by the women's colleges of Cambridge and Oxford and Westfield College, London. The settlement movement aimed to provide a place where future leaders could live to experience at first hand the lives of the poor and seek practical solutions to some of the many problems that confronted them. They could then, it was hoped, carry these ideas forward when they became leaders of the country.

Margaret Llewelyn Davies thought it would be a splendid idea if the Co-operative Movement could develop a similar scheme, where the very poor, who had so far been excluded from the movement, could be taught about the value of the co-op and what it had to offer. A leaflet entitled 'Co-operation in Poor Neighbourhoods' was circulated so members could explore the idea. To her disappointment, the idea received only a lukewarm reception, except for the Sunderland Co-op, which was rather more enthusiastic. It is easy to imagine the stolid, hard-working, well-organised members of the Guild questioning the need to spend more money on the poor, who could not manage their own money adequately.

Sunderland, however, was different. Miss Llewelyn Davies was personally involved in setting up this shop in a poor area of the town. The aim was to sell small amounts of wholesome food, and savings for its customers would come by way of lower prices rather than high dividends. It also intended to have a loans department, which would fund customers' purchases when a family fell on hard times. This, they hoped, would eliminate the need for loan sharks and the pawn shop. A clubroom would be provided where people could learn about the Co-operative Movement and could be a centre for various social gatherings. This, they thought, might wean people away from public houses where many of them wasted what little money they had.

The store was opened in 1902 with a grocery and cooked food department, while upstairs there was a hall that could accommodate 500, a kitchen and scullery and two bedrooms for community workers.

Miss Llewelyn Davies organised the first three months of community work and took an active part in the running of the place. By early 1903, there were six meetings a week with a total attendance of 300 to 400. Miss Llewelyn Davies sat behind the counter taking deposits and enrolling members. She sold cake on Christmas Eve, held meetings, helped with clubs and concerts and visited people in their own homes to tell them the good news about the co-op. However, precipitated by the resignation of the resident worker because of ill health, by 1904 the directors of the Sunderland Society suggested that the settlement part of the shop should no longer be funded and only the store should remain open.

Health and Welfare Issues for Families

As part of its drive to improve the health of mothers and children, the Guild conducted a campaign to encourage local authorities to provide school clinics. Margaret McMillan, the pioneer of nursery education in Bradford, was one of the speakers involved in the Guild's campaign. But it is fair to say that one of the most important aspects of the Guild's work was its campaign for improved care for women in the pre- and post-natal periods of their lives. It culminated with the publication in 1915 of their experiences in a book edited by Margaret Llewelyn Davies with a preface by the Rt Hon. Herbert Samuel MP, Home Secretary at the time.

While many organisations were pressing for an improvement in the care of expectant mothers and their babies, the great value of the Guild's evidence was that it came from first-hand experience. Seebohm Rowntree had been the first to examine the effects of poverty on the poor of his native city, York, and his work, published in 1901, had provided a template for others who came after him, Eleanor Rathbone and the Guild included. In 1902 the Guild conducted a survey that demonstrated the health problems of poor working-class mothers and their children.

Rowntree's advice to the Liberal government of the time resulted in the 1911 Insurance Act, which introduced schemes of health and unemployment insurance. When the Bill was still in its formative stages, the Guild submitted a scheme of maternity benefit, fully costed by an actuary, to the Chancellor of the Exchequer. They also had the results of a survey conducted among Guildswomen about health care. A deputation was summoned to the Treasury to discuss the matter, and when the Bill was published it included several of the Guild's proposals. Their main aim was to ensure the suggested maternity benefit should be paid to the mother and that the scope of the health insurance proposals should be widened to include dependents. They also wanted an increase in medical care for women and children. After all, Miss Llewelyn Davies pointed out, 'by her work as mother and housewife, the woman contributes equally with the man in the upkeep of the home and the family income in reality is as much hers as his'.

Initially Miss Llewelyn Davies carried on a vigorous debate with Lloyd George, the Prime Minister, via the letter pages of *The Times*. The Guild's request for the maternity benefit to be paid to the mother was rejected, so having lost the first round in the battle the Guild focused on the amendment stage of the Bill. In 1912 the Central Committee set up a small group to keep an eye on what was happening in politics. There were only four members of this committee, one of whom was Margaret Llewelyn Davies and another Margaret Bondfield, who later went on to become a Labour MP and Cabinet member. They arranged for the Guild to lobby MPs, they wrote to the press and various public officials. Although the clause that would have made the maternity grant payable to the mother passed the committee stage, it was rejected by the House of Commons as a whole. So the Guild organised a petition appealing to MPs to support their plea. The government response was to submit an amendment making it possible for the husband's signature to be accepted only if authorised by the wife and allowed a free vote on the issue. This was passed by a majority of twenty-one.

Miss Llewelyn Davies embarked on a series of lecture tours in which she pointed out that infant mortality was higher in poor, working-class areas than in other parts of the community and that the reason was a combination of low incomes so the mother did not get enough to eat during pregnancy and ignorance of pre- and post-natal hygiene. She thought the solution to this would be for there to be maternity units within easy reach of working-class women and that there should be more maternity hospitals, since in some areas the only available hospital care was in the workhouse.

In 1914 a deputation from the Guild discussed the matter with Herbert Samuel, the Home Secretary. The Guild suggested a maternity grant should be £5, though the government were only offering £1 10s. This provoked some acerbic responses in the pages of the *Co-operative News*. As Mrs Haworth of Accrington said, 'If the state can provide for Dreadnoughts and pensions for those who serve in the army then why not raise the ideals of motherhood and take care of mothers?' A government circular was sent out to public health authorities offering a 50 per cent government grant for any project developed by them and stipulating that representatives on the managing boards should be representatives from working women's organisations.

The following year, in spite of the exigencies of war, *Maternity*, a collection of letters from 160 Guild members recording their experiences of pregnancy, childbirth and post-natal life, was published. The 160 letters were chosen from many more of the same ilk. They make sad reading. They tell of poverty, ignorance, illness and, above all, acceptance of all this as their lot as women. These letters are not from the very poor. They are from

Guildswomen, survivors of these conditions, those who by the time they wrote these letters had the organisational skills, the ability to express themselves and the confidence to do so. The book contains not only the letters but also the method of enquiry, a list of the husbands' work, an analysis of the number of stillbirths and miscarriages suffered by the correspondents, a local government board memorandum about maternity and child welfare, a summary of the Notification of Births Act of 1915, an outline of the administrative powers of local authorities and finally a national scheme proposed by the Women's Co-operative Guild.

The method of enquiry consisted of a short questionnaire of five questions with a covering letter, which went to women who were or had been officials of the Guild. The letter asked these people to stress what they 'have felt about the difficulty of taking care, the ignorance that has prevailed on the condition of pregnancy, and how these conditions result in lack of health and energy, meaning that a woman cannot do justice to herself or give her best to her husband and children'.

The questions were:

How many children have you had?
How soon after each other were they born?
Did any die under five years old, and if so, at what ages and from what causes?
Were any still born, and if so how many?
Have you had any miscarriages, and if so how many?

There were 386 replies covering 400 cases. A second letter was sent, asking for particulars of wages and the occupation of the husband.

Analysis of the data showed that of 348 mothers, 148 (42 per cent) had stillbirths or miscarriages, one woman had had 10 miscarriages and one poor soul had suffered five stillbirths. The total number of live births was 1,396 and the total number of deaths of babies less than one year old was 122 (more than 11 per cent).

The letters, written with outstanding honesty and in straightforward language, recount their lives as young women and the consequences of their many pregnancies. At a time when speaking of such things as menstruation, incontinence, men's sexual appetites, abortions and mental ill health was unheard of, they tell it how it was for them. The use of abortifacients, called 'drugs', is admitted, though while contraception is admitted, and thought of in the same terms as abortion, there are no details of methods given.

The accounts highlight the difficulties the women faced when their husbands were ill or out of work. Thirty shillings a week was reckoned to be a good wage for a labourer, but it was barely adequate to raise a family and, in any case, in heavy industry accidents were rife, so the family income could suddenly plummet. One of the family expenses was contributing to a Friendly Society, which would pay money, albeit a small amount, in cases of illness or accident. The men's occupations varied from skilled crafts such as watchmaking and scientific instrument making to unskilled roles such as agricultural labourer or navvy. There was a smattering of white-collar workers such as civil servant, or telegraph clerk on the railway.

Women's health was a subject in which the knowledge of the medical profession was rudimentary. The cost of a consultation was also something that had to be taken into account: two shillings and sixpence is quoted in one letter as the price of a consultation. As the family income in one particular case was between fifteen shillings and thirty-two shillings, this was, at best, a twelfth of the weekly income and at worst a sixth. A family could be in debt for years paying off the medical bills incurred at times of illness.

It is obvious from reading these accounts, even to a medically untrained eye such as mine, that most of these women suffered from anaemia. In letter 73 the writer says, 'During the early stages of pregnancy, with first baby, I was very much subject to a fainting condition, which I was informed was a perfectly natural condition during such a period, and could not be avoided.'

In letter 74 the woman was told by her doctor that her miscarriage was caused by heavy washdays, so concludes that expectant mothers should not be doing heavy physical work such as this, at least in the first three months of pregnancy.

Letter 20 is a vivid description of the sheer exhaustion many mothers feel even today, but then compounded by lack of money, lack of help with caring for the many children who followed one after another every fifteen or sixteen months. Lack of sleep was no doubt made worse by anaemia. Doctor's bills are another source of anxiety.

The writer of letter 20 has a fine turn of phrase and a vivid way of expressing herself. 'I was married at twenty-eight in utter ignorance of the things that most vitally affect a wife and mother.

My mother ... thought ignorance was innocence and the only thing I remember her saying on the subject of childbirth was, "God never sends a babe without bread to feed it." Dame Experience long ago knocked the bottom out of that argument for me.'

After her third child was born, she goes on to say that after suffering from dreadful eczema, which prevented her from going out to work, their income suffered. 'Many a time I have sat in daddy's big chair, a baby of two and a half years old at my back, one sixteen months and one month on my knees and cried for very weariness and hopelessness.' Then she had a fourth child who was delicate. 'I watched by her couch three weeks, snatching her sleeping moments to fulfil the household tasks. The strain was fearful, and one night I felt I must sleep or die – I didn't much care which, – and I lay down by her side and slept and slept and slept.'

She complains about the monotony of life and how the lack of stimulation means she has little in common with her husband and she feels they are growing apart. 'I could give no time to mental culture or reading and I bought Stead's penny editions of literary masters and used to put them on a shelf in front of me on washing day, fastened back the pages with a clothes peg and learned pages of Whittier, Lowell and Longfellow, as I mechanically rubbed the dirty clothes and thus wrought my education. This served a useful purpose; my children used to be sent off to sleep by (my) reciting what I had learnt during the day.'

She concludes her letter by writing:

So here I am a woman of forty-one years, blessed with a lovely family of healthy children, faced with a big deficit, varicose veins, and an occasional loss of the use of my hands. I want nice things, but I must pay that debt I owe. I would like nice clothes (I've had three new dresses in fourteen years) but I must not have them yet. I'd like to develop mentally, but I must stifle that part of my nature until I have made good the ills of the past, and I am doing it slowly and surely, and my heart grows lighter, and will grow lighter still when know that the burden is lifted from the mothers of our nation.

Included at the end of the letter, as with all of them, is a note of how many children, how many miscarriages and how much their income was. Wages: 32 shillings to 40 shillings; five children, one miscarriage. The wages were higher in this family than in many, and five healthy children and only one miscarriage is much better than many of the other contributors.

Another letter hints at the hidden violence lurking in some marriages. She had seven children and suffered two miscarriages and managed on thirty shillings a week. She writes:

> I do wish there could be some limit to the time when a woman is expected to have a child. I often think women are worse off than beasts. During the time of pregnancy the male beast keeps entirely from the female; not so with the woman; she is at the prey of a man just the same as though she was not pregnant. Practically within a few days of the birth and as soon as the birth is over, she is tortured again. If the woman does not feel well she must not say so, as a man has such a lot of ways of punishing a woman if she does not give in to him.

When these letters arrived on Margaret Llewelyn Davies' desk, she must have realised that she had in her hands a collection of accounts of working-class life that was unique. The writing had an immediacy and freshness of language that spoke more directly than any synopsis she could devise. She showed them to her friend Virginia Woolf, who immediately realised their potential and said, 'You must publish these.' The book included a foreword by Margaret Llewelyn Davies in which she explains the background to the letters. 'It might justly claim to speak with greater authority than any other body for the vote-less and voiceless millions of married working women of England.'

She makes the point that the women who have written these letters live in better conditions than the average working woman but that they nevertheless give an impression of perpetual overwork, illness and suffering. She also notes the lack of self-pity and the lack of support from the medical profession and that at a time when she is pregnant a woman should be well fed but is not. She makes her meal off 'the scraps which remain over'.

Miss Llewelyn Davies also underlines the difference in working conditions between factory work and that done in the home. To some extent, factory work is regulated. It is an offence, she says, for an employer to knowingly employ a woman within four weeks after confinement. 'People forget that the unpaid work of the working woman at the stove, the scrubbing and cleaning, at the washtub, in lifting and carrying heavy weights, is just as severe manual labour as many industrial operations in factories'.

Relations between husband and wife are a delicate matter, but Margaret Llewelyn Davies underlines the fact that most of these wives have continued to maintain good relations with their husbands in spite of their ordeals, though the position of the wife in the family is seen by these women as being inferior to the man. 'In plain language, both in law and in popular morality, the wife is still the inferior in the family to the husband.' She attributes this to the lack of financial independence and because for many people a woman's roles in life are to care for the household, satisfy a man's desires and bear children.

The International Scene

A further development of the Guild, just as Miss Llewelyn Davies was considering retirement, was the establishment, in the aftermath of war, of contacts with co-operatives on the Continent that had formed an international association. Emmy Freundlich, a democratic socialist member of the Austrian parliament and a keen co-operator, had already established warm relations with Honora Enfield, who was to succeed Miss Llewelyn Davies as Secretary General of the Guild and who was also secretary of the International Guild of Co-operative Women.

Retirement

As General Secretary of the Guild, Margaret Llewelyn Davies had set the agenda for the Guild for thirty-two years when she retired in 1921. Her retirement was partly caused by and partly a result of reorganisation within the Guild. As the Guild grew, it had become very difficult for the individual branches to keep in close contact with the central administration. Miss Llewelyn Davies had been known personally to many of the branches and was much loved by many because she cared about them as individuals but it was difficult for the secretarial staff, overseen by Lilian Harris, to cope with the volume of work.

Members of the Central Committee, the advisory body to the General Secretary, proposed that electing the General Secretary should be moved from the individual branches to the Committee. This was rejected by the 1920 congress, but it was agreed that in future the Committee would supply a short list for the branches to vote on, and that the post of Secretary should be a full-time official who could be dismissed by the Central Committee. Miss Llewelyn Davies wisely decided that this arrangement would not suit her and retired. Individual members of the Guild felt they had lost a friend. At one branch the announcement of her resignation was read out by the branch secretary, who was in tears. There was a genuine sense of personal loss. However, the warmth of her personality, the interest she showed not only in the business side of the Guild but in its members, meant that her values and insights lived on in the Guild for many years.

When she retired from being the Guild's secretary, she and Lilian Harris were living in Hampstead, having moved there on the death of her father in 1916. She was able to devote more time to her other abiding interest, the pacifist movement, whose attitude she had passed on to the Guild in no small measure.

The Growth of the Pacifist Movement

The illusion that the British Empire was entirely a 'good thing' and that the world should be grateful to be run by the Brits, who knew how to do these things, had received something of a blow in 1902 when Emily Hobhouse revealed that in the aftermath of the Boer War in South Africa, the British administration had set up concentration camps to accommodate the womenfolk and children of Boer farmers, who had retreated into the bush and were waging a guerrilla war on the British. The civilian inmates of the camps were being very badly treated, she reported, and both children and their mothers were dying from disease and lack of food. Millicent Fawcett had been dispatched by the British government to provide a less emotional account, which she duly did, and which many people called a whitewash.

There was, therefore, some unease about war and its consequences. It was no longer a case of men in red uniforms going off to fight other men in different-coloured uniforms in a nice, clean, wholesome war, with the ladies left at home swooning over the handsome men in their clean, glamorous uniforms. As Jane Austen's Mrs Bennet said in *Pride and Prejudice*, 'I remember the time when I liked a red coat myself very well – and indeed so I do still in my heart.'

A substantial number of women in the suffrage movement, and in wider society, thought that belligerence had no place in a woman's thinking. Men were the aggressors; women were the ones who produced the babies who grew up to be the men who had to fight. Women did not produce children so they could be mown down by enemy fire after all those years of nurture that had gone into their upbringing. An anti-war stance, they thought, was the natural position for women to take.

Miss Llewelyn Davies and the Guild took a rather different view but arrived at the same conclusion: war was unnecessary and should be opposed. They considered that a co-operative Commonwealth, transcending national boundaries, would lead to a more fair society in which war was unnecessary and everything could be negotiated through arbitration. Miss Llewelyn Davies wrote that 'the brotherhood of nations is the religion of Co-operators, and under an International Co-operative system of trade and industry, the material interests of nations are no longer in opposition, but the resources of the globe are pooled and divided in the interests of all'. A somewhat idealistic, though stirring, view.

In 1913 the International Suffrage Congress was held in Budapest. Many of the Continental delegates spoke of the importance of women having the vote so they could act as a bulwark against war. On the very day that war was declared by Britain, on 4 August 1914, the women's movement was holding a meeting in the Kingsway Hall to support Sir Edward Grey, the Foreign Secretary, who they thought was against the war. At the same time as the meeting, there was a pro-war rally in Westminster, with anger against the Germans being whipped up by the press.

In September, several Labour MPs sent a letter to various newspapers urging that there should be democratic control of foreign policy, the creation of an international organisation that would resolve conflict by negotiation rather than aggression, would be careful not to humiliate any defeated powers in future peace settlements, and would avoid an artificial reorganisation of frontiers. It was signed by E. D. Morel and various other Liberal MPs, and they were soon joined by suffragists from the Labour movement, among them Margaret Bondfield and Margaret Llewelyn Davies. It became known as the Union for Democratic Control (UDC).

One of the things that shocked the members of the UDC was the way truth was subverted and conveyed by the press to a gullible public so there was no possibility of any informed discussion about the issue of war. (What a sense of *déjà vu* that conveys!) The UDC was described as a German organisation funded by the Kaiser, and as such was the target of physical violence and abuse.

At one meeting called by the UDC early in the war there was a commotion in the hall because of the influx of a great many Australian and Canadian soldiers, organised by the *Daily Sketch,* which supplied them with forged tickets. The young soldiers were brutal towards the young men in the audience. The speakers were unable to reach the platform. The UDC women remained calm throughout, with one Quaker woman going down on her knees to pray in the midst of the conflict while the rest tried to salvage their pamphlets. A report given to Parliament by the Provost Marshall, head of the Military Police, was a complete fabrication but was accepted as the truth and circularised in the newspapers. The speeches were subsequently printed and sold as pamphlets but, by this time, the police had informed managers of meeting halls that they were not prepared to keep order at rallies the UDC might organise, which made it impossible for them to book meeting halls.

In 1915 Mary Sheepshanks, vice-principal of Morley College, a further education college for working men and women, published an open letter to the women of Germany and Austria in which she said, 'Do not let us forget that we are passing together through the same experience of pain and grief. We pray you to believe that come what may we hold to our faith in peace and goodwill between nations.' It was signed by a hundred British women pacifists, including Margaret Llewelyn Davies. It precipitated the split in the NUWSS because of Millicent Fawcett's attack on Mary Sheepshanks and those who had signed the letter. Ten of the NUWSS committee resigned, including Maude Royden, Kathleen Courtney and Helena Swanwick.

Out of this letter and a reply carrying 'warm sisterly greetings' from 155 German and Austrian women was born the idea of a congress of peace activists from both sides of war, with the American peace movement also involved. A meeting place was something of a problem, but The Hague was offered and a peace congress organised for three months hence, in April 1915. Organising it was an assemblage of some of the foremost suffragists in the country, among them Maude Royden, Kathleen Courtney, Margaret Ashton of Manchester and, from the Guild, Margaret Llewelyn Davies and Sarah Reddish. A total of 180 women said they wanted to go. Some already had passports but the Chief Lord of the Admiralty, Winston Churchill, put paid to the possibility of their going by closing the North Sea to shipping. The women waited in Tilbury for a week before realising that there was no possibility of them crossing to Holland. *The Daily Express* carried the headline 'All Tilbury is laughing at the Peacettes'.

Margaret Llewelyn Davies continued in the peace movement throughout the 1920s and '30s. She thought war yet another example of capitalist exploitation, since it lined the pockets of the arms manufacturers at the expense of the workers. She encouraged the Guild to take a stance against imperialism and militarism in schools, and when in 1934 the Peace Pledge Union was created by the Canon of St Paul's, the Reverend Richard Shepherd, she was one of its staunchest supporters. Indeed, prompted by the then Secretary, Eleanor Barton, it was the Guild who first introduced the white poppy as an alternative to the red poppy worn on Armistice Day. The white poppies signified remembrance not only of the soldiers but also the civilians who had perished in the war.

In 1917, when the Russian Revolution resulted in the Russians withdrawing from the conflict, Margaret Llewelyn Davies, like many on the left of politics, was full of optimism and keen to promote good relations between the two countries. Between 1924 and 1928, she chaired the Society for Cultural Relations with the USSR, whose founder members were E. M. Forster, Julian Huxley, Maynard Keynes, Bertrand Russell, Sybil Thorndike, Alexei Tolstoy and Virginia Woolf. Their aim was to promote British–Soviet relations on a non-political basis through meetings, lectures, film shows and exhibitions. They also arranged tours of the USSR for British members and visits to Britain for Soviet cultural and public figures.

Many musicians had fled Russia following the revolution. And the *Ballets Russes*, managed by Diaghilev, which had always performed in the West, never returned to the USSR. Opera too was disrupted. However, as Madame Kamenova, the representative of the USSR Society for Cultural Relations with Foreign Countries, said, 'The October Revolution, whilst pulling down old traditions, was at the same time the creator of a new culture and a new life in the country.' There was still a vibrant culture to be explored and enjoyed. Unfortunately, when Josef Stalin forced Trotsky out of the

Central Committee in 1927, connections with the West were cut off to a large extent and the USSR became isolationist.

Miss Llewelyn Davies' forceful personality and firmly held beliefs remained a guiding force in the Guild for many, many years. Her socialism, her conviction that co-operation was the way towards lasting peace, and her faith in the strength of working-class women to improve the lives of their contemporaries, carried on.

A testimony to the power of her ideas is exemplified in one woman's loyalty to the Guild: Vera Binns, *née* Reynolds, born in Leeds in 1909. When Vera left school, denied an apprenticeship because she was a girl, she nevertheless learned all there was to know about printing, her chosen trade. She followed her mother into the Women's Co-operative Guild and, unswerving in her loyalty to the Labour Party and the Co-operative Movement, took part in marches in the 1930s to support the thriving Jewish community in Leeds. She was a staunch supporter of CND from its beginnings in 1957, and though unable in later years to visit the peace camp at Menwith Hill, she supported it with gifts of food and money. When Peter Sutcliffe, the Yorkshire Ripper, was waging a war on women in the late 1970s, and the police were advising women not to go out at night on their own, Vera was furious. 'It's not a woman who is doing the killing,' she thundered. 'It's a man. Tell the men to stay at home!'

Though crippled with arthritis in her old age, Vera was still a fervent supporter of the Guild. She wore her white peace poppy every year, read the *Co-operative News* regularly and until she declined into dementia in extreme old age organised the monthly meeting of her branch of the Guild. The greatest accolade she could award anyone was that they were 'a good socialist and a good co-operator'. While she was alive, the spirit of those earlier years still lived. She died at the age of ninety-two in 2001.

3

Helena Deneke (1878–1973) and the Women's Institute

A quiet, unassuming woman, Helena Deneke was a follower rather than a leader, so only the sketchiest of biographies exists, and she had the misfortune to outlive all her contemporaries so that by the time she died there was no one who could write about her achievements and her hard work. Fortunately, she has left a rather rambling unpublished autobiography running to five volumes and a war diary for the first two years of the Second World War.

She was a friend of Grace Hadow, co-founder of the Women's Institute, who could rely on Lena, as she was known to her friends, to do the boring day-to-day administration that a successful organisation relies on.

She was of German stock. Her father had arrived in England in the 1860s to work for a German bank where 'a man's word was his bond and taking an unfair advantage was unthinkable'. If only this admirable sentiment had survived into the twenty-first century! Mr Deneke met his future wife, Clara, when she was visiting her sister in London. The Denekes lived the rest of their lives in England, though they maintained contact with German visitors to London, and later Oxford, and went on regular visits to Germany. Mr Deneke was a generous father. His advice to his daughters, Helena and Margaret, was 'give but don't lend', presumably to indicate that personal loans can sour personal relationships. They seem to have followed this advice. They and their mother gave to Lady Margaret Hall, but they also encouraged others to give as generously as themselves.

They were great collectors. They collected the manuscripts of Felix Mendelssohn, which they subsequently donated to the

University of Oxford Library, the Bodleian. They also 'collected' people, in particular visiting Germans, in much the same way as some people might collect autographs. Lena's account of her life is full of the names of important people she and her family knew well, unfortunately most of them unknown nowadays. Einstein is an exception. When the girls were young, it was musicians such as the violinist Joachim, and Marie Fillunger who, to quote Lena, was 'debarred from opera by her ugliness but sang divinely'.

Mr Deneke was very happy in England and felt the country had served him well. Long before the First World War he decided to become a naturalised Englishman. His wife clung more strongly to her German roots but when her fourth child, a girl, died at the age of eighteen months and was buried in England, Clara's longing for her homeland – Westphalia – disappeared. Helena and Margaret were bilingual, as was their older brother Charles, and, being educated at home, asked to have an English governess rather than a German one.

Mrs Deneke retained her contact with Germany. She was a good friend of Clara Schumann, wife of the composer Robert Schumann, and the Schumanns' daughter, Eugenie, who lived in London, and taught Margaret Deneke, Lena's sister, to play the piano.

In 1900, a new century, Lena made a momentous decision. It was time to take control of her own destiny. She wanted to join the ranks of the bluestockings at Oxford. Her father was mystified and must have felt it was on a par with entering a convent. 'Do you want the companionship of highly intelligent women? You need only remember that your mother is not easily equalled,' was his comment.

Lena was adamant. She wanted to study English literature, and having surveyed the possibilities, which were fairly limited, thought her best chance of being accepted, seeing as she believed she was not particularly gifted, was the poorest college: St Hugh's in Oxford.

Dame Elizabeth Wordsworth, great-niece of the poet and principal of Lady Margaret Hall (LMH), had founded St Hugh's expressly for young women who could not afford the higher fees of LMH. Acknowledging this, Miss Annie Moberly, who became principal on its inauguration in 1886, exclaimed bitterly that Miss Wordsworth had started St Hugh's as a rubbish dump for LMH!

The fees per term were £18–£21. For that, Lena found herself in a very shabby house, badly furnished and with wallpaper hanging off the walls. She had a small room under the eaves, with a camp bed, a table, a chair, a chest of drawers and a view of the trees in the university parks. When her mother arrived and saw the room, she immediately went out and bought a combined wardrobe and chest, and matching washstand, while her father sent an oriental carpet to cover the bare boards.

Lena was worried that all this ostentation would upset Miss Moberly but Mrs Deneke had a warm, outgoing personality and made friends easily – and in any case, there was no way Miss Moberly was going to take umbrage at a rich woman buying furniture for her shabby college. The two women became the best of friends. It did result in Lena being known as 'the princess', however, and she freely admits that the thing she learned most from her three years as a student was not English but learning to live at close quarters with other women.

The academic community of women was very small. Lena was the first of nineteen or twenty students to arrive for the start of the academic year. The girls were friendly, but Lena says of herself that she was 'both diffident and ignorant'. There were rules of college etiquette of which she was completely unaware. The seven or eight freshers had to wait to be invited to tea by the older students but Lena didn't know this and invited the second- and third-year students round to her room in a bid to appear friendly. Her tutor offered to show her the shops but she was not interested. Why would she be? She had come down from London where there were shops aplenty and money provided by papa.

Once a week there was a social evening when the tables were pushed back and Miss Moberly played the piano for them to dance. There was very little contact with men, of course. Miss Moberly, one of the fifteen children of the Bishop of Salisbury, also took Bible classes every Sunday evening when all twenty-two students would crowd into her room. 'Questions and discussion were not invited,' writes Lena. Miss Moberly impressed on the girls that they were in Oxford on sufferance and their behaviour should be impeccable. Even a failure to wear gloves would be severely looked upon.

At one of the lectures on English literature, Grace Hadow was pointed out to Lena. Grace, unlike Lena, was a leading light of university society. Her brother, sixteen years older than she was, had been appointed Dean of Worcester College twelve years before, and Grace's life was a flurry of social events. In lectures she took few notes, Lena observed. Lena must have been astonished a short while later to receive an invitation to tea from Grace. What had she done to come to the notice of such an august personage? The answer was that she had entered an essay competition, which Grace had also entered. Grace wanted to discuss the topic with her but frustratingly, Lena does not tell us who won the competition. Her obituary, however, records that she won both the Junior and Senior English Essay Prize awarded by the Association for Promoting the Higher Education of Women (AEW) so it is quite possible it was she who won the prize on this occasion, though she thought she had done so badly that she tried to withdraw her entry.

Lena took her final exams in 1903, and with Grace Hadow got a Class 1 grading. No woman could graduate, since none had been allowed to matriculate – that is, join the university, a rite that occurs at the beginning of the first term of the first year. (This right was not granted by the university until 1920.) However, having acquitted herself so well, she was asked to stay on as a tutor at St Hugh's. For this she was not paid a salary but was given a room and her board. She became the college librarian, which was not very onerous as there were not many books. She then started teaching German at Somerville College, paid not by the college but by individual students.

Lena valued Miss Moberley's friendship, but when Miss Moberley appointed Eleanor Jourdain as vice-principal, problems arose. Lena instinctively distrusted Miss Jourdain. Lena once observed her with her ear to Miss Moberley's locked door and thought Miss Jourdain was manoeuvring to get rid of Miss Moberley and take her place. If so, it took her a while to achieve her aim. Annie Moberley remained head of St Hugh's until 1915, when she was indeed succeeded by Eleanor Jourdain. Lena's dislike of Miss Jourdain was reciprocated, and life at LMH must have been difficult. The relationship was not helped by the publication in 1911, ten years after the event, of *An Adventure*, an account by Miss Moberley and Miss Jourdain of a supposed event at Versailles that Miss Moberley interpreted as entering into the reverie of the Queen of France, Marie Antoinette, as she languished in the Bastille awaiting execution. Whatever Miss Moberley experienced and Miss Jourdain purported to have shared, Lena thought the two women's exploration of the subject was unhealthy, and she was very embarrassed about the whole affair.

Grace Hadow came to the rescue. In 1913 she arranged for Lena to transfer from St Hugh's to Lady Margaret Hall as bursar and tutor. There was no official appointment, not even a letter. Winifred (Freddie) Moberly, Annie's sister, was resigning the bursarship of LMH and, to quote Lena herself, 'the staff wished her to be untrained' like Freddie Moberly. They wanted someone who would 'get on with an old established set of servants and who could work with the house treasurer Mrs Toynbee', who had held that position since 1887. The decision to appoint her was made by the vice-principal of LMH, Eleanor Lodge, a close friend of Grace Hadow. Lena's obituary notes that she was 'singularly and amusingly unfitted for the role of Bursar'.

Lena found that being bursar had its challenges. She was very unsure of what to do if any student was ill. One young lady records that if you were ill, Miss Deneke would poke her head round the bedroom door, look anxiously at the patient, and ask if she would like a little gruel. Lena records that the cook always underestimated how much food was needed to feed the young ladies, and only by being taken into the dining room and shown how every crumb had been eaten could she be persuaded to provide more.

The months before 1914 were days of plenty. There were chicken legs for breakfast and large joints of meat, though it was not easy to decide on puddings that would be suitable for mass catering. It was not helped by Lena's well-known indifference to food. She was reputed to have once mistakenly made a meal of the scraps saved for the college dog.

Lena was a supporter of the Oxford Women Students' Suffrage Society (OWSSS) so in 1913, when the women's suffrage pilgrimage was passing through Oxford, Lena stole out of LMH to do door-to-door canvassing.

Eleanor Lodge, vice-principal at LMH, had warned her that members of the conference then in progress were well-brought-up Victorian daughters who would want to distance themselves from such activities. Lena was also in no doubt about her father's attitude to women's suffrage. He disapproved, though her mother was a personal friend of Millicent Fawcett. 'When we first lent a room for one of her conferences,' Lena reminisces, 'he came into the hall to greet Mrs Fawcett.' 'You are a heretic, I know,' said

Mrs Fawcett, 'but an amiable one.' Millicent Fawcett was a regular visitor to the Denekes' house, Gunfield, when the family moved to Oxford.

The Pilgrimage started from various places in Great Britain, the branch that passed through Oxford began in Carlisle and was led by Edith Picton Turbervill, a future Labour Party member and an advocate of more participation by women in the hierarchy of the Church. While some stalwarts of the suffrage movement managed the whole of the walk, which ended in London, and Eleanor Lodge and Grace Hadow between them carried the Oxford banner the whole way from Oxford to the capital, Lena joined the procession in Summertown, on the northernmost edge of the city, and accompanied it through the city centre and out to the east, along the London road.

The principal of LMH was Miss Jex-Blake, great-niece of the pioneer doctor Sophia Jex-Blake. Unlike her great-aunt, Miss Jex-Blake was a shy and retiring woman who had never been to college and took very little part in the running of the college. She had been appointed to keep Miss Jourdain out of the post. The day-to-day decisions were made by Eleanor Lodge, who held the Senior Common Room (SCR), the teaching staff, together.

At this time Grace Hadow was a part-time tutor, living in Cirencester with her ailing mother. Grace visited Oxford once a week and the SCR arranged for the OWSSS to hold its weekly meeting on that day. With Grace Hadow as chair, it fell to Lena to be secretary. The minutes of their meetings, which are still extant, show that in January 1917 they decided to send two workers as soon as possible to work in canteens for French soldiers and that £100 should be paid from the general account specifically for the canteens.

There were only two occasions when Lena remembers Miss Jex-Blake ever discussing with the SCR what they should do. One was when Lena and Madge Skipworth, tutor in French, approached her to ask for a relaxation of the rules on smoking. Neither of them were smokers but the rules were being broken so consistently they felt it would be better to be less stringent. The second occasion was on the outbreak of war, in August 1914, when the SCR was called together to discuss whether or not the college should close for the duration of the war. They decided to stay open but to be as flexible as possible to allow staff to take time away to help the war effort when needed.

The members of the SCR threw themselves into war work with a will. They expected air raids from Zeppelins so a blackout was enforced, which had to be monitored every evening by the dons. Patrolling the college was better, they thought, than being shut up in the basement waiting for bombs to drop. Coal was limited so Lena had to work out each person's ration of coal per scuttle; by 1918 food was in short supply and was rationed. This involved ration books, which had to be collected from the food office and distributed. On one memorable occasion, Lena accidentally sent the coupons off to America.

Lena initiated the War Savings Association to which sixty members belonged, each paying three pence a week. In the same year, 1916, there was a Zeppelin alarm, and everyone obeyed instructions, dressed warmly and retreated to the kitchen. The supply of biscuits ran out at four in the morning so at that point everyone went to bed.

Lena was also secretary for the Millicent Fawcett Hospital for Russia. *The Common Cause* reported that the maternity hospital in Petrograd financed by this fund

> ... would open up much wider spheres of work. The hospital established such a reputation for thorough and disinterested work on the part of British women that their help, in co-operation with the Great Britain and Poland Fund, was sought by the Zemstovs (Local Administration Units) in Middle Russia and Galicia... A much-needed children's hospital for infectious diseases was opened at Kazan ... and is now combating diphtheria and a severe epidemic of scarlet fever, the forty-bed hospital being filled with refugee children from two to ten years of age.'

These hospitals and others like them were supervised by Freddie Moberley, who travelled ceaselessly between hospitals by unreliable trains, troikas and military vehicles with her tea basket and candles. The only thing that worried her in the many buildings in which she lit her candle and made her tea was a dirty floor.

Freddie Moberley is an example of just how tough, resourceful and brave many of this generation of women were. Lena Deneke was not like that. She was quiet, cautious, and unwilling to stand in the limelight. She was, however, a prodigious worker who would undertake the boring, routine, background jobs that the more glamorous work of people such as Freddie Moberley relied on. Without the fundraising of Lena and hundreds like her, these hospitals could not have been run.

In the city, they set about organising to receive Belgian and Serb refugees. Madge Skipworth, the French tutor at LMH, and Lena learned Flemish so they could communicate with the refugees; they scrubbed floors and washed down the paintwork in houses in preparation for receiving them.

In the long vacation, LMH sent teams of five in relays to a farm near Sudeley in Gloucestershire to help with haymaking and weeding. Lena and Eleanor Lodge were among them. Four of the young women would work on the land while the fifth kept house. They had a small, clean cottage where they lived and worked from 8 a.m. till dusk for 14 shillings a week. Coal and milk were supplied by the farmer. In the evening, Helena Deneke wrote, 'a little family at a cottage on the opposite hillside would invite us to make music by blowing on combs'. It must have been an eye-opening experience for Lena to compare the few resources that family had with those of her sister, but who nevertheless contrived to make music.

Madge Skipworth and Lena travelled up to London in the evenings to work for the War Trade Intelligence Department in Westminster. The aim of the department was to pool intelligence on commercial trade, gathered from postal communications. On the outbreak of hostilities, Britain had severed Germany's six undersea cables running through the Channel so they were forced to communicate with their allies and neutral countries through other countries' networks or via wireless, which made them more vulnerable. Lena's and Madge Skipworth's job, as fluent French and German scholars, was to correct a register being compiled by secretaries unused to foreign languages.

There were upheavals within the Oxford colleges. Women tutors shared the teaching with the senior men who were too old to serve in the forces. There was, therefore, much closer communication between men and women dons than before the war, which proved an advantage for the women as the men found their female colleagues reliable and nothing like as scary as they had expected. By 1920, the university agreed to award degrees to women and Queen Mary accepted an honorary degree in law from the university.

In 1920 Lena became secretary of yet another organisation, the Oxford Committee for the Help of Universities of Central Europe. The whole of Europe had been devastated by the war and there were such levels of starvation and general lack of goods of any kind, made worse by the embargo on trade instituted by the victors, that representatives from all the Oxford colleges met together to try to organise help. They tried to channel food and clothing to the universities and arranged for members of the University of Vienna to come to Oxford to recuperate from the horrors of war. They sought to co-operate with the Imperial War Fund, a short-lived humanitarian charity that was overtaken in popularity by Save the Children, founded by another LMH graduate, Eglantine Jebb, and her sister Dorothy.

In 1915, with the government being very concerned about food supplies, the idea of an organisation that would support and raise the morale of country women and encourage them to produce more food had been mooted. The movement began in a small way in Anglesey and slowly began to spread through the hard work and dedication of a Canadian woman, Mrs Watt. When the war was over, and votes for women over thirty had been gained, many of those who had been active in the suffrage movement moved over to the Women's Institute: the treasurer, Mrs Auerbach, had been treasurer of the NUWSS, and Grace Hadow became vice-president. The organisation wisely asked Lady Denman, who was both rich and generous, to be its principal, and she proved to be a decisive and clear-thinking leader.

The structure of the Women's Institute closely followed the model of the NUWSS, and had local branches, supported by a county federation, with the National Federation based in London to represent the whole movement.

The women schooled in the politics of the suffrage movement immediately saw that here was a vehicle for educating women not only in food production, but for taking their place in a society where women were moving towards parity with men. Country women could be educated on how to run meetings, how to stand up in front of a group of other women and speak their minds, and the importance of using their new-found political clout. They could do for country women what Margaret Llewellyn Davies had done for working-class women through the Women's Co-operative Guild: they could give them a voice and increase their skills and confidence. Country women could be given lectures on food hygiene, on improving their domestic skills, on literature and on the world outside their village. The skills they already had could not only be nurtured, they could be judged and ranked and the best examples praised so they could see that the work they did at home was valued by the wider community. And they could have fun while they were doing all this.

With branches springing up all over the county, a co-ordinating body was needed and Grace Hadow was instrumental in setting up the Oxfordshire Federation of Women's Institutes (OFWI). She suggested to Lena that she might like to help with running the Federation, so Lena became the honorary secretary, and later president, posts she held until 1945. The inaugural meeting of the Oxfordshire Federation was on Saturday, 3 February 1919 at 2.30 p.m. at Barnett House, a centre for social organisations and charities in the centre of Oxford, where Grace Hadow now worked. Their first task was to organise an exhibition of handicrafts, planned for the following July, and held at New College, one of the oldest university colleges, where Miss Spooner, sister of the Reverend Spooner of 'spoonerism' fame, welcomed representatives from all the branches. The first exhibition made about £50 for the federation.

They set up a propaganda fund for promoting the WI. One of Lena's many responsibilities was to travel the length and breadth of the county, setting up branches in villages where, until the First World War, society had retained much of its feudal system, the kind of places where, if someone had a toothache, they would be told, 'Squire, ee draws 'em well. Why go into Oxford?'

Lena was invited by Susan Buchan, wife of the writer and publisher John Buchan, to join the Elsfield branch of the WI, and since the branch was very small (as was the village), Lena's sister Marga and her mother Clara also joined. When the Buchans went to Canada in 1935, Lena reluctantly took over as president of the Elsfield branch only because Mrs Elkington, the vicar's wife, asked her to take on the job to prevent Miss Parsons, another village worthy, from doing so. Unbeknown to Mrs Elkington, Miss Parsons had also approached Lena to prevent Mrs Elkington from becoming president.

Susan Buchan and Madge Skipworth, Lena's colleague at LMH, were on the executive committee at that inaugural meeting of the

Oxfordshire Federation of the Women's Institute. Once the OFWI was up and running, there was a great deal for the newly installed secretary to do. In 1921 they broached the idea of a countywide library scheme. The county council was unhelpful, and unwilling to provide any funding because, they said, 'Oxfordshire people don't read.' Grace Hadow's response was, 'Then we must prove that they do.'

She and Lena organised a travelling library to go round to each WI branch, with each member paying one penny a month subscription. Barnett House also provided plays suitable for women's groups. In Elsfield, Mrs Elkington offered to be village librarian. This literary aspect of the Federation was supplemented with literary competitions and folk songs sung at the annual exhibition.

Lena whizzed around the county setting up new branches wherever village people felt there was a need. By 1922, the Federation could report that there were now forty-five branches in the county, a tribute to the secretary's hard work. All the topics tackled by the WI in Oxfordshire generated correspondence, which passed across Lena's desk as she sat in Barnett House.

She dealt with the Clean Milk Society – an organisation headed by Waldorf Astor, which aimed to improve the hygienic production and handling of milk. The Society was not just interested in raising public awareness of the dangers of poor-quality milk – they told you how you could do something about it. They suggested asking to inspect the methods of handling milk and visiting the farm at milking time with a 'Score Card for Dairy Farm Inspection'. Perhaps this idea might have worked in towns but the idea of Susan Buchan or Mrs Elkington issuing forth armed with one of these cards to inspect the milking process in the three farms carrying dairy herds in Elsfield village just defies the imagination. It would have set off feuds to rival the mafia!

Lena carried on correspondence and organised the itinerary of a variety of speakers, including a Miss Hope who was based at Reading and would give demonstrations on the preparation of a variety of foods. She charged ten shillings and sixpence, plus expenses. At this time branches often had neither electricity nor running water in their meeting rooms and Miss Hope was very specific about her requirements. For every demonstration she needed:a firm table and paper to cover it, a jug of water and towel, four large plates, a cup and saucer, three small basins and a mixing bowl, and a board and rolling pin. For meat she also required a three-burner stove with a two-burner oven, and for bread and cakes she would like a Valor Perfection stove with a large oven. She could make cold sweets without the aid of a stove.

One project Lena organised was a competition to produce a village history. Forest Hill compiled an excellent one, as did Islip and Headington Quarry. Elsfield had no need of an amateur compilation because John Buchan had encouraged his friend George Clarke, later Sir George, to write a professional history of the Manor of Elsfield. It is interesting and historically accurate but not nearly so lively as the amateur compilations, which had photographs of the WI, local people dressed up in old costumes, accounts of local haunted houses. Sadly there were no pictures in the Elsfield book and no haunted houses.

Lena was also on the national executive of the organisation, so headed up to London on a regular basis with Grace Hadow to help steer the NFWI in the way Grace Hadow and Lady Denman decided it should go.

Her home life too was a very full one. In 1916 Mr Deneke had bought the house called Gunfield, next-door to LMH, and the family, by this time consisting of Mr and Mrs Deneke and Margaret since their older brother Charles had died in 1906, had followed Lena to Oxford. It was a large house with many bedrooms in which the generous and outgoing family accommodated their many friends on a short- or long-term basis. The first musical event they gave was for the workmen who had done all the modernisation of the house. One of their friends wrote a piece of doggerel verse about the men, which was so popular with the audience it had to be repeated time and time again. In fact the two boilermen came back at the end of the evening and requested a copy of 'their song'.

Lena and her family used Gunfield as a base for all kinds of social events, which tied in with their support for LMH and Lena's responsibilities there as German tutor and garden supervisor. Their contacts with renowned musicians of the day meant their musical soirees, to which students were invited, became a well-known aspect of Oxford life, and their propensity for 'collecting' famous people meant that Albert Schweitzer and his wife, and Millicent Fawcett were regular visitors.

Even Einstein himself was lured to the house by promises of being able to play Mozart and Beethoven quartets with the violinist

Marie Soldat, cellist Arthur Williams, and Erna Schutz. Einstein had heard them all in either Berlin or Vienna so was pleased to come and join them for an evening of music and a substantial dinner. He made three visits in the three years he was resident at Christchurch College – in 1931, 1932 and 1933. The Denekes recorded the conversations they had with him and described his behaviour, which they seem to have found eccentric in its non-observance of what they considered the normal rules of society. Margaret notes that he had a disconcerting habit of laughing heartily at his own jokes, which no one else found funny. He also confided that Mozart was his first love – the supremest of the supreme, he said, but for playing the great Beethoven 'I must make something of an effort. I never practice.'

On his first visit, the Denekes were invited to the Sheldonian to watch Einstein receive his DPhil from the University. He admitted afterwards that he had not understood a word as it was all in Latin. The Deneke sisters were keen for him to give the Deneke lecture at LMH, a yearly event commemorating Mr Deneke, who had died in 1924. They offered him the statutory £25, though Margaret stipulated: 'No maths.' Einstein grumbled that the day would never come when he would *want* to give a talk. The talk was all right but having to stick to what he had said and written was the awful part.

On his third visit in 1933, Einstein arrived the day after the funeral of Mrs Deneke. Marga records that on the day she died, Clara Deneke had finished an elaborate piece of embroidery, checked the household accounts and her game of Patience had worked out. She had been crippled with rheumatism, which made her life a misery at the end, but the sisters – and many people in Oxford and beyond – would mourn her passing. Einstein was upset not to have had the chance to say goodbye but agreed to give the Deneke lecture, though he asked for it to be brought forward from 1934 to that year, 1933, and the lecture duly took place on 13 June. The room was crowded, and the £25 he was paid for his services he gave to a friend in financial distress.

Margaret spent a great deal of time and effort raising money for LMH so extra accommodation could be built for the increasing number of students who wanted a place there. She did this by making extensive lecture and performance tours of America, which she found exhausting. She made friends with a Mrs Harkness, a well-known benefactress, who warmed to Margaret's innocence in the field of fundraising, and when Margaret was too tired to eat lunch one day pressed her to abandon the rest of her tour and gave her a cheque for £35,000. Mrs Harkness' portrait hangs in the dining room at LMH, though she was not pleased with the likeness, commenting that it was only fit for an Institution for the Blind. She asked for the building built with her money to be called the Deneke building in memory of Mrs Deneke, whom she had liked enormously when she visited in early 1933. Mrs Deneke, a very skilled needlewoman, had embroidered a pink silk bed-jacket as a present.

Lena took Mrs Harkness to meet Dame Elizabeth Wordsworth, the first principal of LMH and founder of St Hugh's. Dame Elizabeth had a dry sense of humour and a lack of reverence for the social niceties, which made Lena nervous, and she warned Mrs Harkness of Dame Elizabeth's eccentricities. At the end of the visit, in spite of being riddled with arthritis, Dame Elizabeth insisted on accompanying the two women to the door, and when assured there was no need, replied, 'I must see you to the door or you might steal my silver teaspoons.'

Of the four buildings erected at that time, the one named after Eleanor Lodge ran into a great many setbacks as it was being built and it is reassuring to know that it was as difficult then as it can be now to have to organise the building trade! Lena records that when building works started, there were builders' strikes that put back the digging of the foundations until the autumn, so they flooded. The foreman failed to test or re-measure the architect's drawing and when the foundations were already substantial, found that they were seven-and-a-half inches out of line when they reached the main building. The Clerk of Works insisted they be demolished and rebuilt. The steel they ordered was the wrong size and had to be sent back and re-ordered. In March 1925 the foreman left. The stonemasons had cut 75 per cent of the stone 'face-bedded', which meant the wrong surfaces would be exposed to the air, so the stone needed to be re-cut. Thirty bricklayers should have been employed but only nine turned up on a regular basis and they knocked off at five o'clock and refused to work overtime. The strongest among them had a party trick – he could dance with a hod of bricks on his back. He ended up in prison for murdering his landlady and Lena met him much later when she was a Poor Law Guardian at the mental hospital. Lena found the night watchman asleep at nine o'clock in the morning and the same man became very friendly with the newly appointed foreman, who shared his love of whisky and whippets. The whippets often spent the day hidden under coats in the night watchman's shed.

In spite of these setbacks, by October the roof was on – at which point a new student who was practising on the organ in the chapel noticed an unusual glow, turned round and saw flames leaping up to roof level on the unfinished building. She left the chapel and made a discreet entrance into the dining room, whispering in Miss Jamison's ear that there appeared to be a problem. Miss Jamison, Lena and the Bursar left the room, summoning the college fire brigade, who could not locate the hydrant. The flames were at roof height and beginning to take hold of woodwork under the edge of the roof. Fortunately Emily, the chief maid, appeared at this point and was able to tell the city fire brigade where the hydrant was located. Miss Skipworth checked that the whippets were not in the shed, where the fire had originated, and the fire was soon extinguished. The builders had been recommended by the architect.

The Second World War
In 1939 Lena had just returned from Canada, where she had been staying with the Governor John Buchan and his wife, now ennobled as Lord and Lady Tweedsmuir. While there, she met up with Grace Hadow, who had been touring Australia and the USA, raising money for the Oxford Home Students' Association. Both Lena and Lady Tweedsmuir were shocked to see how tired Grace looked, but Grace boarded the last boat to sail down the St Lawrence before the winter, assuring everyone that she was in good health and spirits. When Grace landed in Britain, she travelled by train to Carlisle, having to stand for the whole journey. She then succumbed to a chill and, with Lena by her side, died of pneumonia in January 1940. Lena decided to write Grace's biography, which was published in 1946, but on 3 September 1939, the day war was declared, she had already started a war diary, which now resides in Box 18 of her papers in the Bodleian.

Lena's war diary for the end of 1939, and 1940, shows just how terrifying this time must have been as she plots the ever-approaching armies of Nazi Germany, the fall of Norway, Holland and Belgium and then the bombing and invasion of the Channel Isles in June

1940. No wonder she threw herself into war work with such energy and dedication.

Lady Denman, the president of the National Federation of WIs, had decided that the organisation should stick rigidly to its constitution and therefore, as an organisation, would not take part in any war work, though individuals could do as they pleased. She herself ran the Land Army.

One aspect of Lena's work as president of the Oxfordshire Federation was to take responsibility for organising jam making and fruit preservation. She notes plaintively that the WI has been asked to take responsibility for growing vegetables and preserving fruit, and for marketing their produce, and that there is an abundance of crab apples but no sugar. There were many other problems too for Lena to sort out. WI members complained about the red tape, filled in the wrong forms or mistook red plums for blue and cooked them too much for them to be bottled successfully, forgot to check the gas meter before they started to boil the jam so couldn't make an accurate claim for the money they were owed, complained that they couldn't take their produce to the centre designated by the men in suits in Whitehall because there was no bus. The grocer buying the jam complained about the stickiness of the jars and the mould that had grown on one jar, but said he was prepared to buy all this substandard jam because he thought he could sell it to schools and the Army. Sorting all this out was not an easy job! Organisers of the centres met at Gunfield to pool information and found, in October 1939, that they had accidentally made a profit!

As if she hadn't enough to do, Lena also joined the Women's Voluntary Services (WVS) and the Air Raid Precautions (ARP). As a member of the WVS, she had a multitude of jobs to do. The day before war was declared, there was a huge influx not only of evacuee children and mothers with babies but also various organisations that had decided moving out of London was the safest option and were looking for accommodation. Lena had a car and an extra petrol allowance, probably because of her WI work, which meant she was expected not only to travel to WI functions, but also to convey people such as evacuees or soldiers returning on leave from the station to their destination. Her first task was to take a nun from the Convent of the Sacred Heart to High Wycombe, to find fifty-three children who should have arrived in Oxford but were stuck in High Wycombe. There was a seething mass of children and a line of mothers with babies who were harder to place. There were twenty-four babies from an institution, with nurses to look after them but no one to do the washing, as the regular washerwoman had refused to leave London. Lena dispatched three people from Oxford to do the washing.

One of the first things Lena became involved with was the searchlight posts, which were positioned on the hills around Oxford. The WVS offered to supply library books to the men occupying these posts. There was usually just one room with a separate cooking shed and at the beginning of the war they were very badly equipped. Typical was an Elsan chemical toilet with no chemicals, and an oil stove with no oil and no authorisation to buy any. The winter was bitterly cold and the men were very bored so the librarybook service was very useful. Lena and Clare Kreyer, a WI colleague, took on responsibility for the whole of South Oxfordshire. Fortunately by April 1940, conditions had improved. Chemicals had been supplied for the chemical toilets, and oil for the heaters. In addition, the men were moved around every six weeks to another job to break the monotony.

Lena lists the work she might do on a typical day at the beginning of the war:

> WVS work: Try to arrange accommodation for the Hospital Almoners' Society which included an interview with the manager of the Electric Company to arrange heat and light.
> WI work: Discuss detailed plans for Women's Institute war work: what the constitution allowed them to include in WI work and what they should not do.
> WVS work: Meet mothers and babies at the station and run them to Witney.
> LMH work: Interview old students who want jobs
> LMH work: Discussion about the best use of Women's Appointments Committee, the university careers service.
> WVS work: Arrange to take a turn at a First Aid Post if there's a raid.

She found the 'odd-jobiness' of it all quite exhausting.

It was easy to unknowingly upset people. The school at Middleton Stoney, near Bicester, had had an influx of schoolchildren and their teachers, and was having to run double sessions to fit everyone in, so the Lord Lieutenant of the County, Lord Bicester, and his wife said they could fit all the children and their teachers in at their country home, and there would be ample room for playing fields if needed. Lena gratefully accepted this offer and, in a reciprocal gesture of generosity, took Lord Bicester's application for a petrol allowance, which he had not yet filled in though the closing date was that day, to the office in Oxford, getting there in the nick of time. What she thought a job well done, however, upset the billeting officer for the area who resented not being involved in the decision and resigned. Lena thought this a very good outcome.

Lena and the rest of the WI were shocked at the filthy state of some of the children whom they were expected to take into their homes. The difference in the standard of living of the slum children when compared to their hosts was also a surprise. One woman told her two charges to go to bed but when she went upstairs they were nowhere to be seen. When she called them they emerged from under the bed. 'Why on earth were you under the bed?' she asked. 'Please, missus, we thought you and mister slept there,' they replied. At Gunfield, however, Lena had two very nice fifteen-year-old girls and their teacher from Hammersmith.

The views of the WI found expression in a questionnaire organised by the National Federation of Women's Institutes (NFWI) which, when collated, was published as *Town Children through Country Eyes*. This was taken up by politicians and informed decisions about social welfare throughout the country.

Lena, with her sister, was also an ARP warden for the area around Gunfield. The ARP post was actually in the pantry of their house but spilled over into other rooms. It was manned twenty-four hours a day. Gumboots were arranged by the sink, rattles on the plate rack, while the pantry cupboards were filled with ARP equipment. The tin hats were stacked on the piano in the music room.

In June 1940, St John's College asked people living in the vicinity to donate their railings to be melted down for metal to make planes. Lena couldn't bear to part with her gate, so kept that, though how that served as a barrier without its attendant railings is something of a mystery. So here was yet another job for her. She collected the donations and took them to the dump.

The first convoy of wounded soldiers arrived in Oxford to be accommodated at the Cowley Road Hospital, a general hospital rather than a military one. Lena was given the job of organising 'comforts' and trips out for the walking wounded. This got rather out of hand as young girls were coming into the hospital at any time and sitting on the beds of the bedbound. They were also very enthusiastically wheeling out soldiers without any idea of the responsibility they were assuming. One girl decided to take her young Frenchman out on the river, which, as he could not yet walk unaided, seemed less than wise. What irony if he were to survive a German attack only to drown in the Isis!

The Local Defence Volunteers, soon to be renamed the Home Guard, comes in for considerable criticism from Lena. 'They are useless,' she says, after recording that three of their number were now in the Radcliffe Hospital with self-inflicted bullet wounds. They had also stopped her on her way back from a WI meeting at Elsfield. They had improvised a roadblock from a pine tree and a set of bicycle wheels, so as she drove down the hill she was forced to stop and produce her identity card. As she had been travelling this way for the last twenty years and everyone knew her and her car, she was not pleased. The following morning the President of Stadhampton WI approached her and said, 'Oh Miss Deneke, my husband held you up last night. He was in Gallipoli and is having the time of his life! He is very proud of his barrier.' Lena does not record her reply!

She does, however, record the difficulty of obtaining first-hand information. Unlike during the First World War, when people visited northern France regularly and could get news direct from the mouths of soldiers back from the Front, most of the information available to people was via the radio and the newspapers.

Lena seems to have felt that in view of the propaganda machines active both in Germany and Britain, what was printed or carried on the airwaves would have been heavily censored and distorted. She and Marga thought that by July 1941, Churchill was becoming a demagogue and they would switch off the radio if they heard his voice.

In March 1941 there was an invasion scare and people were told of the likelihood of incendiary bombs and gas. They were told to find even more recruits to the ARP, but Lena says wearily that there is no one – all the able-bodied people are fully occupied.

Milk was now rationed and the WI market got into trouble and feared they might be prosecuted because they had sold five dozen eggs to Worcester College above the retail price. A young man came from the Board of Trade to try to explain clothing coupons but got short shrift from his audience who, having read and committed to memory what the *Daily Sketch* had published, knew more than he.

Egg marketing was running into trouble. The regulations had been made, said Lena, by people who knew nothing about hens, eggs or the housewife. Anyone keeping more than fifty hens had to send their eggs to packing stations, but retailers said customers were returning them because they were addled.

Lena herself said the war had turned her into a hen keeper. She began in 1940 when wire and hen houses could still be bought, and put up three runs on the lawn. She started with eight Rhode Island Reds, six Light Sussex and four whites, which produced an abundance of eggs. She held the ration books for four customers but gave many of the eggs away. Marga bred rabbits to pass on to other people who might wish to grow rabbits or to sell for meat at the WI market stall. Lena and Marga also grew most of their own vegetables, except potatoes, and Gunfield was registered as a smallholding under the War Agricultural Committee.

The War Diary stops after Christmas 1941 and one gets the impression that Lena was very weary of the daily grind of driving people hither and thither, worrying about food and air raids, and physically tired after so many broken nights. Perhaps she was also wondering just why she was recording so much of what was happening. Maybe so there would be an honest account of the day-to-day doings of people during momentous times. She certainly reread the diary years later when she added a short section on how Marga had reorganised Gunfield to accommodate evacuees. So perhaps she recorded what was happening so she could remember a very important time in her life.

Lena's Visits to Germany after the Second World War

When the Second World War ended in 1945, Germany was divided into four parts, each run by one of the Allied countries: Russia, America, France and Britain. The gender balance of the population was heavily skewed towards women, with 121 women to 100 men in the British Zone. This was not only because many of the men had been killed but also because, at least in the British zone, there were a great many German prisoners of war who were still in Britain and could not be released until the harvest had been completed.

British politicians were keen to foster self-help groups of women who would work to improve living conditions and they were also very aware of the political setup in the Russian sector, where women were much less encumbered with old-fashioned ideas of what constituted the role of women. The vigorous women's policy pursued in the Russian sector led to the formation in the west of the Women's Affairs Section, run by Jeanne Gemell, an ex-pupil of Lena's.

The role of women under the Nazis had been very clear, summed up in the term: *kinder, kucher, kirche*: 'children, cakes and church'. Their work was to provide children for the Fatherland, who would be brought up believing in National Socialism rather than Christianity, women would run their homes well and acknowledge the position of the man as head of the household. Some historians think this is a gross oversimplification, however, and that women could find opportunities in or through the Nazi Party for greater influence and self-expression than they had experienced before. While it is difficult to know the true situation, there is no doubt that women's organisations that had been independent of the government were absorbed into the Nazi system, as the Women's Institute found to their embarrassment when they invited a German delegation to their annual meeting in 1939. The speaker ended her speech with the Nazi salute 'Heil Hitler', rather against the ethos of the studiously non-political WI.

The main aim of the British occupation policy in 1945 was to secure peaceful and democratic development and to get production going, to take the pressure off the British economy. Not only did they want to rebuild the economy and the infrastructure – bridges, roads and railways – but it was felt to be crucial to the future of both Germany and Britain that the German population should be educated in democratic government so that the nightmare of Nazism, or any other form of dictatorship, could never happen again.

As there were many more women than men, educating women to take an interest in their civic duties was of prime importance, so the British looked for models of women's participation in civic life in Britain that were independent of government. They decided that the Women's Institute, the Townswomen's Guild and the Women's Co-operative Guild were three movements German women could usefully study and model themselves on. They chose a representative from two of these three – Helena Deneke from the WI, and Betty Norris of the Townswomen's Guild – to join the Women's Affairs Section, to visit and talk with German women about how best to help them reconstruct the social life of the country.

Since she could not be in two places at once, Lena resigned her post on the executive of the Oxfordshire Federation of WIs and was presented with a really beautiful collection of homemade pictures, one from each WI in the county, which demonstrate just how much affection everyone had for her and how they appreciated all the work she had put in to make the WI so successful.

Both Lena and Betty Norris were fluent German speakers, though Lena's German language skills were rather out of date. She still spoke the German of Goethe, and needed to update her vocabulary, which she duly did with extra German lessons, and they were drafted into the Army at Lieutenant Colonel level. Their uniforms, Lena noted, were very similar to the ARP uniforms she and Marga had worn during the war, but with different buttons.

A large part of the files of the Women's Affairs Section of the British Military Government were destroyed after the Section was closed down after the end of occupation in 1955. Fortunately, Helena Deneke kept a great deal of the paperwork that passed through her hands during her long life, and these reside in a multiplicity of boxes in the Bodleian Library in Oxford.

The two women set off in August 1946 to start their seven-week tour of the British Sector. They spent their first four days in Bunde, a quiet provincial town in Westphalia. They lived in the English enclave, where conditions were markedly different from that of the general population. The calorie intake for Germans calculated by the military government was 1,500 calories a day, but by 1946 this had been reduced to 1,015 calories. The Germans saw this as punishment and accused the British of adulterating the grain to produce sterility. Lena and Betty Norris saw that in spite of slight increases in the food allowance, the Germans were still seriously undernourished. The military government provided midday soup for the children, which was appreciated, but often much of what food there was was given to the father, if there was one, to keep him working and it was the mother who suffered most. This contrasted with the conditions in the English enclaves where there were ample rations.

Lena and Betty Norris found that the religious societies had managed to survive the Nazi era by concentrating purely on religious matters but the independent women's organisations had been absorbed into the 'Frauenschaft' under Hitler, where they lost all autonomy.

Lena and Betty's tour had been well organised. They were given the use of a Volkswagen and driver and told to visit all the main towns in the British Zone, and also to take note of conditions in the countryside. In Westphalia, Schleswig-Holstein and Hanover, the countryside appeared not to have suffered from the war except that there was a shortage of manure and the fieldwork and harvesting was mainly being done by hand. There were 'footsore and burdened travellers' at the roadside, probably part of the influx of refugees from the east who had fled before the Russians.

The first city they visited was Munster, where the local bishop, Bishop von Galen, had been outspokenly critical of the Nazis. This had resulted in large numbers of Nazi troops being stationed in the city. Their presence and the artificial oil development centred there resulted in bombing by the Allies, which destroyed the major part of the old city. When Lena and Betty visited, the cathedral was a shell but at the east end the sand had been raked, two prie-dieux had been placed and a single row of begonias had been placed round the flat stone marking the grave of the bishop, who had died at the beginning of the year. A large wooden cross was fixed into a pile of rubble in the city centre.

They visited many places and wherever they went spoke to women – in small groups, in large groups, talking with individuals and addressing formal meetings. They held discussions with women representatives of welfare and religious groups, and of the German Red Cross, and the political parties. When asked much later if she had found this tiring, Lena said, 'Of course not. You were transported like a parcel and just spoke at meetings as required, much less tiring than doing several different jobs in England.'

In their report the two women stressed the physical difficulties German women were facing, with a total lack of resources of any kind. There were no textiles or sewing materials available and while some people could wear the clothes they had had before the war, those who had had their homes destroyed had nothing.

The population of the Zone had increased from 20 million to 22 two million because of the influx of refugees from the Eastern zone. They often arrived barefoot with only the clothes they stood up in, the majority being women, young children and old people. They were compulsorily billeted on farms and in private houses, but where these were full they had to live in ill-equipped camps, not always weatherproof. The amount of floor space allowed per person was four square metres, the size of two double beds. Because of all this overcrowding, there was no space for children to play and nothing for them to do. They got far too little schooling and, as Lena and Betty point out, 'They run wild in the streets or are sent into the country to collect wood or food. Begging from Allied soldiers, barter with one another and all the temptations of the Black Market develop from this lack of supervision and control.' Approved schools and homes for children on probation were all full. Lack of food, soap and medical supplies resulted in children losing weight and being unable to fight disease, and tuberculosis was spreading.

As well as talking to people, they witnessed first-hand some of the living conditions people were subjected to. At Rheda, two old Army huts were being used as a transit camp.

A contingent of ninety-eight refugees had just detrained from Poland and were to be moved into billets. One mother had a group of twelve young tousle-headed children clustering round her at the rough table for a meal of soup. Close by were other small children with their mothers. There were no younger able-bodied men. One elderly couple, barefoot and scantily clad, told of their forcible expulsion from their own little homestead. It had been robbed and raided for months. Fortunately they had not been separated from their elder daughter and a child of seven or eight. They asked to be billeted on a farmer for work. The temper of these refugees was hopeful. They were relieved from threats of attack and the hardship of travel and did not yet know the further troubles impending.

These were not feckless people, Lena and Betty were keen to point out. Some of them showed remarkable resourcefulness. At one camp they visited a family had patched up a neat cabin and planted a vegetable garden, and helpers were on hand to organise activities. A kindergarten was planned.

'If these women of the German Red Cross were given authority to direct repairs and reconstruction, we feel confident these would be done economically and efficiently, and one urgent local problem would be solved, but there must first be an allowance of essential materials' was Lena and Betty's assessment.

A severe lack of building materials was holding everything back. In Hamburg people were living in dark, dank, rat-infested cellars where even the cats could not be relied on to rid the hovels of rats since there was not sufficient food to entice the cats to stay. When the working-class quarters of Hamburg had been bombed, the inhabitants had been moved to Bavaria to be safe. After the war, refugees from Sudetenland pushed out the people from Hamburg, who had moved back to their old homes only to become refugees in their own city. The military government had given Nissen huts to house these people. 'The wooden ends of these huts will not resist the winter cold,' Lena and Betty's report pointed out, 'but materials are scarce and have been rigidly allocated yet a modicum of bricks from the many ruins of Hamburg should suffice to put this right.' The military government, however, would not allow Germans to help themselves and however much the ladies of the Red Cross pleaded, their pleas were ignored.

The German women they met assumed that living conditions were better in England, especially when they saw how well the British lived in their enclaves in Germany. Lena and Betty had to tell them in quite forceful terms that although conditions were not as extreme in Britain as they were in Germany, there were nevertheless acute shortages of building materials, clothes and food, and that the occupying forces lived better than people back home in England.

Having attended innumerable meetings while in Germany, Lena and Betty concluded that the democratic constitution of a society, as run in Britain, was not understood by the Germans. Individuals were not expected to bear any responsibility, nor to be more than passively interested in the activities of the committee. They also found that the accepted form for meetings in Germany also did not allow for individual members to take an effective part. It was usual for there to be a number of set speakers and the chairman left the stage immediately after the introductory speech, which made it difficult for any discussion to develop. This, they found, contrasted markedly with meetings of the WI and the Townswomen's Guild, where members could build up their skills and talents. 'A member learns democracy in practice, for the varied programmes of these meetings provide a demonstration in which she shares,' they wrote. 'These and similar bodies have proved themselves as a training ground in citizenship and have taken a notable part in discussion of public questions.'

They thought the British model might usefully be adopted, but only when living conditions had been considerably improved. Exhibitions and craft demonstrations, so necessary to make talks interesting and engaging, were impossible without materials. The growth of democratic organisations, they stressed, must be slow and spontaneous, which would happen once physical conditions in Germany had improved. 'We are convinced,' they continued, 'that the non-sectarian and non-party-political basis is the one on which democratic conviction is likeliest to take root among German women ... that women of different, even opposed convictions can work together for a definite common end. We therefore think that development should come through the *"Ausschuss"* (committee) of a non-party-political and non-sectarian character, such as we have described.'

The two women suggested changing the military government's attitude to the provision of some essential materials – for repairs to buildings, the supply of utensils and the repair or replacement of worn-out clothing. They acknowledged the goodwill of the occupying forces but spoke sternly about the need to meet local needs from local resources without referring at all times to international agreements. 'In insisting on unconditional surrender before hostilities ceased we also made ourselves responsible for these affairs,' they said. 'The Germans are not a work-shy people, but two basic needs of theirs remain unsatisfied: a ration for the ordinary consumer that allows of full work, and sufficient fuel. Without material aid to support relief work it is difficult to see how our teaching in democracy can be made to hold good.'

They then go on to lambast the government for preaching at women, who will react by turning away from any ideas presented in this way. 'As long as the vote has no real power to influence the Government, political activity is no more than beating the air. Women of good sense are aware of this.' Education in democracy should not be given in English, even if it is then translated. It will not engage women. A body of women of outstanding ability should be engaged to teach, women of broad sympathies and with a wide experience of informal education. They should have a university education, or equivalent, and speak fluent German.

'There are many women of an older generation who would welcome the opportunity to take a lead in the reconstruction of their country but, like all the women we have met, they are set about with fears: fear of revision in de-Nazification, fear that their homes or furniture may be requisitioned, fear for the future of Germany, fear of inflation, and failure of all supplies.' And, they add ominously, there are two greater fears: the coming winter and the uncertain fate of prisoners of war and missing persons. 'Democracy works more slowly than a dictatorship, it cannot be established overnight. Success in our education demands great patience and proof that the system works.'

Lena was particularly interested in the *Landfrauenvereine,* the Organisation of Countrywomen, which she thought offered an opportunity for moving forward with the democratisation of German organisations. One problem was that young women had no experience of anything but the Nazi system, while the older women might well be set in their ways.

Lena identified three points of importance in the reconstruction of the *Vereine.* Under the old constitution, the membership had been restricted to farmers' wives only. It was difficult for individual members to participate in the group and Lena thought it would be healthier for membership to be extended to a much wider group of people. The groups should also be financially independent of government, as the WI had been since 1919, and the third change she thought necessary was to change the attitudes of the leaders. They should also have more fun at their meetings. She was perhaps thinking here of the parties where they had tried to eat jelly with a knife and fork, or seen how many biscuits someone could eat in a minute and remembered what Madge Watts, founder of the English and Welsh WI, had said about meetings: they should be 'fun but not frivolous'.

To show German women how the WI was run in England Lena organised a series of visits between the two countries. This was not easy because the women had to be able to speak English, which only applied to the better educated among them. It was also impossible to find English families who would accommodate women who had belonged to the Nazi Party, so possibilities were extremely limited. It was also very expensive and the government did not cover all the costs of a visit. Nevertheless some women did come and enjoyed their visit, though how much they learned is impossible to guess.

They were impressed with the standing of women in the home and how much husbands helped their wives with household tasks such as washing up.

Lena carried on working with the *Landfrauvereine* and revisited Germany in 1948. She found that women were working so hard on the farms that they were too tired to attend meetings. Lena suggested educating men to share the work more evenly, and importing labour-saving machines, thereby showing that the old unpractical Lena still lurked within the lieutenant colonel's uniform.

Inevitably, the lead in the *Landvereine* was taken by the middle classes, as indeed had been the case in the Women's Institute, though sometimes refugees from East Prussia and Silesia would seize the initiative, as they had more experience of such organisations.

Alongside her work with the *Landfrauvereine,* Lena continued to play a role in the National Federation of WIs and, with Lady Brunner, drafted the resolution promoting the idea of a national college dedicated to educating women of the Women's Institute. This idea came to fruition in March 1948, when Marcham Park, near Abingdon, was bought and became Denman College.

Marga died in 1969, and after that Lena was lonely. Towards the end of her life she moved to a nursing home and gently declined into dementia. She died in 1973, leaving a substantial amount of money, £76,025, the bulk of it going to LMH. Along with all her papers, the family collection of Mendelssohn manuscripts, drawings and memorabilia were left to the Bodleian Library, where some of them are now on display.

4

Eleanor Lodge (1869–1936) and Higher Education

Eleanor Lodge was the youngest of nine children, the only much-longed-for girl, who was so small and delicate as a baby that she was wrapped in cotton wool and was not expected to live. Her eldest brother Oliver, who was to go on to be a Professor of Physics at the newly established Liverpool University and a founder member of the Society for Psychical Research, admits that as a child he barely knew Eleanor, as he was eighteen and ready to leave home.

She had a very fragmented education and a life disrupted by tragedy. The two adults who were most important to her, and of whom she was not afraid, were her mother, who died when she was nine, and her nurse Thyrza, who was dismissed from her post when Eleanor was sent to the first of several unsatisfactory schools. 'I was not told till she had gone, and it would have been better to let me know and say goodbye to her. I minded so dreadfully that I could not bear ever to go to see her. To see her with other children was more than I could face. I cried my eyes out at school and I hated coming home'.

The casual cruelty of many Victorian parents and the complete non-recognition of their children's feelings are astonishing to us today, but we have the benefit of Freud's insight into the importance of childhood experiences, which was not available to the late Victorians. Determined to toughen up his daughter, her father would send her to entertainments and the circus on her own, where she was hopelessly scared and miserable, terrified of being the last one left in the building and being locked in. At the age of eight, she went on a nine-hour journey alone, involving three changes of trains and one of stations, was too shy to ask the guard about her trunk, which got left in the guard's van, and encountered a group of drunken fishermen on the train to Lincoln. She nevertheless arrived unscathed, though embarrassed that she had left her trunk behind. Obviously the Victorian protectiveness towards children was very far removed from today's attitudes.

Her education left much to be desired. At her uncle's school in Lincolnshire, 'There was a lot of learning by heart of poetry and French and German grammar, Kings and Queens of England, books of the Bible, names of the nine muses and so on', she says, though one wonders what the 'and so on' includes, given the long list of facts she had already committed to memory! Times tables, perhaps?

From there she proceeded to another school in Wolverhampton where they did sums every day but there was no explanation and it was only when she was at home in the holidays that her brother Charles explained the whys and wherefores of the numbers. The schoolchildren learned most things by rote from appallingly dull books and were questioned about them in class.

Some of the older girls bribed the younger ones with food to get them to copy out their work for them. Eleanor was happy to do that for an extra slice of bread at suppertime, though the bread was very dry – like chaff. Dry bread was supposed to be better for them than fresh, but yesterday's stale loaf would be cheaper than fresh, so it was the finances of the school that benefitted rather than the children.

There were two slices of bread for breakfast and at eleven, a plate of dry bread was handed round with water to drink. Dinner was predictable. Meat and a pudding, with the menu varying according to the day of the week. They were only allowed spoons to eat with, no forks being provided and when it was the day of the week for jam tarts the crusts, being very hard, shattered and flew in all directions. Tea was the same as breakfast with an occasional treat of bread and treacle, while supper was again two slices of bread, unless you had earned an extra slice from one of the big girls. They were sent to bed at eight o'clock and slept five or six to a room, with lights out at nine o'clock.

The worst part of the school, Eleanor reckoned, was not the food or the teaching but the stuffiness and lack of fresh air and exercise.

They were supposed to take a walk – an hour allotted for this which included putting on hats, shoes, coats, scarves – after which they proceeded on the dullest walk imaginable, in a crocodile with the supervisor at the back making sure nobody swung their arms! It was so abysmally boring that Eleanor often developed a cold, or some other expedient for staying at school.

In summer, they were confined to a play area with a small plot of grass. They were not allowed to play tennis, as this would make one shoulder higher than the other, but they could play croquet. A croquet mallet in the hands of a bored thirteen year old is not a good idea. Eleanor used it to hit another girl on the head.

Then her cousin Clara came to keep house for them, which improved life considerably. Clara dressed her properly in simple, good dresses instead of the strange creations that Thyrza had had made and Eleanor had, for the first time, the thrill of an Ulster, an outdoor coat with a cape, and gloves with two buttons. But then Clara left to prepare for her wedding to Eleanor's brother Frank, so Eleanor was at a loose end for twelve months while the family decided what to do with her and where she and her father should live.

It was a very productive year, academically speaking. She divided the day into six working hours and did six different topics in order: French, German, History, Geography, Arithmetic, and Music, this without any input from adults to advise her or to mark her work. She allotted half-an-hour a day for reading French and German and half-an-hour for translating from English, to correct which she translated back to English from the French or German.

Eleanor's father decided to move to Oxford, a sensible choice given that her brother Richard had now married and was a Fellow of Brasenose College. Eleanor was enrolled at the Girls' High School. Then her father died. This left the family wondering what on earth to do with Eleanor. She was taken out of the high school and sent to be educated, if that is the right term, by a Mrs Lovell, who took in several young ladies and employed a governess for them.

Eleanor's overall impression of the time she spent with Mrs Lovell was not a happy one. Mrs Lovell was extremely conservative in both politics and habits, had lived for many years in India, and as a consequence found Oxford cold and damp. The windows were never opened and there was little opportunity for exercise. Worst of all were holidays when she was passed around from one brother to another making her feel 'always in the way and absolutely useless'. The teaching at the school was so bad her brother Richard took it in hand. He set and marked examinations, and lent them books and Mrs Lovell made them copy down and learn by heart any text that Richard had underlined.

After two years with Mrs Lovell, Richard had arranged for Eleanor to take the entrance exam for Lady Margaret Hall and she lived with him and his wife while preparing for it. She admits that she took the preparation far too seriously and overworked. She also, for the first time, could take as much exercise as she wanted. Richard and his wife thought she did both to excess. They did their best to help – they took her to cricket matches, which she found seriously boring, they invited students from Brasenose to dinner, presumably so she could meet a suitable husband or at the very least have some fun. She sat mute through all the meals and social events and says that she must have been difficult to deal with.

She passed the entrance exam easily, but then had a breakdown. She was depressed – hardly surprising when one considers the kind of childhood she had experienced. Though she probably did not know the word, she was obviously suffering from anorexia. Her brother Oliver records that at one point in her life, and this must surely have been that point, she was five feet eight inches tall yet weighed only five stone, eight pounds.

The nursing home where she went was not unpleasant. She was allowed to read as much as she liked, providing she ate. Following her stay at the nursing home, she went with one of her many cousins, Sissy, to a convalescent home in Brighton to take the waters, where Sissy, who was excellent company, kept an eye on how much she ate and made sure she was enjoying herself. Whether it was the water, Sissy's company or the fresh air and exercise, Eleanor recovered her health, though, as her brother Oliver remarked, she never felt tired even when at her worst, and could walk or cycle many more miles than he could.

Then she went to Liverpool to look after the first six of Oliver's children. Another six would follow. She loved Oliver and his wife Mary and would have liked to stay with them, caring for and educating their children, but she was working too hard and was advised it was not a good idea to work for a family member so decided in 1890,to move on to Lady Margaret Hall. Her connection with LMH was 'the opening of a new world to me and the beginning of much happiness'.

Lady Margaret Hall

'I can never think of a university education as just a means to an end', Eleanor writes. 'I feel it is an opportunity and an inspiration which is of incalculable value.' She was to spend the rest of her life making that opportunity available to as many young women as she could.

> The very fact of having a room of one's own, a place where one not only could work but were expected to work, the possibility of independence, of arranging one's time for oneself, of getting up and going to bed according to one's own ideas and not those of others, made each day an adventure and a joy.

She had finally found a home, a place where she could be herself. Every day began and ended with a chapel service. There was an abundance of coal so the rooms could be adequately heated, though there was no electric light and each student had to provide herself with an oil-lamp. Morning chapel was compulsory every day except for Sunday morning, when it was optional, but students were not allowed out of college on a Sunday evening when Miss Wordsworth, the principal, gave an address.

The chaperone rules were strict, though beginning to be less so than previously. No college room could be visited by a man, even a brother, unless you were accompanied by a don or 'a relative of a suitable age'. Expeditions to watch the university boat races were chaperoned, as was May morning when Magdalen College choir sang at dawn from the college tower. Many of the men's colleges had now opened their lectures to women, though at Balliol the women had to access the lecture hall via a private staircase. No one was allowed to attend a tutorial with a male tutor alone but soon that was to go by the board. Today this seems the only part of Victorian chaperoning that is sensible, though Eleanor obviously found it as silly and irksome as the rest of the rules.

There was no tutorial system within the women's colleges. All the administrative work was done through a central body, the Association for the Education of Women (AEW). Everyone beginning her Honours work was put in the charge of a tutor from one of the men's colleges. The secretary of the AEW arranged the academic itinerary for each girl, paid the fees, and collected progress reports of the individual students. Gradually tutors were appointed to individual women's halls. At first, there was only one tutor for all the women's halls – then Somerville appointed a History tutor of its own, then a Classics tutor, and gradually the number increased.

Social life was somewhat limited, though that did not disturb Eleanor very much as she preferred to work. No dances were allowed during term time but during eights week, held over four days in May, when the colleges competed in rowing, there were college concerts. One event that gave Eleanor 'passionate joy' was the Christmas play written by Miss Wordsworth, with titles such as 'The Apple of Discord', a skit on university life, and given by the students. A couple of performances were given in Oxford, after which the actors decamped to London and travelled round the various university settlements. What the audiences made of the in-jokes and university references is anybody's guess, but the students enjoyed themselves enormously.

As well as theatricals, the girls were allowed to play hockey – for which they wore skirts that were no more than six inches above the ground. Miss Wordsworth went down on hands and knees and measured them. The next new craze was bicycling. They were allowed to bicycle providing they did not ride over Magdalen Bridge. Boating was one sport Eleanor was very good at, and she was very quickly made boat captain. Boating was a curious hybrid between punting and canoeing. The boat was a punt with one girl sitting on the platform while the rest, either sitting or kneeling, used oars to paddle the boat along. Speed cannot possibly have been of the essence!

She introduced another form of amusement – long walks with sandwiches. Considering she could out walk her brother Oliver, I imagine she must have been out ahead of everyone else from the beginning of the walks. Wherever they ended up, they were supposed to go to church, since Miss Wordsworth thought a day of unmixed pleasure was not a good thing.

Eleanor was expected to get a First but, in the event, obtained only a second class degree, which did not disappoint her as she had expected no better. She was very sad to be leaving LMH but had decided to become a nurse and would start training as soon as she was old enough.

The secretary of the AEW sent her some pupils so she began to teach history, which she enjoyed very much. LMH was growing, with extra accommodation being built for the greater number of pupils, and Miss Wordsworth approached Eleanor with a view to her helping with the extra students. It was not an advertised post and Eleanor felt that it was offered to her purely because she was on the spot. She was asked to take over responsibility for the library and to do any teaching that was needed so, in 1895, she was delighted to be able to return to LMH as a staff member. She was to remain there until 1921.

While there she took a year's sabbatical to study at the Sorbonne in Paris and settled on studying the condition of the peasants in Gascony during the Hundred Years' War, not exactly a mainstream interest. Just as she was finishing the work, a message came from Richard, summoning her to Glasgow because of a family crisis, so she finished the thesis by working fourteen hours a day for the last two weeks of her stay in Paris. 'I never enjoyed writing anything more,' she says, 'beginning at five in the morning and dashing out at intervals for coffee, fresh air and exercise'.

On her return from Paris, she was officially employed as History Tutor and supervised all the women history students and in 1906 was made vice-principal of LMH, again, one supposes, without an interview. She was put on the council of LMH to represent the staff and sat on the council of the AEW and later on the Delegacy for Women Students, a University body presided over by the vice-chancellor, to which members of the women's societies were elected. This proved to be a stepping stone to the full admission of women to the University, as the men, from the vice-chancellor downwards, realised that they could work with women who were as clever, knowledgeable and clear thinking as they. During the war, there was a distinct shortage of academic men in the colleges so flexibility was forced upon this most conservative of institutions. Because of this, Eleanor was asked to lecture, a task she had never done before, so became the first woman to deliver a lecture at the University. She was president of the Tutorial Body in 1918 when the University carried the decree conferring membership on women.

There is no account in all her writings of her involvement with the suffrage movement because she wanted her autobiography to show how important higher education had been to her and could be to other women. Her wartime experiences are similarly omitted. She had an adventurous time, however, both as a suffragist and aiding the war effort funded by the suffrage movement.

She is listed on the committee of the Oxford Women Students' Suffrage Society (OWSSS) along with Helena Deneke and Grace Hadow, and was on the platform at Oxford Town Hall on 19 March 1912 when the suffrage meeting was addressed by Lord Haldane. She also walked from Oxford to London on the Suffrage Pilgrimage in 1913, when she and Grace Hadow carried the OWSSS banner.

Eleanor spent many holidays doing research on the history of Gascony, so became conversant with Paris, Boulogne and the Basque country, all of which she explored on her trusty bicycle. The long vacations during the First World War were taken up with other events, however.

War Work

When war was declared on 3 August 1914 Eleanor was in hospital in London recuperating from an operation and 'it was a terrible feeling to lie helplessly and listen night after night to the tramp of men marching off to military camps'. On her return to Oxford she found the colleges filling up with cadets while every able-bodied young man had left the city. Academic dress – the ubiquitous cap and gown – had disappeared, to be replaced with khaki.

Somerville became a hospital with its students dispersed to Oriel College or into digs in the city while the idea of LMH being used as a hospital for shell-shocked soldiers was soon abandoned because of the parade ground noises – barked commands and bugles – issuing from the adjacent university parks. LMH had decided to stay open rather than devote itself to war work though both staff and students were given permission to take as much time off as they might need to support the war.

After returning to LMH after her operation, she really struggled to keep going until Christmas, when she was urged to go abroad to recuperate fully. Oliver gave her £50 and she set off for the south of France, finally ending up in Cannes, then nearby La Napoule, but the war intruded even this far south as trains of wounded men came through La Napoule on their way to hospitals in Cannes, their gaunt faces and bandaged heads visible through the train windows. She returned via Avignon, where the papal palace had been turned into barracks.

On her return she found that her companion, Janet Spens, editor of her autobiography, was still recovering from illness. Together, however, they managed to put some time in helping Belgian refugees. Mountains of clothing donated to the refugees needed sorting and distributing. Eleanor and Janet found the work quite distasteful at times. They were shocked that people could actually donate dirty linen and clothes which were too battered and threadbare to be of use to anyone. In spite of this, they turned up regularly twice a week to deal with the needs of the refugees. Eleanor would 'haunt the cheap shops in town for bargains of all sorts' to make the most of the money they had been allotted. They were not only entangled in linen, clean or otherwise; they also dealt with placing people in suitable accommodation and Eleanor even attempted to learn Flemish, though soon gave it up as a bad job.

One undertaking she really did enjoy, though it is questionable how useful it was to the Belgians, was a summer camp organised by her in the summer of 1915. It aimed to teach English women to live in primitive conditions so when the war was over, they could move to Belgium and help rebuild the country. Eleanor was asked to organise it and 'with the courage of ignorance I consented'.

They chose a site in the Cotswolds, near Broadway, where they assembled tents; made arrangements for food to be brought in; found teachers who could teach camp cooking, first aid and camp construction; and organised local farmers to demonstrate how to dig latrines. The camp was run on military lines with a strict timetable, which had to be adhered to and with two people detailed to be on watch all night. Eleanor had a lovely time, as possibly did the other forty or so women who had volunteered. Though the experience was not directly useful to the Belgians, it was probably of use to women who went out to do war work on the Eastern and Western Fronts.

The next summer Eleanor arranged for groups of students and staff to help on the land. Mr Brocklehurst of Sudeley Castle was one of the first people to employ women on the land and took four extra workers for July, August and September, one of them being Eleanor's colleague Helena Deneke. As already noted, they were each paid 14 shillings a week and were supplied with a cottage, free coal and milk. Butter in limited amounts was available for a shilling a pound, and there were free vegetables from the garden. Their cottage was attached to that occupied by the shepherd and his wife. Their children were very useful as they did the women's shopping on their way back from school and helped with picking up wood for the fire. There was also one small boy who took it upon himself to protect the Oxford women from the bull. Armed with a stick he would march past the bull and keep it in order while the women scuttled along at his side.

The first week they spent cutting thistles and pulling up docks. Having had a good breakfast of porridge cooked in a hay box, they were surprised to be told to stop work at nine-thirty so that the labourers, – men and women alike – who had not had breakfast, could have lunch – bread and cheese or bacon and home brewed ale. After the first day the Oxford women took along biscuits and cold tea for a lunch break. They were disappointed not to get a half-day holiday on the Saturday and found that there is no such thing as a half-day holiday in farming, especially at haymaking and harvest time. The women on the estate started work at eight in the morning and were allowed time off on brewing and washing days. The Oxford women enjoyed the haymaking but hated the hoeing, which gave them a crick in the back.

Eleanor spent the summer of 1917 caring for Janet Spens, who was at that time of her life quite poorly. But in the last year of the war, Eleanor took the summer term off work to go to France, not as a holiday but working for the war effort.

Early on in the war, Madge Skipworth, tutor in French at LMH, had spent some time in the north of France, near Bar-le-Duc, and was appalled at the lack of provision for the French soldiers travelling to and from the front. Sometimes they were so tired they just lay down in the road to sleep and there was no possibility of finding refreshments. When she came back to England, she set up a fund to remedy the situation, tapping into the network of women who had worked for the suffrage movement and aiming to raise enough money to set up a *cantine anglaise*. The OWSSS passed a resolution to send out two workers as soon as possible to work in canteens for French soldiers and decided that £100 should be set aside for that purpose. The French Red Cross was contacted and their offer of help was accepted.

Lorna Neill, just out of boarding school and writing back to her mother in England, gives a vivid picture of one such *cantine anglaise*. She worked in the *cantine* at Revigny, south of Verdun. The lights from the long wooden barraquement lit up one corner of the square and shone on three big notices showing in white letters the words '*Cantine Anglaise*' '*Café gratuit*' '*Bouillon gratuit*'. Lorna wrote to her mother: '10,000 men pass through the entrance before the windows every twenty-four hours' and said that in February they gave out 250,000 cups of coffee, 15,000 cups of tea, 15,000 cups of chocolate, 22,000 cups of soup; 302,000 cups in total. They also gave out 63,000 cigarettes, 3,500 presents, 600 loaves and 310 tins of beef.

In the spring of 1916, the French Red Cross responded to the suffrage movement's offer of help and asked OWSSWS to take responsibility for a canteen at Dormans, a small village with a large railway junction between Chalons and Epernay. The OWSSWS, of course, agreed to this and sent Miss Wilson, the organiser of the canteen at Bar-le-Duc. The new canteen was opened in August. It had a covered foyer outside the building and could sleep 500 men while 2,000 men were being fed every day. The walls of the canteen were whitewashed, with red and white checked curtains at the windows, and a dresser holding a collection of French pottery, and they soon acquired a pig called Jeanette to eat up the scraps. In the kitchen, open from 7.30 a.m. till midnight, there was one cook and three orderlies, who cooked and served regular hot meals twice a day, as well as eggs, cheese, coffee, chocolate, beer, cider and other light refreshments, which were available the whole time. It was a serious undertaking and the men were delighted at the cheapness of the food. They played cards and draughts and liked to practise their English.

In April 1918, Eleanor went out to inspect and consider extending the work. The boat she travelled on from Southampton to Le Havre plotted a zigzag course to avoid German submarines so took longer than in peacetime. Having landed safely in Le Havre, she made her way to Paris and then on to Dormans on the Marne.

The canteen was functioning so well that Eleanor decided to open another canteen at Pargny les Reims. The general in charge in that area, General Gouraud, agreed and she was driven to Pargny in the general's car. On the way, she saw a strange sight. She saw what seemed like a brown serpent curling along one side of the road and a blue one on the other. The brown snake was the line of British soldiers, in khaki, winding their way towards the Front, while the blue one was the French, with all their possessions, coming in the opposite direction. When she asked for an explanation, she was told the British soldiers were being sent up to rest on what was thought to be a quiet sector after the horrors of the Somme. When asked if they would be glad of a rest, they shrugged their shoulders. 'The Bosch won't leave us quiet for long,' they prophesied.

Eleanor returned to Dormans and began planning for the new canteen but as they sat at supper, they saw an unusual sight at the station. Small trains with the usual open carriages seemed to be coming along the line looking unusually black and presently there emerged from the trains a black line, which was making its way from the station towards their camp. They realised with sinking hearts that these were refugees, women and children mostly, carrying what they could salvage from their homes. The Germans were advancing, having gassed and shelled the town of Fimes. The soldiers in the camp moved out of their beds to make way for the refugees so they could rest before leaving by train for Paris.

The next day, Eleanor toured the town to discover that most of the refugees had got away. She commandeered two orderlies and a wheelbarrow and collected as much pâté and meat as she could. The cook did not turn up for duty so the orderlies did the cooking while Eleanor and an aide, Miss Goddard, made vast quantities of coffee, chocolate and *bouillon*. Their customers were mostly British soldiers, wounded and dropping with fatigue, part of the brown snake she had seen earlier. They could offer no resistance to the Germans. Their officers were lost, they had no ammunition. They were just retreating apparently without order or hope. The hospital was full to overflowing but the patients got away on the last train before the line was destroyed. Eleanor would have liked to telegraph home to say she was fit and well, but the telegraph lines were down so communication was impossible.

The lack of food meant that the canteen would have to close, so Eleanor went to the general to tell him so. He obviously had no idea what to do, so Eleanor returned to the canteen and they continued to serve what little they had until the evening. They emerged from the canteen to find the town deserted. At their lodging the house door was open, bedrooms got ready as usual, nightgowns and slippers laid out on the bed and a saucer of milk for the cat. But no landlady. Like everyone else in the town she had disappeared. The general had been instructed to evacuate the town but had forgotten to tell the English women.

At this point an RAMC unit turned up and commandeered the canteen, so the British soldiers could start cooking the beef they had brought with them. The Colonel took Eleanor on one side and confided that the Germans were getting very near and that they might have to move at any moment.

Eleanor and Miss Goddard lay down, fully dressed, in the canteen to try to get some sleep. 'The night was the noisiest I have ever spent', Eleanor wrote. There was the roar of artillery and occasional bombs. At 2.30 a.m. a message came from the Colonel to be ready to start in half-an-hour. They collected as many personal possessions as they could carry and left the town with the Colonel in his ambulance. There were six other cars plus men and baggage travelling with them as they retreated to Montmirail. 'The road was full of troops travelling forward for the defence of the Marne and a continuous stream of refugees in the other direction with their cows, mules, wheelbarrows and what little bits of furniture they had managed to salvage, some with carts but many on foot, all just going to no known destination but simply away from the on-rushing enemy,' she wrote.

They felt they must get to Paris to consult with the *Croix Rouge* so managed to board a train overflowing with refugees going to Esternay. The town was full of soldiers who pooled their rations and cooked a banquet for the refugees. 'They fed us at midnight on the village green at tables lighted up with candles flaring in the wind with soup, meat and beans and cheese and coffee, waiting on us hand and foot and with no thought of gain or payment,' Eleanor said.

In Paris there was a shortage of nurses since nurses who had gone on leave to England had been forbidden from returning to France. The following morning Eleanor and Miss Goddard found themselves at the Hotel Astoria, which had been turned into a hospital chiefly for French soldiers.

Paris was a strange place for anyone who had known it before the war, as she had. The streets were deserted, except for American servicemen practicing their baseball skills in the Champs Elysees while all the well-known monuments were covered in sandbags. There was the constant thump of the German heavy artillery gun known as Big Bertha, which had smashed its way into the history of the war by flattening forts at Liege, Namur and Antwerp.

The little contingent of English women wondered if they would ever get home. One of their number, Mrs Bailey, was learning to drive and offered to drive them out of Paris but her recklessness behind the wheel was almost unbelievable and they felt they would be safer staying within earshot of Big Bertha. Meanwhile Miss Stout, a Shetland girl who had been sent out to join the canteen but had never got there and was part of the nursing group, made excellent marmalade by mixing it in her washbasin and cooking it up on a gas stove, though we are not told where she acquired the oranges and it must have been quite sour, as sugar was rationed, as was bread.

Eleanor worked at the Hotel Astoria till it was time to go back for the October term. She confesses that she was humbled by the experience. She found it a great strain, seeing such terrible injuries and not being such a good nurse as she would have liked to be. She never got used to the suffering. Eleanor stayed in Paris three months.

Peacetime

On her return from nursing, she found herself in an Oxford overwhelmed by the virulent influenza that was to kill more worldwide than even the slaughter of the war years. At first Miss Jex-Blake, an excellent nurse, took care of the first students to succumb. One died but the rest, though seriously ill for some time, survived. In Old Hall, the original building, all twenty-eight students fell ill as well as the maids, all of them nursed by Janet Spens and Eleanor and as they were getting better, Janet herself fell ill. Eleanor began the rounds at five a.m., taking temperatures and washing people, ready to pass on the list to Miss Jex-Blake. Together she and Janet made the beds and Janet brushed everyone's hair, quite a task as everyone still had long hair. Food had to be carried across from the dining room and there was no possibility of leaving the college, so four of the students who had escaped infection were detailed to do any shopping that was needed.

As the infection waned and invalids were dispatched to the country to fully recuperate, normal life was resumed. Students would come back from lectures expressing surprise that there had been more men than women present. Numbers in the history faculty soared and various societies for both men and women were started. These societies now held meetings at men's and women's colleges in turn. In 1918, the university voted to accept women into full membership and women who would be presented for their degrees were trained in curtsying by Miss Jex-Blake. Queen Mary was awarded an honorary degree and visited the women's colleges, which was not only an excitement for the individual colleges but also a marker showing the Establishment's approval of higher education for women.

In the summer term of 1921, Miss Jex-Blake decided to retire, and Eleanor very much wanted to follow in her footsteps as principal so she applied for the post, feeling that she would probably not be given the job. Realising that if she were unsuccessful she would be working under another principal with all the difficulties that might entail, she applied for the post of assistant lecturer in history at Westfield College in Hampstead. It was a small post but the salary was not much less than she had been earning. The principal wrote back to say that she was looking for someone to take her place, as she was being pressed to take the post of principal of Girton College, in Cambridge, and that if Eleanor really wanted to leave LMH, she would be delighted to discuss her appointment as principal of Westfield.

Westfield College

The way people were appointed to important positions in the early twentieth century is quite astonishing today, but we have to remember that the world of university women was very, very small. The numbers attending women's colleges at the turn of the century stood in the hundreds and if anyone had done a substantial amount of work, either administrative or academic, it would have been noticed.

It is no surprise then that Eleanor Lodge, having made enquiries about an assistant lecturer's post in history should have walked into a job as the woman running the college. She was well known for her academic work, her high-achieving academic family and her energy. She did, however, have an interview, which came in the middle of LMH's scholarship week so Eleanor was so busy she had no time to prepare for it. She managed to buy a new hat for the occasion but had no respectable clothes to go with it and no time to acquire any. Janet Spens dashed out and bought her a coat, which would hide the shabbiness beneath, and she departed for London. There she caught sight in a shop window of a horrible scrawny neck, realised it was hers, and dashed into a shop to buy a fluffy scarf to cover it up. She must have made a good impression, scrawny neck or no, because she was asked to come for a further interview. In the meanwhile, she dropped a heavy fender on her foot, so attended the second interview with one foot clad in a size eight velvet boot. Notwithstanding the boot, they offered her the job, which she accepted. They were lucky to get her, and no doubt knew it.

Westfield College had begun life in 1882 as an Evangelical Christian establishment funded by an American woman, Miss Dudin-Smith, to the tune of £10,000. This had enabled an organising committee to set up the college, under the leadership of Miss Constance Maynard, an alumna of Girton College, Cambridge, who had teaching experience gained at Cheltenham Ladies College. The college began with six students and by this time, the aims of the establishment had changed slightly. Miss Maynard intended that young women should be prepared for the London degree according to Christian principles, the emphasis on evangelical Christianity having been somewhat muted.

Miss Dudin-Smith's money had enabled the acquisition of two houses in Hampstead, which were duly knocked into one. As knowledge of the college spread, more students were taken on and Miss Dudin-Smith's money was no longer adequate. Grants were available from the London County Council, but they were dependent on the college being un-denominational, so the strict Church of England bias of the college had to be abandoned.

By 1919, the college had become a full member of the University of London and its finances were on a sound footing. When Eleanor assumed her duties in 1921, she found an establishment of about a hundred students, most of them living in the college. This was an unusually small college for the University of London, but about the same size as LMH, and was different from the majority of London colleges in being residential. Lectures were given in the morning, with the afternoons free for games or walks, and work resumed after tea until dinner, and after dinner till cocoa at bedtime. The main teaching took place in the college with no inter-collegiate lectures, as had happened in Oxford. Again this was different from other London colleges, which were geared to students who mainly lived at home or in digs, so had lectures in the afternoons and had the evenings free so they could get home.

Miss Maynard paid a visit to the College in the December after Eleanor had taken over. It was not a happy visit, though Miss Maynard does not seem to have been a very happy person, preoccupied as she was with her religious life and the approach of death. (She was now in her early seventies). She was upset to find that her divinity lectures had been given to other people and that Eleanor did not keep control of the content of the lectures. 'All protection has vanished and students are allowed to know everything, even the very blackest, and take their choice,' she wails. 'No man cares for their individual souls.'

She was astonished that there appeared to be no social distance between Eleanor and the students. Why, Eleanor actually played in the students' hockey team looking no older than them. And the students were asked for their opinions! Miss Maynard concluded that Eleanor was afraid of her students, as were other members of the staff, though she found Eleanor courteous and gentle. The visit made her wonder if she had completely wasted her life at Westfield trying to instil values that had been tossed overboard without a second thought. Eleanor calls the time she spent at Westfield the happiest time of her life, so we must assume that Miss Maynard's assessment was wrong.

There is no doubt that Eleanor brought a breath of academic fresh air into the stuffiness and old-fashioned ways of Westfield. To prevent the college from becoming too inward-looking, lecturers were brought in from the outside world, often, it has to be said, Eleanor's relations, Sir Oliver and Sir Richard Lodge; Professor Paul Vinogradov, the Russian-born historian, unknown now but revered at the time for his work on the peasantry in medieval England; Lawrence Housman, who came twice to lecture on poetry. Mrs Fawcett chaired a meeting where the speaker was Eleanor Moore of LMH who spoke about Jerusalem High School. Divinity lectures, a regular feature of the curriculum, which had been given by Miss Maynard herself, Eleanor delegated to anyone she thought suitable. One year it was Maude Royden, who would surely not have met with Miss Maynard's approval.

The drama group was very active, giving a spirited performance of *Pygmalion*, which upset some of the audience because of the swearing. The heroine, Eliza Doolittle, says 'Not bloody likely', when asked if she is going to walk across the park. At its first performance it was thought by many people to be so risky for the actress concerned, Mrs Campbell, that it might damage her career.

Sport was an important part of college life, as one might imagine. Tennis, swimming in the Finchley Road baths, hockey and lacrosse and also boating in Regent's Park. In the inter-college competitions Westfield College performed very creditably, with Eleanor noting in the log book when they did particularly well against rivals such as Bedford College or Holloway. The college facilities were made available to outside groups too, such as the Girls' Realm Guild, the Church Army Girls and the Federation of University Women, showcasing the college to women who might speak well of it.

In 1924 there was a mock election where the Conservative Party was the winner. Unsurprising, therefore, that two years later, when the General Strike paralysed the country, many students opted to help the country in its hour of need, though the striking men would have interpreted their actions rather differently. The students' exams were postponed until that September because they had lost so much time by helping break the strike, though Eleanor pleaded with the University establishment to move the exams forward to July, so students would be less distracted, without the summer break to divert their attention away from academic studies.

Probably one of the most important things Eleanor had to do in her time at Westfield was to give evidence to a Royal Commission, which was considering the constitution of the University of London. If previous reports had been followed, Westfield would have been reduced to the position of a non-university college, preparing students for external degrees. In 1925 Eleanor and the head of governors, Sir Thomas Inskip, were interviewed about the college and its characteristics. Westfield's academic achievements were a crucial factor in persuading the Commission that a residential college such as Westfield had an important part to play in the University of London, and it became one of the eight colleges to form the central part of the university. This gave it the right to be represented on the Senate and Collegiate Council, which decided the way the university was to be run.

As head of the college, Eleanor, along with Miss Gedge, the very reliable finance officer, were often interviewed by the University Grants Committee and by the Court, which controlled the finances of the university, and by the Education Committee of the LCC. Eleanor never had any qualms about these situations since she had great faith in Miss Gedge's control of the money. Between them, they showed that the money from the various grants was being well spent and well accounted for. As a consequence, they were able to gain extra grants for the library, to improve staff salaries, and to take on extra staff where needed.

Eleanor found there was more sharing of work between men and women teachers in London than in Oxford and the opportunities for research were easily to hand in the British Museum and the Record Office, but the quality of students was perhaps not so high as at Oxford. Eleanor was introduced to the History Board of the University, where men and women history scholars could meet and it was cheering, she said, to see with what complete equality men and women worked together. Membership of this Board meant that she was involved on other committees, all of which she took up with enthusiasm. She believed that the higher profile a woman could maintain, the better it would help the cause of women's emancipation.

She was president of the Association of Women Teachers – a trade union founded in 1909, and also of the Students' Career Association, both, as she points out, 'very useful from the point of view of women students'. She also became president of the London branch of the British Federation of University Women.

'All these committees and societies did take up a good deal of time,' she admits, 'but I think they were worthwhile: they made the college better known and I generally found that going to prize-givings brought us students, and some very good students too.' What pleased Eleanor enormously and what she worked very hard to achieve was an increase in the numbers of women who proceeded to higher degrees, so the college went on to have what she calls 'a respectable number who have taken MA, MSc and PhD degrees, either through Westfield itself or through other institutions.'

The most important social event while Eleanor was head of the college was a visit by Queen Mary, which made everyone very nervous, especially as it was very cold and wet, and the sleet and snow made some of the surfaces slippery. Undaunted, the queen visited every bit of the college, chatted to everyone and seemed reluctant to leave. As she left, the whole college heaved a collective sigh of relief that the visit had gone so smoothly.

Not only did Eleanor participate in much of university life, she also took a very active role in the affairs of Hampstead Borough

Council, of which she was a member and through which she became chair of the public library committee, and was involved with the building of a museum in the garden of the poet John Keats' house.

Eleanor returned to LMH for its Jubilee in 1927. Elizabeth Wordsworth, the founder of the college, had been made a dame – though she said she was too old to go to Buckingham Palace to receive the insignia. The Duchess of York came to lunch, therefore, and brought Dame Elizabeth's insignia with her. There was a dinner for 600 students, ex-students and university staff, which included three of Eleanor's brothers. Eleanor herself received a D.Litt from the University of Oxford in 1928, thus was entitled to wear a splendid red gown so she could at least vie with, if not outshine, many of her staff.

In the final chapter of her autobiography, Eleanor Lodge lays out her feelings about a university education. She says: 'I hold that a university education is an inestimable benefit, whatever may be the walk of life to which a student turns later. I think it makes them better nurses, better shopwomen, better secretaries, better teachers, better wives'.

Her list of jobs women were likely to take up is illuminating. They are all service work. Support roles, they might be called, which shows how limited her own experience of work was and how limited was likely to be the careers on offer for girls who attended Westfield College.

She goes on to say, 'I have no sympathy with those who think University work is only for "high-brows" (whatever that may be) and that it prevents women from being charming or practical.' She warns however about lowering standards of entry into higher education. 'Leniency in the entrance examination is very cruel kindness'. And university training should not just be a means to earn a better living. 'It will do far more by its effect on her mind than by the actual detailed knowledge which it has helped her acquire.'

She sees diversity as being a key element of student life: a mixture of the social classes, with rich and poor meeting and making friends across the class divide; a juxtaposition of different disciplines so students of the various disciplines could benefit from each others' expertise; and a mixture of mature and young teachers and students so different age groups could contribute their different experiences.

Eleanor Lodge retired from her post at Westfield in 1932 to live with Janet Spens in a house only a stone's throw from LMH. She was made Commander of the British Empire in that year, and died of cancer four years later, still learning to the end, studying Spanish as she lay in bed and planning for a future that was not to be. Her autobiography, as Janet Spens has pointed out, was not so much the story of her life but about what she thought university education might do and ought to do for women. 'She was very anxious that it should be published, regarding it as a duty to express her gratitude for all that it had meant for her'.

Westfield College eventually became part of Queen Mary University in the East End of London, a far cry from the heights of Hampstead. Eleanor Lodge would be astonished that there are six Nobel prizewinners who have gained their education at the university, but disappointed, no doubt, that none of them are women, though the fact that one of the vice-principals is a woman would assuredly have delighted her.

5

Maude Royden (1876–1956) and the Anglican Church

Born in Liverpool in 1876, Maude Royden was the youngest of eight children of a shipbuilding father, Sir William Royden. She was one of his five daughters and, having inherited her father's brains and charm, was closer to her father than her mother. She thought her mother 'ignorant' but understood why and wrote to her very good friend, Kathleen Courtney, 'It's not fair, is it, to keep women boxed up, and then complain they are foolish.' She also felt sorry for her mother, who had borne eight children in ten years. 'Our mother was exhausted,' she commented.

It may have been this exhaustion that prevented the family realising that Maude – a name she hated – had two dislocated hips, which were not diagnosed until she started to walk. Understandably, as a child she cried a lot because of the pain. X-rays had not yet been invented so eventually her parents took her to a bonesetter, who 'broke down some lesions', which made walking easier and pain-free, though she was lame for the rest of her life.

Very early on she rejected the idea put forward by her parents that her lameness was sent from God, but it did give her a feeling for the underdog, and she knew the frustration of being unable to keep up with her older brothers and sisters. In later life, also, it may have made her less threatening when she visited the poor, whose company she enjoyed and who seemed to like her enormously.

She had a good relationship with her brothers but pointed out: 'Every boy who grows up thinking that his sisters are of less importance than himself is put into the position of one who has a right to exploit them'.

Maude chose to go to school. The school she decided on was Cheltenham Ladies College, which cost as much as one of the boys' public schools, though she did not realise it at the time. When she arrived there in 1893 she found six hundred other girls, all following Miss Beale's ethos of combining rigorous educational standards with high religious and social ideals. She came out near the top of the Cambridge Higher Local exams and went as a history student to Lady Margaret Hall (LMH), Oxford.

The principal of LMH at that time was still the founder, Dame Elizabeth Wordsworth. She was a formidable woman who never really took to Maude. She perhaps distrusted her immoderate enthusiasms and found her family background of manufacturing and Unitarianism, which fostered independence of spirit, less congenial than a safe, quiet academic or Church of England upbringing. Maude, in her turn, found LMH very small. Compared with Cheltenham, there was only a handful of girls, who were carefully chaperoned wherever they went. Maude could never really forgive Dame Elizabeth for her lack of interest in the cause of women's equality. She thought she was not suited to the job.

The ruling passion in the 1890s at LMH was hockey, which of course Maude could not join in. The one thing she loved was having her very own, private room. The other great advantage was the friends she made. Her particular friends were Evelyn Gunter and Kathleen Courtney. They talked about everything under the sun, except one subject – sex. Kathleen Courtney wrote: 'We made great and lasting friendships but they were not lesbian. (Of course *we* did not know the word in those days)'. As Sheila Fletcher, Maude Royden's biographer has pointed out, Maude's generation was the last of the pre-Freudians. They may not have been lesbian but they were exceedingly romantic and used endearments and emotional language in their letters to each other that we would find strange today and which is easily misinterpreted.

Maude had become a devout Anglican in Cheltenham. She came to equate God with beauty and loved the whole experience of a church service – the incense, the lights, the music – and in Oxford attended the very high church of St John the Evangelist. In 1899 the use of incense was forbidden in the Church of England, which was trying to distance itself from the Roman Catholic Church, and this move away to a simpler form was to pose something of a problem for Maude in later life because she enjoyed the ritual and appeal to the senses of a High Church service.

Maude joined the Oxford Students' Debating Society, the women's equivalent to the men's Oxford Debating Society, and when she spoke in 1898 her hands shook so much she could hardly hold the paper her speech was written on. She and Kathleen revived 'sharp practice' at LMH where the main speaker had five minutes to speak to a motion, after which the meeting was opened to everyone else in the room, only the most determined and loudest voices among them being heard. It stood them both in good stead in later years when they were campaigning for women's suffrage.

The students divided themselves into two groups, those who needed to earn their living when they left college, and those who did not – the 'Home Sunbeams'. Evelyn belonged to the first group and obtained a post on the Oxford University Extension Delegacy, which ran classes for people out in the community, thus reaching many working-class men throughout the country. Having gained only a second class award, Maude felt there was no place for her in Oxford and reluctantly decided to go home. Her mother suffered from depression and needed her there. Kathleen, also with a second, intended to work at the LMH Settlement in London.

The Settlement Movement had been started by Canon Barnett, who opened Toynbee Hall in the East End in 1884 so that privileged people could live among the poor and befriend them. His wife Henrietta was an heiress and keen on social reform, though she and Octavia Hill, pioneer of social housing, with whom she had worked, both thought that giving out money and goods to the poor was counterproductive, breeding dependence instead of self-reliance.

Spending time at a settlement was very popular with Oxford men graduates, who tried to bring cultural activities to their neighbours. They provided evening lectures on art, literature and music, but the women's settlements that followed soon after were geared more to practical philanthropy, such as put into practice by Octavia Hill. LMH had started its own settlement in Lambeth in 1897, and Maude did consider working there with Kathleen but decided against it because of her mother's health.

Having moved back home and now in danger of becoming a 'Home Sunbeam', Maude was very pleased to discover there was a settlement in Liverpool, the Victoria Settlement, which Eleanor

Rathbone was also to become involved with. Maude joined it and started working there on a Monday morning, collecting money for the Provident Fund, in which people could save for any emergency that might occur. In the afternoon, she visited people in the workhouse infirmary.

She rather disliked her fellow workers, who 'play chess badly, crack foolish jokes and eat apples with steel knives' but showed remarkable empathy with the poor women she visited and was amazed at their lack of resentment of her visits. The area she visited was very poor, with a mixture of Protestant and Catholic Irish. The police warned her stabbings were not uncommon. Her great difficulty was that she could not distinguish between deserving and undeserving poor. She was surprised at the wit and resilience of the people she visited and found herself laughing a lot. 'If I were living in those conditions, I'd very likely take to drink,' she said. She was full of admiration for their stoicism. The work at the settlement showed her the many problems that confronted the poor of Liverpool – housing, the migration from country to town, and most important, to her way of thinking, the position of women. The settlement, however, was badly run with staff having little idea of how to help the poor and never staying very long.

Maude was also struggling with the problem of whether or not to convert to Catholicism. She missed very much the ritual of high church services so when she was visiting Evelyn in Oxford, Evelyn suggested she might like to discuss the matter with George William Hudson Shaw, known as Hudson, a short, stocky man with a pronounced Northern accent who had a reputation as a charismatic and spiritual churchman with the flexibility of thinking that might help Maude come to a decision. Seventeen years older than her, she nevertheless found him 'the most understanding soul alive'. He advised her to 'let the Eternal Problem rest for a while'.

She returned to Liverpool determined to work harder for the settlement and started a girls' club for the roughest girls in the neighbourhood. She also began a series of lantern lectures at the Seamen's Institute. She felt, however, that her life and the settlement were going nowhere and discussed with Hudson whether or not to leave. He offered her a three-month placement, working in his parish of South Luffenham as his wife was an invalid and could not undertake any parish work.

Hudson Shaw was an interesting man and because of the part he played in Maude's life, is an integral part of her story. His father had been a civil engineer with mental health problems who died when Shaw was only twelve years old. The boy expected to leave school and earn a living but his mother remarried and emigrated to Australia, leaving him in the care of her sister, who adopted him and paid for him to attend Bradford Grammar School. From there he went to university in Oxford. He had planned to be ordained but had no money and as he had just got engaged to be married, thought his best plan might be for him and his bride to emigrate to Australia, as his mother had done before him. He was obviously a very gifted man, a powerful speaker and meant for higher things, and an unknown benefactor came forward and offered him an allowance to keep his talents in England.

A friend of Hudson's, Michael Sadler, had been appointed secretary to the Oxford University Extension Delegacy, which needed to recruit lecturers. Sadler persuaded the delegates to appoint Hudson on a three-year salaried contract. There was a great hunger for knowledge among working men, who had been known to walk considerable distances to and from lectures after a hard day's work, and Hudson's lectures were so popular among the millworkers of Lancashire and the West Riding that he could draw in a thousand men to his classes with lectures on Imperial Rome and Ruskin, and had to turn off the gas at ten o'clock to persuade the men to leave.

His first wife died in 1888 and his widowed aunt cared for him and Arnold, the son born of the marriage. Two years later, he married his first cousin Effie, with a view to supporting both her and her mother and providing a stable background for Arnold. Unfortunately, Effie had mental health problems and the birth of her son Bernard upset her mental equilibrium, turning her against the physical side of marriage. Hudson suffered from bouts of depression, hardly surprising in the circumstances. He was then offered the living of South Luffenham in Rutland and as Effie was in no state to undertake the duties of a vicar's wife, it was at this point that he asked Maude to come and help. Maude was given permission to spend a short time there. The Roydens' flexibility where Maude was concerned may have been because her mother thought that, being lame, there was little chance of her marrying, so normal rules did not apply.

South Luffenham was a village of about three hundred people, with the wages of the farm labourers being twelve shillings a week. Maude's situation was very much what it had been at the Victoria Settlement. She took the Mothers' Meetings, where she bought a quantity of flannelette and sold it in smaller pieces so the women could make petticoats more cheaply. She ran a weekly girls' sewing class and a night school in domestic economy, but also arranged talks about Shakespeare and gave lantern lectures.

She got on well with the younger Shaw boy, Bernard, but was less sure of her feelings about Arnold, who soon emigrated to America. Effie, Hudson's wife, was a strange person. She was terrified of life. She once confided to Maude that 'if she knew what she was frightened of, she would not be frightened'. She was very shy. If she realised anyone was listening to her play the piano she would immediately stop, close the piano lid and, as often as not, leave the room. She also retreated to her bedroom if there were visitors. But Effie liked Maude and Maude liked her. Together they would tease Hudson. On one occasion when the two women were talking, or more likely when Maude was talking and Effie listening, Effie's mother had said, 'Hush. Hudson is going to speak'. 'After this', wrote Maude, ' whenever Hudson opened his mouth, Effie and I were liable to raise our hands in admonition and say to each other, 'Hush. Hudson is going to speak.' No wonder Effie liked Maude, who said of her: 'The idea that conversation cannot be a monologue was one Effie never got hold of.' Maude and Hudson argued all the time, mostly about 'the woman question'. Hudson thought, like Ruskin, that women should not have the vote because they could not bear arms and fight for their country. Naturally, Maude disagreed.

Useful as she felt she was to Hudson, Effie, and the village, Maude found the place lacking in stimulation. In 1903 when Hudson returned from one of his lecturing tours to the US, he suggested she should speak about Shakespeare at a University Extension course in Driffield. She spoke about *Hamlet,* which was a great success among the audience of sixty-eight. The Mothers' Union in Derby then asked her to speak on introducing Shakespeare to children and after that, she was asked to deliver a course on Shakespeare. She obviously had the knack for getting people's attention and conveying information in an engaging way. Hudson then raised the question of her lecturing on an Extension Course in Oxford.

He was met with the usual response from the University: the work was not fitting for a woman, it was too hard and there would be too much travelling. Hudson said that if they would employ her, he would resign if she was not up to the job, so they agreed to give her a trial lecture at the Summer Meeting. Hudson was surprised to meet her two friends, Kathleen Courtney and Evelyn Gunter, and was intrigued by this three-cornered friendship and how it worked. 'We just love each other,' Maude replied.

The Summer Meeting saw a collection of some of the most prestigious speakers in England, among them Ralph Vaughan Williams. It was inaugurated by the American Ambassador, and presided over by Michael Sadler, the secretary of the University Extension scheme. Maude was the only woman lecturing, and spoke on Faust. She continued to give lectures and, in 1905, moved to Oxford because of the difficulty of travelling between South Luffenham and Oxford.

By this time Effie, whose life had been immeasurably improved by Maude's presence, had pointed out to Hudson and Maude that they were in love. 'How ridiculous!' they both exclaimed. Their edginess with one another increased until, after one outburst, Effie burst into tears. 'You're spoiling one of the loveliest things in the world,' she sobbed. They realised that Effie was, in fact, right. There was no question of the relationship between Hudson and Maude being consummated. He was a married man and a priest, but he had seen that Maude could perfectly well maintain a three-cornered friendship with Kathleen and Evelyn. Perhaps it would be possible for the three of them – Hudson, Effie and Maude – to sustain a similar friendship.

Being in Oxford, Maude threw herself with her typical exuberance into work for women's suffrage. She joined the 170-strong Oxford Women Students' Suffrage Society and, with Kathleen Courtney, was on the executive committee. In the Oxford History archive there is an announcement of a Votes for Women meeting at the Corn Exchange in Oxford at 3 p.m., chaired by Miss A. Maude Royden of Lady Margaret Hall, the date unfortunately not given. The speakers were the Reverend William Temple, Fellow of Queen's College and future Archbishop of Canterbury, and Miss Helen Wodehouse, PhD, of Birmingham University. 'Admission free', the paper announces, but there would be a collection for the funds of the Women's Suffrage Movement.

Professionally matters were going well. The University Extension scheme offered Maude a higher grade with the strong recommendation that she should refuse it, on the grounds that if she accepted a higher fee she might price herself out of a job. Maude refused to refuse the offer and accepted the higher fees. She did not price herself out of a job, because she was good at it.

She was also involved with the Workers' Education Association (WEA), an offshoot of the University scheme. The WEA was interested in the question of suffrage, but were not working specifically for women to have the vote. Rather, they wanted universal suffrage for anyone over twenty-one. Maude contributed articles for their journal *The Highway* and also wrote for the *Common Cause,* the magazine of the NUWSS. She took part in the electioneering for the 1910 election and was asked to take classes in public speaking for the WEA.

Hudson had, by now, changed his mind about votes for women. Being in such close contact with Maude, he could hardly have maintained his anti-suffrage position, though an anti-suffrage society had been formed in1908 so he would not have been alone. Hudson joined the Church League for Women's Suffrage, founded in 1909 with Maude acting as secretary. Hudson then had one of many bouts of depression, which left him unable to work, so Maude took over his classes for the Extension Scheme.

In 1911 she was elected onto the NUWSS Executive Committee and in the same year embarked on a speaking tour of the USA, combining the unlikely topics of women's suffrage, Shakespeare and the Romantic poets. Hudson's son Arnold organised the tour for her with a great deal of bombastic advertising, which irritated Maude. She spoke with wit and passion about the plight of many working women, paid seven shillings and sixpence a week, working long hours in cramped and unhealthy conditions, some of them forced into prostitution to scrape together enough money to live on. Many of these women, she said, were employed by the government. They were exploited and kept in their servitude by the lack of training for other kinds of work. The involvement of the government was meant to improve the lives of its citizens but 'what is the use of building hospitals and jails and tying up wounds and binding up sores when the great canker is at the heart of the country?' she asked.

When Asquith's Liberal government failed to grant the franchise to women in 1912, at a time when member of the WSPU were throwing stones through shop windows, Maude did not approve. They smashed the windows of Oxford Street shops 'behind which,' they imagined, 'stood Lloyd George and Churchill, when in fact there was nothing but Dickens and Jones' was Maude's acerbic comment.

Following the refusal of Asquith's government to grant the vote to women, Maude's reaction was that rather than throwing stones through windows, they must work harder: go on handing out leaflets, speaking in market places and at tube stations, in drawing rooms and at white elephant stalls. She herself crisscrossed the country, no journey being too long or arduous, but in 1912 she spoke mainly in London, basing herself with the Shaws, who had now moved there, with Hudson's parish now being St Botolph's in the City. They had found a flat in Bedford Square, which Maude shared with them. With Hudson working in the City and unable to be at home all the time, Effie was extremely unhappy. Maude, however, was very busy indeed. Following her own recommendation to work harder, she made 267 speeches in 1912. A typical day for her at this time might include a morning class on public speaking, an afternoon speech on working women and the vote, and ending the day with a drawing-room meeting in Kensington. She said you must be prepared to stand up on a chair on a street corner in London and say to two children and a dog, ' People of England ...'. So she had no illusions about the speaking she did and how little effect it might sometimes have.

In April of 1913, she took on editing the weekly suffrage paper *The Common Cause*. This was at the time of the Cat and Mouse Act, which provoked even more violent actions from the WSPU, and in the same month that the Pilgrimage was organised, a long-distance walk from seventeen towns and cities in Britain culminating in London to be held in July. Eleanor Rathbone, Kathleen Courtney, Millicent Fawcett and Margaret Ashton, all members of the committee of the NUWSS, were among those who walked, as were Eleanor Lodge and Grace Hadow, but because of her lameness this was not possible for Maude. Determined to be of use to the Pilgrimage, however, she joined the flying corps of speakers who went by train to various places en route to draw the fire of the mob before the pilgrims arrived. A thousand of them attended the service in St Paul's where, of course, Maude was not allowed to speak. She spoke in the Ethical Church nearby. However, Maude was one of the delegates who met Asquith to try to persuade him to grant the franchise to women. She told him: 'Women have become politically conscious and when that happens to any class it can never be sent to sleep again.'

Many suffragists were transferring their political loyalty from the Liberal Party to the Labour party, newly formed in 1900, which promised to support votes for women. In February 1914, there was a joint meeting in the Albert Hall of members of the suffrage movement and the Labour Party. Some suffragettes were disruptive but, on the whole, the meeting was good tempered and the mood euphoric; £6,000 was raised to press for suffrage at the next election. Arthur Henderson, newly-elected leader of the Labour party, was cheered to the rafters; and Maude gave a rousing speech, pointing out that contrary to some people's opinions, women were actually members of the human race. Fenner Brockway, a founder member of the Labour Party, said it wasn't rhetoric or gesture but 'the sheer conviction of her personality' that got through to people. She could pack the Albert Hall and no one would leave till they had heard her speak.

Maude and Sex
By this time Maude was also seriously engaged with the campaign for social purity, which had formed in the aftermath of Josephine Butler's campaign against the Contagious Diseases Act. There was a stream of thought within the suffrage movement that getting the vote was only one aim and they needed it so they could work more effectively to improve the lives of working women, get protection for children and replace the double standards for men and women pertaining to sexual *mores*. It was not right, they thought, that men should be allowed to have sex with any woman without any smirch on their reputation, while women were expected to be chaste. There was a practical angle to this, quite apart from the moral one. Venereal diseases were prevalent, and could be picked up by men and passed to their perfectly innocent wives. Syphilis was a dreaded disease because of its consequences. It affected foetuses, leading sometimes to death, or blindness in the baby, and could lead to insanity in adults.

Maude was a brave woman who was prepared to speak out on the one topic that many people considered taboo: sex. By being outspoken about sex, she made it easier for other women to follow suit. In 1913 she was asked to speak to Oxford undergraduates – men, of course – about the white slave trade. This was followed by a request from the Bishop of Winchester who asked her to speak at the Church Congress and again the following September in Southampton at the International Conference on the White Slave Trade.

The message she had, as expressed several years later in *Sex and Common-Sense,* was that sex was nothing to be ashamed of. 'The first essential is to realise that the sex-problem is the problem of something noble, not something base. It is not a "disagreeable duty" to know our own natures and understand our own instincts: it is a joy.' One of the problems was: 'Boys and girls are allowed to grow up in ignorance. The girls perhaps know nothing till they have to know all. The boys learn from grimy sources.' She cited a talk she gave at one university where many young men had come up to her afterwards and said with hardly a single exception that 'our parents told us nothing. We have never heard sex spoken of except in a dirty way'.

While Maude had no personal experience of the joy of sex, she certainly knew about the less than joyous consequences for many women, who had talked to her unreservedly while she was at the Victoria Settlement in Liverpool, and she had the experience of Hudson's chastity to reinforce her message that men could control their sex drive if they chose to do so. She also knew about the difficulties a life of chastity imposed on both men and women. When they were returning one evening from a ride on Dartmoor, the lights of cottages in the vicinity were beginning to shine out into the darkness when Hudson burst out, 'Every peasant in the land can have tonight what I must never have!'

They wrote letters to one another constantly, even when they were not apart and sometimes several times a day. Maude sometimes tried to imagine what life would have been like if they had never met, but couldn't. 'At the heart of all we did and thought was this passion', she wrote in *The Threefold Cord,* published after Hudson's and Effie's deaths.

Maude reviewed Marie Stopes' book, *Married Love,* published in 1918, and strongly approved of its message. She particularly liked the fact that Stopes acknowledged that women, as well as men, had physical needs. She wrote:

People often tell me, and nearly always unconsciously *assume*, that women have no sex hunger — no sex needs at all until they marry, and that even then their need is not at all so imperious as men's, or so hard to repress. Such people are nearly always either men, or women who have married young and happily and borne many children, and had a very full and interesting outside life as well! ... Now, the point at which this problem hurts many of us lies in this, that women have been taught, by a curious paradox, first of all that they ought not to have any sexual feeling, any hunger, any appetite at all on that side of their natures; and secondly, that they exist solely to meet that particular physical need in men. The idea that woman was created, not like man, for the glory of God, but for the convenience of man, has greatly embittered and poisoned public opinion on this subject ... I think with bitterness of that age-long repression, of its unmeasured cost; of the gibe contained in the phrase 'old maid', with all its implication of a narrowed life, a prudish mind, an acrid tongue, an embittered disposition. And all these cramped and stultified lives have not availed to make the world understand that women have had to pay for their celibacy!

Both Maude and Stopes attributed an almost mystical significance to sex, which Maude considered to be a sacrament, though she felt it was perfectly possible for a single woman to lead a happy, fulfilled and useful life without marriage. Maude thought sexual relations should be confined to marriage, and that a female lover was no substitute for a husband, though, unlike Stopes, who found the idea of homosexuality and lesbianism repulsive, Maude modified her attitude to gay sex as she grew older.

Maude was also surprisingly relaxed about divorce. She writes:

Young people should know what sex is and involves: what marriage is: how necessary to the welfare of the race, their children and themselves are fidelity and love. They should know that unless they believe that their love is indeed for life they ought not to marry.

If, nevertheless, a man and woman believe that their marriage is a complete and hopeless failure, their claim to be released from it should not be granted in haste. A period of years should in any case elapse before divorce can be obtained, and every effort should be used to reconcile the two... If, however, it is clear that for no worthy consideration can they be induced to take up again the duties and responsibilities of marriage ... they should be released. And this because it is not moral but immoral, not Christian but unChristian, to pretend that a marriage is real and sacred *when it is not.*

She was also in agreement with Stopes about the need for women to have access to contraception. Stopes' position stemmed from her views on eugenics, which led her to the belief that the nation's genetic stock should be improved. Maude's views on contraception grew from her knowledge of the burden imposed on women by numerous pregnancies. 'I know a woman who at the time I met her had borne eight dead syphilitic babies and was to bear a ninth,' she wrote in 1922. 'Will anyone suggest that it was her duty to go back to her husband and conceive other children until such time as I or somebody else succeeded in convincing him that he ought to cease entirely from marital relations with his wife?'

In 1924 a deputation about contraception lobbied John Wheatley, Minister of Health in the new Labour government, but he was a Roman Catholic and refused to do anything, citing the sanctity of life as a reason for his refusal. Maude preached a scathing sermon in which she pointed out that women died in childbirth four times more often than men were killed in the mining industry. What did he mean by the 'sanctity of life?'

Peace and Politics
With the imminent outbreak of war in 1914, the split in the NUWSS over what to do in that event saw Maude on the side of the peace activists. At a Caxton Hall meeting at the end of March 1914, Maude spoke about the forthcoming international conference on peace in the Hague organised by WILPF. There would be two societies of German women who would attend and about a hundred British women. 'It is not anticipated that there will be any difficulty about passports', said Maude, which was reported in the *Morning Post*. This was read by Lady Jersey, vice-president of the National League for Opposing Women's Suffrage, who promptly took herself round to the Foreign Office and spoke her mind about Maude. 'She is a singularly inaccurate sentimentalist', she pronounced and warned against allowing British feminists to travel abroad. She suggested that the passports not be refused till the last minute, which would make it impossible for the women

to make other arrangements. Three British women managed to be there, among them Kathleen Courtney who was helping to organise the event. A hundred and eighty women were prevented from travelling. Some already had passports, but Winston Churchill, First Lord of the Admiralty, closed the North Sea to shipping. The women waited in Tilbury for a week before realising that there was no possibility of crossing to Holland. The *Daily Express* carried the headline 'All Tilbury is laughing at the Peacettes'.

Maude feared her stance on pacifism would alienate her family. Her eldest brother Tom had organised the embarkation of the British Expeditionary Force and her sister Ethel had helped to establish the WRNS. Another sister, Daisy, had three sons in action. Hudson was not a pacifist and was proud of his appointment as chaplain to the Honourable Artillery Company.

One of the organisations working for peace was the Fellowship of Reconciliation, founded by a Quaker and a German Lutheran, which held its inaugural meeting in July 1915. Its aim was to support pacifists in times of conflict and, if possible, to convert the country to Christian Pacifism. They organised a march – yet another! – through the Midlands to London. They had a rough time of it. Maude could not, of course, walk or cycle but she travelled by caravan alongside. The popular mood was very anti-German, aggravated by the sinking of the Lusitania, the bombing of London, and the shelling of seaside towns such as Scarborough and Hartlepool. In Mansfield, a crowd of soldiers and civilians jeered and scoffed at them, so they cut short their visit and went to Nottingham, then Loughborough. There were rumours in the Press that they were spies, which made matters worse, and when they reached Hinckley – on payday when there was money to spend on drink,– two of the peace marchers were attacked in the street. The tents and the caravan were also attacked. The caravan was tipped over and set alight. The goods strewn about the field were smashed up and one man grabbed Maude by the throat but let go without doing her harm. Police reckoned that the mob that attacked them was probably in the region of two or three thousand. This event shook Maude and made her question her previous conviction that she must speak 'in season and out of season' without taking public opinion into consideration. Hudson urged her to be careful what she said, and to whom she said it, and she heeded his advice.

The Church and City Temple

Maude Royden is chiefly remembered for her insistence that the Church should admit women to the priesthood. It is from this point on that she began to focus her attention in this direction. Having lectured on the University Extensions courses, tackled the thorny question of sex education for young people and the popular idea that sex was something to be ashamed of, she knew she could hold people's attention, that she was a powerful speaker and saw no reason why she should not speak about her faith, which was what motivated her entire existence. She had once preached at South Luffenham, but not in the church. She and the congregation had had to relocate to the Sunday school room. This was a nonsense, in Maude's view.

The Church had, however, modified its attitude to some extent over recent years. In 1897 it was agreed that women could vote on parish church councils, though not stand for office; in 1914, women were allowed to stand for office on the parish council and, in 1918, allowed to participate in higher councils.

Women in the Church were supported by the Church League for Women's Suffrage, of which Maude was chair. In 1915 they began to campaign in earnest. Women's work in the mission field had proved their right to an equal vote in church matters and nothing but equality on governing bodies and ultimately in the priesthood would satisfy women, they said. The *Church Times* stated that ordaining a woman as a priest 'is so absolutely grotesque that we must refuse to discuss it! The monstrous regiment of women in politics would be bad enough but the monstrous regiment of priestesses would be a thousandfold worse!' 'The really pleasant and devout communicant does not speak where she has any single man (brother, husband, father) to be her spokesperson,' wrote one correspondent.

In the face of views such as this, Maude recommended going slowly. Then began the struggle for women to be allowed to participate fully in Church life.

Whatever moves the women made, whatever tiny step forward they wanted to make, they were blocked by the conservative hierarchy of the Church. The National Mission of Repentance and Hope, which aimed at spiritual revival throughout the country, came and went, as did the promises to investigate the position of women by various bishops. At this time, a time when men were given communion before women, Maude wrote a pamphlet about the Church in which she looked at the offices of the Church of England and concluded that every single office was closed to women. 'Are there, then, untouchables in the religion of Christ, after all?' she asked.

She was surprised at this point to be asked to speak at the City Temple. While this was a nonconformist church, and she had often spoken in nonconformist churches, this was the big one. Catherine Booth, co-founder of the Salvation Army, had preached there in 1888 but in spite of this, even Anglicans recognised it as a 'real' church. The City Temple was between ministers and the gap was being filled by a series of preachers. When one fell ill, Maude was asked to fill the gap for the morning and evening of 18 March 1917. Elizabeth Wordsworth, Dame Elizabeth as she liked to be known, retired principal of Lady Margaret Hall, said: 'Fancy Maude Royden at the City Temple! However, one can't call it preaching in a *church*. I dare say she was very good in a sort of way, and of course the novelty went for a good deal. I don't think she is quite as wise as she doubtless is well meaning.' However much Dame Elizabeth damned with faint praise, the public thought differently. Police had to be called out to control the queues of people waiting to get in. It was described in the *Daily Express* as 'Woman crank's sermon'.

Maude was upset by the way she was portrayed in the Press as a German-loving pacifist and concerned that the Press was very occupied with what she was wearing – a black cassock with a white net collar and a small hat like a biretta, visible in all parts of the church as she stood in the pulpit. The ladies in the choir were dressed in mortar boards and blue academic robes over white dresses, while the male singers stood behind, also dressed in blue academic robes and mortar boards. She had Hudson's approval and her brother Tom and sister Daisy were in the congregation to support her. Her theme was the need to put as much faith in spiritual laws as we put in scientific laws, as both kinds come from God. 'The laws of God work in the same way as the Laws of Science,' she said. 'You cannot break them – you can only break yourself against them'. She thought the congregation was more struck by the fact that the building was still standing when she finished speaking than by anything she said. Clara Butt, the famous contralto, came into the vestry afterwards to congratulate her, as did the Bishop of Lincoln.

Some Anglicans were upset that she had preached in a nonconformist chapel, interpreting this as her desertion of the Church of England. Maude reassured them, however, saying she spoke wherever she was asked to speak. She felt no sense of wrongness about preaching there. There was no part of the service that did not come out of either the Common Prayer Book or the Bible and she thought her preaching in a nonconformist church might open the way for nonconformists to preach in an Anglican church.

Two weeks after her preaching debut, the Russian revolution took place. There was a rally in the Albert Hall where Clara Butt sang the Russian National Anthem, George Bernard Shaw sent a message and many greetings were sent to the Democrats of Russia. Maude, speaking from the platform, said that the people had passed from bondage to freedom. 'Tonight we know that everything is possible', she concluded.

At home there were changes. Bernard, Hudson and Effie's son, aged twenty-three, had been killed by a gas bomb, a grievous loss that stayed with them for the rest of their lives and which they were unable to speak about. An aged aunt came to live with them so there was no room for Maude, who moved out to live in Poplar. Evelyn Gunter gave up her job at the Oxford University Extension scheme to keep house for Maude.

Then Maude was offered the post of 'pulpit assistant' at the City Temple. She didn't know what to do. She was already committed to a group called 'Life and Liberty', a ginger group set up by Reverend Dick Shepherd, vicar of St Martin in the Fields, aiming to sort out the internal problems of the Anglican Church and work towards freeing it from the domination of Parliament, which had to debate every change the clerics proposed to make. Freeing the Church from this constraint would speed up any decision they decided on and make the structure more flexible.

The Life and Liberty movement organised a big meeting at which William Temple, a supporter of women's suffrage, but too cautious for Maude's liking, gave the opening speech to an audience of 2,000, three quarters of them women. Maude seconded the motion that the archbishops be asked to ascertain 'whether and on what terms Parliament is prepared to give freedom to the Church ... to manage its own life'. Archbishop Davidson received a deputation and promised to deal with the matter 'with all reasonable speed'. His idea of 'reasonable speed' differed from that of Life and Liberty. He said he would discuss it when the next Representative Church Council met some time in the future.

Maude was under pressure from the City Temple to make a decision on whether or not she would take up the post they had offered, a post specifically created for her and with a six-months contract. She decided to take the job and preached her first sermon on 17 September. The following Sunday, she christened four children and immediately received a letter from the Reverend Seaton, a member of Life and Liberty, telling her that her presence at a forthcoming conference would no longer be acceptable.

Maude was very upset. She pointed out that the babies would not have been baptised into the Anglican Church as their parents were nonconformists, so she was not denying them access to the Church of England and the practice of the laity baptising children was as old as the Church. She also pointed out that proceedings at the conference would be invalidated if she were not present. The Reverend Seaton replied that she could come providing she did not sleep at the college where the event was taking place. William Temple poured oil on troubled waters and got her to agree that she would come to the conference, put her point of view then leave. Maude offered to resign from Life and Liberty and Seaton said he might be prepared to change his decision if Maude promised not to baptise any more children. Maude refused.

Life and Liberty did manage to obtain more autonomy for the Church in the Enabling Act of 1919, which gave the Church delegated legislative power exercised through a national assembly. It was much more conservative than Maude would have liked but women could now serve in the new assembly and on all other church councils.

Maude's work at the City Temple was highly valued and she was offered an extension to her contract. Her work expanded. She led one Sunday service and sometimes the Thursday service as well. She started a clinic particularly for young women in need of advice, thus extending her pastoral role. When she had been appointed to the City Temple by the leader, Fort Newton, Maude wrote in fun that she had walked round the church to see how many places he could forbid her to stand and that perhaps he might ask the congregation to go down into the crypt before she began to speak, for it was a consecrated building, or suggest that all male persons should go out before she began to speak. Of course Newton did none of these things. Instead he left her to develop her own style. She soon instigated an after-service meeting, where she would leave the pulpit and sit among the congregation to discuss issues.

Having strong views about sex, Maude was outraged when the government suggested the idea of setting up 'maisons tolerees' in France where prostitutes would be kept for the use of soldiers and receive health checks, in an attempt to curb the incidence of venereal diseases. She preached against it and Newton said 'I have never seen such flaming wrath of outraged womanhood against the degradation of her sex'. Maude herself said:

> To any woman who believes the sacrifice to be necessary, I would say that she ought herself to volunteer! The men who urge regulated prostitution on grounds of national necessity ought to invite their wives and daughters to fill the places left vacant by the women who are worn out... As a woman in a Christian pulpit I cannot be silent in the presence of such infamy.

The government backed down on these proposals.

In January 1918 when women got the vote, the NUWSS marked the event with a celebration in the Queen's Hall. Mrs Fawcett was in the chair, Lord Lytton, Arthur Henderson and Sir John Simon representing the three political parties were on the platform. Maude gave a speech, and *Jerusalem* was sung by the Bach Choir with Parry himself conducting. Maude congratulated him on the music. 'That was a good hymn' she said. 'That was a better speech,' he replied.

Tired of waiting for the Church to soften its attitude towards women's participation in services, Hudson took the bull by the horns and asked Maude to read the lesson at St Botolph's. The first time, he noted that her lips trembled as she started reading and he was angry that she should feel so nervous. He started his sermon by saying, 'Today for the first time in this historic church you have heard a woman's voice proclaiming the good tidings of Christ's gospel. Some of you may have objected to the innovation. I think you should call yourselves Jews, not Christians.'

By September 1918, not having heard a word about women preaching in church, Hudson lost patience again and asked Maude to speak at St Botolph's. She spoke on 'The League of Nations and Christianity'. Hudson wrote to Bishop Ingram and told him the church was packed from end to end, both galleries included, with some people standing. The bishop asked him not to arrange any women speakers on a Sunday, though Thursdays would be all right. Hudson replied that it was too late. He had already announced that Maude would speak on a Sunday but tried to pacify the bishop by saying that her sermon would be separated by an organ recital from the service, which he would take himself. It would, he said, be suicidal to lose Maude's talents and those of other like-minded women.

Hudson asked Maude to preach at the Three Hours Service on Good Friday. It not being Sunday, Maude accepted. On Maundy Thursday, however, the day before Good Friday, a message came from the bishop forbidding her to speak. Hudson closed the church, stuck a notice on the door and invited people to attend a service in the parish room. It was a very uncomfortable service, with no room to kneel because of the crowds and some people peering in through the windows to hear what she had to say. A petition was sent to the bishop telling him that there was something seriously wrong when an Evangelical like Maude should be harassed and impeded by people who should be her chief supporters.

The following year the League of the Church Militant, which had been the League for Women's Suffrage, arranged a march from St George's church in Bloomsbury to Trafalgar Square. It must have been a splendid and colourful sight. Maude gave a speech to the assembled crowd, then the procession moved off, a crucifix at the head, followed by banners of St Theresa, Joan of Arc, and St Catherine of Sienna. A band in red coats led clergy in their surplices, including Hudson, and the choir of St Botolph's in purple singing *Onward Christian Soldiers*. The procession paused and laid a wreath before the monument to Edith Cavell, shot by the Germans for caring for both Germans and English soldiers during the war.

The bishops under such prolonged badgering gave in and said that women could become deaconesses, and laywomen should be allowed to speak in consecrated buildings though men should have priority and deaconesses would not be on the same level as deacons. Their declaration was in vain. Convocation limited their decision, saying that women could speak only to women and girls.

Hudson was very disappointed. He asked Edith Picton-Turbervill, a stalwart of the suffrage movement and a staunch Labour supporter, to take midday services in Holy Week and Maude to take the Three Hour service on Good Friday. He went to discuss this with the bishop, who said that he could not forbid it since the Three Hour service was non-statutory. Maude said teasingly, 'Are you not bound to obey the bishop, Hudson?' 'Only in his godly judgements and this is not godly at all,' he replied.

The church was crowded, with men, women and children arriving long before the service started. When the church was full, the doors were closed to prevent latecomers from gaining admittance and before the service started, Hudson reminded the congregation of the Brawling Act of 1860, and asked anyone who wished to protest to do so at the beginning then leave. No one did. When she heard of the event, Dame Elizabeth Wordsworth said, 'I am sorry Maude Royden defied the bishop. Even if it was defensible on legal grounds it was not behaving like a lady.' No wonder she and Maude had never got on.

Hudson's stance did not make life easy for him. When he spoke at the London diocesan conference, he was howled down by his fellow clergy. The motion that 'it was inexpedient and contrary to the interests of the church that women ... should minister in consecrated buildings', was carried by two to one.

Maude said it was a question of sex. The idea of women as ceremonially unclean because of menstruation, conception, and childbirth, was still prevalent though unexpressed. 'Is motherhood in any way less spiritual, more animal than fatherhood?' she asked. And Maude pondered whether the Virgin birth would have been a doctrine of the Church if women had been in charge.

In 1918, at the age of forty-two, she adopted a baby girl, Helen. This was eight years before the Adoption of Children Act, which gave adopted children legal standing and outlawed such practices as baby farming. In 1918, matters were much less formal and anyone could adopt a child who needed care. It was common practice at this time for middle-class women to take on the care of abandoned babies, many born out of wedlock because of the war. Emmeline Pankhurst had adopted four such children and given one to her daughter Christabel to bring up. By this time, Maude was earning enough to support not only Evelyn, who did most of the caring for Helen, but a nanny, a chauffeur and a cook. Maude admired mothers, especially working-class mothers and was enraged by society's response to war babies and illegitimacy. 'There are no illegitimate babies, only illegitimate parents,' she said. The State must try to make up for what these children had lost: two parents and a stable family life. It was owed to those who had died. She also took in Friedrich Wolfe, an Austrian famine victim, aged four, who stayed in Maude's household till he was adopted at the age of eight.

There were a great many children like Freddie as the British blockade under the terms of the 1918 peace treaty made famine conditions commonplace. WILPF protested against the blockade, and several of their members, including Maude, joined the Fight the Famine Council, begun by Eglantine Jebb who, with her sister, went on to form the Save the Children Fund. 'All the world has trespassed against that child', Maude said, speaking of Freddie and was shocked by post-war attitudes, not just to starving children but to both men and women after the war. She felt there was a role for the Church to play in politics. She was outraged at the contempt shown by the government for ordinary people: brothels in France, the treatment of pacifists in prison, its attitude to discharged soldiers, and women who had now lost their jobs. She said: 'We took men for whom their country had done nothing and sent them into the hell of war... On Wednesday I watched a march of the unemployed going through the streets of London... It is not enough to tell them 'You can go and mend roads' or to women turned off from the assembly line "Mistresses are shrieking for domestic servants".'

But the overriding question, she felt, was peace. 'We know that if you injure one nation, the others suffer... Do you think it belongs to peace to starve a generation of children in Austria? Or to force from Germany what Germany cannot pay? You cannot get peace out of war, any more than you can get grapes out of thistles.' She pointed out that Germany was paying back 140,000 milch cows to Belgium and France while German children were dying from lack of milk. How was that supposed to generate peace?

The Guildhouse
In March 1920 she resigned from the City Temple as she felt her work there had run its course. Percy Dearmer, who later went on to edit the well-known collection of hymns *Songs of Praise,* and

at the time occupied a chair in Ecclesiastical Art at King's College, London, suggested she should set up her own establishment. He had no church of his own so offered to help Maude in what became known as the Fellowship Guild. Its centre was a disused congregational chapel, four minutes from Victoria Station. Maude thought it was dreary and excessively ugly, but in Dearmer's hands it was turned into a place of beauty. He was excited by it. 'No sham Gothic!' he exclaimed. 'Excellent!' He had the whole of the interior whitewashed and introduced touches of bright colour in the lanterns, pulpit cushions and stewards' blue cassocks. Percy Dearmer fashioned the service – mainly Anglican, with a period of silence borrowed from the Quakers, and the congregation was encouraged to talk to one another when the collection was being taken. Their spiritual aim was to try to create a more vivid sense of Christian fellowship, to involve the laity and even, if possible, to draw in sympathetic nonconformists. There was an advisory council, which included Mrs Fawcett, William Temple and Sir Thomas Royden, Maude's brother. A branch of the League of Nations was established there, there was a dramatic society, a children's rally and a music club as well, of course, as regular religious services. When people asked what drama and music and the League of Nations had to do with religion, Maude had a sharp answer. 'Religion is everywhere and is in everything. If not, it is nowhere', she would say.

Percy Dearmer began what he called 'Five Quarters' every Sunday afternoon. It consisted of a lecture by someone well known such as Lady Rhondda, ex-suffragette; or Sir Tom Royden; Mrs Wintringham, MP; and speakers from different faiths: Hinduism, Buddhism, the Jewish faith, Roman Catholicism. Politicians were asked to speak on the ideology behind parliamentary measures, not party politics, and the general ethos of the talks was on tolerance, enlightenment, and an enlarged awareness of current trends. A favourite theme was the impact of science on religion and society.

Most of the lectures were extremely popular, regularly drawing audiences of up to 500. The building was always busy and in multiple use, with events on most days – although Saturdays were usually kept free as it was the day when poor children were taken to play in the park and the Ramblers Club rambled. There was a constant stream of fundraising events, recitals and bazaars because money was always needed for good causes – Christmas tea, garments and presents for poor Bermondsey children, 'unemployed' suppers, donations to the South Wales miners, Stratford Memorial Theatre, Dr Schweitzer's hospital at Lambarene. Clara Butt gave several recitals and Sybil Thorndike gave poetry readings. Maude herself preached about politics, explaining why she had left the Tory Party and joined the Labour Party – because she thought it most clearly expressed the Spirit of Christ.

Peace and Politics
In 1921 the country was in recession and the government had decided, following the report of a Committee on National Expenditure chaired by Sir Eric Geddes, to cut defence and social spending. The Geddes Axe, as it came to be known, cut government spending on education and unemployment pay, by £27.7 million. 'But there is always money to kill with,' Maude reflected bitterly.

Her preaching crusades in South Wales, the Rhondda, Newcastle and Durham had put her in touch with the mining communities and when the miners were locked out of the mines in 1926, she spoke eloquently about their plight. 'These are the men whose sons and brothers have shed their blood and left their bones where your sons and brothers left theirs,' she said to her London audience. 'Miners are not a race apart... They are people exactly like you and me.' The Trade Disputes Act of 1927, the political response to the general strike of the previous year, which banned secondary action, made mass picketing illegal and the political levy of the trade unions optional. Maude described it as a savage piece of class legislation.

Maude and Kathleen Courtney were disappointed at the role of the League of Nations, thinking that because it was closely tied to the 1918 peace treaty it was more a club for the winners of the war rather than a genuine instrument for peace. The work of the WILPF, however, looked more hopeful, and when Helena Swanwick resigned as chair of the British branch in 1923, Maude took her place. She immediately embarked on a speaking tour of America, where she hoped to persuade the Americans not to abandon Europe since they had not yet ratified the Peace Treaty nor joined the League of Nations. She travelled 9,000 miles and made 75 speeches in 57 cities. She stayed with the Rockefellers for part of the time and loved New York, but her visit to Washington was a waste of time. Congress was no longer sitting and the President was not there, a shortcoming of the itinerary for which she could perhaps have blamed Hudson's son Arnold, who had organised the whole thing.

Shortly after her return to England in 1923, Percy Dearmer decided to leave the Guildhouse. Maude was very sad because she realised how much she owed him, but they were both charismatic people with decided views. There was not really room for two such people. The Guildhouse continued to function perfectly well without Dearmer, with Hudson and Dick Shepherd offering to share the religious services and a board being set up to administer the Five Quarters. Maude felt the setup at the Guildhouse was democratic, as indeed it was, up to a point, as policy was under the control of an executive committee. But she took it for granted that the committee would endorse any decisions she made. She was well aware, however, of the danger that the congregation might start to worship her rather than God, and fought against her own vanity. She started the 'Little Company of Christ', a small devotional group dedicated to prayer and meditation, which the wife of Martin Shaw, the musical director of the Guild, refused to join. 'Too much Maude', she said.

The congregation at the Guildhouse was made up mostly of poor people, with a number of independent middle-class women who travelled in to the centre. In the late 1920s, the Guildhouse was at its peak of success. It continued its support for Lambarene and the League of Nations and there was a group that took an active part in peace campaigning. A contingent took part in the first Women's Peace Pilgrimage in 1926, when they joined women from all over England and Wales walking towards London. The Guildhouse women walked from Southend, but Maude walked for three days with the South Wales contingent. She was too tired to speak when she reached London and her place was taken by Mrs Fawcett. It must have been a splendid sight. At the head of each column was a woman in a blue cloak painted with the silver dove of peace riding on horseback, followed by women carrying banners, every pilgrim wearing a blue arm-band. The women from the Guildhouse wore blue cassocks with white collars. Eight thousand women assembled in Hyde Park to hear eight speakers, whose aim was to encourage the government to take the lead at the Disarmament Conference proposed by the League of Nations.

Maude was elected to the National Church Assembly, which met for the first time in 1920. She watched carefully to see that nothing interfered with the work on the new Matrimonial Causes Act, which proposed to equalise the grounds for divorce for women and men. In 1923 there was a battle about the revision of the marriage service. Maude proposed that the bride's promise to obey her husband be removed from the service, but this was defeated. 'Many women do really believe that, having promised to obey their husbands, their bodies cease to be their own', Maude pointed out. NUSEC, the organisation that had evolved from the NUWSS, under Eleanor Rathbone, thought that this battle was one worth supporting. The League of Church Militant led the campaign and in 1924, Maude spoke during the Church Congress on the subject. The marriage service was substantially revised, with the causes for which marriage was ordained being modified and the 'obey' clause taken out. However, in 1928, the revised prayer book was rejected by the House of Commons and the revised edition was neither overthrown nor withdrawn. Even today, there is still the option for a woman to promise to obey.

Although it was disappointing that women had made so little progress towards being received into the priesthood, Maude felt they had made quite a lot of progress in shifting the Church's ideas. The Dean of St Paul's had supported the women's position; Lady Barratt, wife of a liberal peer, had preached in Bristol Cathedral; and women could now be found serving as choristers, churchwardens, servers and sidesmen. The Anglo-Catholic pressure group, the Church Union, was against women taking part in church services, and protested when Maude was asked to speak in Liverpool's Anglican Cathedral. The cathedral was packed with people prepared to scoff at a woman preaching, but it was noted by one cleric that the congregation was transfigured by the effect of Maude's spirituality.

Although Maude had taken to preaching because that was all that was available to her as a woman, she felt that her work was flawed because she was not ordained. Her work at the Guildhouse she thought was a failure because although her congregation thought of her as their priest, she did not.

In 1928 she left the Guildhouse for three months to embark on a world preaching tour, along with her secretary Daisy Dobson. She kept in touch with the Guildhouse by monthly reports, printed in the newsletter. They went first to the USA where the money she earned there paid for an extension of the tour to New Zealand

and Australia, Japan, China, Ceylon, and India. She was a great success in the USA, in spite of being a smoker. One newspaper headline called her 'The smoking, flirting, tippling Evangelist' and the account and her name appeared under the picture of what Maude described as 'a charming girl in little more than a string of beads and smoking a cigarette'. In great embarrassment, the editor apologised but Maude replied that 'if the young lady was hoping to win fame with a photograph of me in a cassock, then any apology should be addressed to her. For myself, I could not but think that if anyone really believed her picture to be a photograph of me, I should have a record attendance!' She did in fact speak to packed halls and churches. She spoke almost every day, sometimes twice a day. She missed taking tea with President Coolidge, but was taught to dance the Valeta by Henry Ford, dined with the Bishop of California, and watched the shooting of a Cecil B de Mille film.

In New Zealand she was met by the Prime Minister, the Bishop of Wellington, and the Mayor. She spoke – from the pulpit – in Christchurch Cathedral, where women travelled from many miles to hear what she had to say. In Brisbane she had a cooler reception because of the large numbers of Roman Catholics in the town but in Melbourne people showered her with flowers. She flew in a tiny aeroplane to Adelaide and was caught in a sandstorm, and answered radio questions sent in from the bush.

She did little speaking in Japan, though she preached in the Anglican Church in Tokyo, from where she moved on to China, where the political situation was volatile. Under the Kuomintang, the revolutionary movement that had overthrown the Qing dynasty, there were a great many social changes happening. Maude noted that 'what has been spread over generations and even centuries with us is taking place in a decade'. She talked to people about Christian marriage, about arranged marriages, birth control and the status of husband and wife within the home. The talks on the League of Nations attracted large audiences.

In India there were no public meetings. Maude had come to India principally to talk to Mahatma Gandhi who, in Maude's opinion, was a supreme example of the triumph of moral over physical force. They talked about politics and about the British withdrawal from India. Maude thought the transformation of colonies to dominions was one of the gifts Britain had given the world. Gandhi said, 'It is time we got rid of this superstition about the political genius of the British. We are not at all convinced that it has produced anything of value.' To which Maude replied, 'You think our arrogance poisons all our gifts?' 'Yes,' said Gandhi.

When Maude returned to Britain, five hundred Guildhouse people met her at Victoria Station. Dearmer had written a welcome song, set to music by Martin Shaw. Maude asked the Guildhouse community if they would be interested in developing a similar organisation abroad, if they would agree to her going on such a long trip abroad again, if they would be interested in sponsoring travel for other Guild members, and if they would help people from abroad to come to England, to all of which the Guild gave a resounding 'yes'.

Perhaps due to all her travels, Maude was seriously ill that year and had to take time off work. Freddie had by this time been fostered by another family and Helen was sent to boarding school. Their house at Rosslyn Hill varied between being extremely busy and too quiet. Everyone ate in the kitchen, even when Dr Schweitzer or Ramsay Macdonald came to dinner, which meant Evelyn could join in the discussions if she wanted to. Monday evenings saw the influx of the Little Company, Maude's prayer group. This irritated Helen, who once astonished the assembled crowd by shouting, 'The house is full of praying women!'

The summer of 1930 was disappointing. Unsurprisingly, the Lambeth Conference had quashed an appeal for women priests; because of Maude's absence, the congregation at the Guildhouse had fallen, and with it the income, so its finances were precarious. When Gandhi came to England for the round table talks on Indian independence that year, he spoke at the Guildhouse and this was one occasion when the crowd was larger than it had ever been. Police had to be called out to control the crowds.

In the early 1930s, Hudson health was deteriorating. He had heart trouble and got depressed, so he and Effie moved to an old cottage he owned in Kent. By great good fortune, the cottage next door became vacant and Maude and Evelyn moved in. At first Effie's terrors were as bad as ever but gradually, with Hudson at home most of the time and Maude next door, her fears subsided, and Effie was happier than she had ever been. But it had been bought at a price, the price being Hudson's old age, which for him was a time of deep depression and physical exhaustion.

Dick Shepherd's health was also poor. He suffered badly from asthma and often had to take to his bed. He nevertheless found the energy to form the Peace Pledge Union in 1934 and the previous year had listened with pleasure to Maude's first broadcast, which he found cheering and comforting.

Maude's health too was not as good as it had been. Her lameness was proving increasingly problematic and she needed a high stool in the pulpit so she could sit rather than stand. When travelling, she needed a companion, and went to India in 1935 with Marjorie Corbett Ashby, an old friend from suffrage days, for an All-India Women's Conference. She no longer aspired to be a priest because she couldn't administer the sacrament and she had grown too far away from orthodox Anglicanism to profess the thirty-nine articles, which define the religious beliefs of the Church of England.

By the late 1930s, it was obvious that the Guildhouse would be unlikely to recover from the decline first shown when Maude was ill in 1931. Maude thought it did not appeal to the young. The lease ran out in 1937 and by that time Maude had resigned to devote herself to the peace movement but she was sad about it and wrote to Dick Shepherd, 'One must be allowed to weep sometimes.' Although the Guildhouse carried on for a further twenty years in a modified form, its heyday was over. Maude also cut her ties to the League of Nations, which she thought was not pacifist.

In 1940 Maude did something that alienated many of her friends, though not the faithful Kathleen Courtney. She broke with the peace movement. Sybil Thorndyke and Vera Brittain were very disappointed. Some of her ex-friends even said, 'What is the use of that women?' Maude was undeterred. 'I believe that Nazi-ism is worse than war. It is more hideously cruel. More blind. More evil,' she said.

At this point she travelled to America, her visit coinciding with Pearl Harbour, the Japanese attack on American ships, which brought America into the war. Many people in the USA were in shock at this and Daisy Dobson, Maude's secretary, wrote to the Guildhouse that Maude was needed in America. One woman wrote to Maude 'Some of us have heard of you ... and have felt a new steadiness because you could bear not to be sure'. The tour, at the invitation of the Federal Council of Churches, was very hard work but successful and the food was good. Maude sent Evelyn food parcels and told her 'Don't keep it or share it with everyone. It is for you – not to gnaw secretly in your room, not to have all the nicest things taken out and sent to Helen! And not to be hoarded for me. I have lived in luxury here all this winter.'

Maude came back to Britain in February 1942, by this time almost immobilised by her lameness. She conducted the marriage service when Helen married a school teacher, Donald Newman, but home life was very difficult. She could only use the car for shopping and by this time, Hudson could not walk from one house to the other. The City Temple and the Guildhouse were bombed, and a bomb fell on the hedge between their two houses. Hudson was increasingly deaf and worried he might reach the stage where he could not hear her voice. Effie died in February 1944, at which point Hudson and Maude suddenly realised they were free to marry. Daisy, Maude' secretary, disapproved. Evelyn was suffering with severe arthritis and both Maude and Hudson were determined her life should not be made more difficult. In spite of the unusual situation, Hudson was determined to marry. There were nine people at the wedding. Maude spent her time moving between the two houses until, two months later, Hudson died at the age of eighty-five.

'Why do people ever want to deny work to women?' asked Maude. 'How can suffering ever be borne without it?' She continued her pastoral work through her broadcasts and wrote her account of the love affair between her and Hudson, *The Three-fold Cord*. It had a mixed reception. Some people likened it to famous love affairs: Beatrice and Dante, Abelard and Eloise. Others thought it should not be published because it would not be believed.

Evelyn became so crippled she moved to live with her sisters in Hertfordshire and Maude bought a house in Golders Green. Evelyn died in 1954, and Maude wrote to Kathleen Courtney, 'We have been "We three" for many years. It is however about ten years since Evelyn's martyrdom began and I thank God it is now over.'

Maude was becoming increasingly deaf and when she reviewed her life, she considered it a failure. She thought she had been selfish and 'I suffer from that special sin of the vain, a desire to find people inferior to myself .... All the crusades I preached beyond my experience', she lamented. She regretted also her lack of empathy with Helen. 'I should have tried harder,' she said. She died in July 1956, aged 79.

"BICYCLING TO HEALTH AND FORTUNE."

The 1898 *Girls' Own Annual* believed in the benefits of bicycling. (Author's collection)

The 1898 *Girls' Own Annual*'s idea of academic life. (Author's collection)

The Women's Co-operative Guild, Lockhurst Lane, Coventry. Margaret Llewelyn Davies became General Secretary of the Guild in 1899. (Courtesy of History Coventry, under Creative Commons)

The Women's Co-operative Guild Annual Congress in Newcastle, 1913. (Hull History Centre)

Above: The Women's Co-operative Guild Jubilee Congress in 1933. Margaret Llewelyn Davies is in the centre of the group. (Hull History Centre)

Right: Margaret Llewelyn Davies' book *Maternity*, first published in 1915. (Author's collection)

Edited by MARGARET LLEWELYN DAVIES

MATERNITY
LETTERS FROM WORKING WOMEN

New Introduction by Gloden Dallas

Vera Binns, *née* Reynolds, and her mother in the 1930s, both enthusiastic members of the Women's Co-operative Guild. (Binns family archive)

Helena Deneke in 1919. (By kind permission of the Principal and Fellows of Lady Margaret Hall)

One of the many prestigious visitors to the Denekes' home. (Library of Congress)

The Deneke sisters at home in the 1930s. (By kind permission of the Principal and Fellows of Lady Margaret Hall)

Elsfield's tribute to Helene Deneke on her retirement from the secretaryship of Oxfordshire Federation of Women's Institutes, 1945. (Author's collection)

Eleanor Lodge and the staff of the Senior Common Room at Lady Margaret Hall in about 1912. (By kind permission of the Principal and Fellows of Lady Margaret Hall)

Cantine Anglaise set up by suffragists in Northern France in 1917. (Author's collection)

Eleanor Lodge with her
brothers Oliver and Richard.
(Author's collection)

Eleanor Lodge in her splendid scarlet
gown when she was awarded her
D.Phil. from the University of Oxford.
(Author's collection)

Westfield College Senior Common Room. Eleanor was Principal from 1921 to 1931. (Queen Mary University Archive)

Maude Royden. (National
Portrait Gallery)

South Luffenham Church,
where Maude Royden began her
parish work with Hudson Shaw.
(Wikimedia Commons)

Portrait of Eleanor Rathbone, painted by James Gunn in 1933. (National Portrait Gallery)

Eleanor Rathbone (third from left) and colleagues canvassing for votes for women in Liverpool in 1910. (University of Liverpool)

Eleanor Rathbone at the BBC. (Author's collection)

Ellen sharing sustenance with the men on the Jarrow march. (People's History Museum, Manchester)

Above left: Ellen Wilkinson with colleagues in 1945. (People's History Museum, Manchester)

Above right: Ellen stepping out during the Jarrow march. (National Portrait Gallery)

Above left: Herbert Morrison, Home Secretary, 1947. (Library of Congress)

Above right: Dr Isabel Emslie. (Author's collection)

Below left: Tented accommodation for the Scottish Women's Hospital personnel in Serbia. (Author's collection)

Below right: An ambulance struggles across the stony scree in Serbia, 1917. (Library of Congress)

Virginia Woolf. (Library of Congress)

6

Eleanor Rathbone (1872–1946) and Politics

Like Maude Royden, Eleanor Rathbone was born into a wealthy family in Liverpool. Her father, William Rathbone VI, married twice. By his first wife he had five children; by his second wife, he had six, of whom Eleanor was the fifth. She was not short of company, then, as a child, but always felt that she lacked many of the social graces that girls of her background were expected to acquire.

Her father was a philanthropist and stressed the need for families such as theirs to ensure the welfare of poorer people. They were Unitarians and as dissenters had never been eligible to enter the colleges of higher education in Oxford or Cambridge, which were open only to members of the established church. It was not until 1889, with the reform of the university of Oxford, that dissenters were admitted. Professions such as the law or medicine having been denied them, their money and energies went on municipal improvements. Eleanor's father had helped the infant Liverpool University off the ground by large donations. He drummed into his children that the pursuit of money for its own sake was not what God had intended. It was meant to be used for the good of the community. To this end, having experienced the importance of good nursing when his first wife died, he set up a training school for nurses. In 1868, he withdrew from the day-to-day management of the company and became a Liberal MP, and a staunch supporter of William Gladstone.

In her teens, Eleanor was duly presented at Court which, given her shyness and lack of interest in social niceties, must have been a painful experience. She became interested in learning Greek and acquired a tutor, Janet Case, who urged her to attend a course of philosophy lectures in Cambridge given by Henry Jackson, a great believer in women's education and a brilliant speaker. Eleanor's mother forbad her to go to Cambridge. One reason may have been that women at Girton and Newnham had the reputation for not marrying. This posed a problem, since marriage was seen by many upper class women as the start of an independent life. With marriage came public recognition, domestic authority and a settlement, the income from which would be entirely under her control.

Eleanor's mother unbent so far as to say that she could go to Oxford. The head of Somerville, Agnes Maitland, was a sensible woman from Liverpool, so known to the family and no head-in-the-air academic but a writer of cookery books. And in addition, Eleanor might be able to restrain the wilder excesses of her brother Frank, who was up at Oxford and causing some concern at home.

Eleanor accepted the compromise and in 1893 went up to Oxford, choosing to study philosophy, the only woman in her year to do so. Until the year Eleanor arrived at Somerville, students had been chaperoned to lectures. There was now less need to do so since the College was now recruiting its own tutors. Girls, however, were still required to consult the principal before accepting invitations and were not allowed out of College after sunset without permission.

'Every possible care is taken of these girls,' Mrs L.T. Meade, author of *A Good Girl Graduate*, wrote in the *Lady's Pictorial*. 'and rules for their guidance, without being in any sense severe, are so emphatic and so rigidly enforced, that the most careful parent need not be afraid to trust his daughter to the guidance which awaits her at Somerville Hall'.

Eleanor loved the life. She revelled in the academic challenge and for the first time found friends among her intellectual equals. She became part of a group who called themselves 'the APs', the Associated Prigs, who met to discuss social subjects and how they might be solved. In her studies she was exposed to the thinking not only of the ancient philosophers but also nineteenth century thinkers such as John Stuart Mill and came to believe that the state had a role to play in ameliorating the worst excesses of society and that religion was not necessarily the only mainspring of ethical behaviour. As one of the first generation of women educated to the same level as their brothers, Eleanor saw no reason why she and her women friends should not have the same rights as men so logic spelled out that women should have a role in guiding the state in the way they wanted it to go, which could be attained, they thought, through giving women the same voting rights as men.

Eleanor took her final exams in 1896. Her tutors had forecast a possible First. In the event, they were all disappointed. Her Greek and Latin were not very good and she was a slow writer. This clarified for her what she should do in the future. If she had got a First she may well have stayed on in Oxford in the hope of getting a tutorship. This blow to her self-esteem ruled out this course of action as she and her close friend, Margery Fry, walked round the garden in Somerville discussing what their future could be. They knew they had good brains. They knew they wanted to put them to the service of their fellow men and women, but how? There seemed no way forward because they were women. 'Parliament was shut to us' they concluded. 'There was nothing worthwhile to be ambitious about.' In their pessimism, there were at least two things Eleanor did. One was to provide anonymous support for a research student at Somerville and the other was to instigate a dinner to be held every November for alumnae of the college, a gaudy night, as the men's colleges all have.

Liverpool

After Somerville, Eleanor returned to Liverpool where she was to live for the next twenty years. At the end of the nineteenth century, Liverpool docks handled half of all the commercial tonnage entering Britain. Builders could not keep pace with the demand for warehousing and housing for the workers, and an army of clerks handled the paperwork for the shipping industry. The local population had been swelled by waves of immigration from Ireland during the potato famines and Russian Jews escaping persecution in the 1880s. For many of these immigrants, Liverpool was the starting point for a new life in the USA but many others stayed in the city where it was easy to make a living in its boom economy.

There were several problems arising from the sudden increase in population and the structure of the economy. Most of the work available was casual labour and few men worked a full week, a situation that was convenient for employers because the competition for work kept wages low. Labourers working on the docks had to live within walking distance of work, meaning accommodation here was always in short supply and very overcrowded, with all the sickness and ill health that implied. There was very little work for women, who had to support their families on a fluctuating wage, depending on when their husbands found work and whether or not they called in the pub on the way home, so the women were forced to try to level out their finances by regular visits to the pawnshop or the money lender.

Needless to say, Eleanor Rathbone did not live in the crowded terraces near the docks. She returned to the family home, Greenbank, on the outskirts of the city, where the running of the home had been ceded by her mother to her older sister Elsie. Her father had resigned as an MP, finding the debates more and more difficult to follow as his deafness encroached. William looked to his daughter to help him with his philanthropic work in the city, though this was not necessarily to Eleanor's liking. She wanted, as Miss Maitland at Somerville had suggested, to use her talents and powers to open doors for other women. She almost immediately joined the Women's Industrial Council, an organisation that collected and publicised information about women's work, with a view to preventing their exploitation in sweatshops. She also became secretary of the NUWSS, which necessitated frequent visits to London.

At her father's suggestion, she began work as a 'friendly visitor' for the Liverpool Central Relief Society (LCRS). This was a society aiming to relieve distress in poor families without causing dependency. Her father had thought the Society unnecessarily bureaucratic and unfriendly. He had seen how similar organisations worked in Germany, using philanthropic almoners to check how the system was working and, when he suggested a similar scheme in Liverpool, the LCRS decided to set up district offices run by volunteer friendly visitors. William Rathbone was keen to see how these worked and Eleanor was given the task of finding out.

Her report was damning. She reported that the scheme did little long-term good. The visitors were sympathetic but untrained and gullible, or with too many cases to deal with any of them properly. The weekly doles of food and fuel kept people from the worst excesses of poverty but had no effect on the long-term aim of improving people's ability to manage their income. It sustained the evils of low pay and casual labour, and reduced the inducement to save. In contrast with the London CRS, the Liverpool Society never provided, for instance, tools for a man to make a living, or a mangle so a woman might earn money from taking in washing or, indeed, training for a boy or girl. They were purely concerned with keeping body and soul together and that, Eleanor said, was not good enough.

The last two years of her father's life Eleanor devoted almost exclusively to helping him with correspondence and with pursuing the work he could no longer do himself. So she wrote to the Mayor of Liverpool, suggesting improvements to municipal services; to wealthy friends, asking for endowments for the university and, at her father's suggestion, began to investigate the problem of casual labour, though she didn't see what use it would be.

Her survey of the situation was to bear fruit in 1912, however. Her description of the working habits of casual labourers and the stress it put on their wives was to lead to her being called to give evidence before the Royal Commission on the Poor Laws on poverty in Liverpool. As a consequence, the Liberal government of 1912 took up the issue of decasualisation of dock labour. 'It is by the wives and children that the hardship of irregular earnings are felt most keenly,' Eleanor wrote. Many of the men were chronically underemployed, their wages varying from week to week, but the needs of their families and the money needed to feed and clothe wives and children did not vary.

When William died, he left Eleanor £5,000 to add to the equivalent of a marriage portion he had already given her so she was now a woman of independent means. The first task she set herself was writing her father's biography. It was the story of his engagement in public life and hardly mentions the family. It was as he would have wished, with public duty at the forefront and his family kept in the privacy they had always enjoyed.

Miss Macadam

Since leaving Somerville, Eleanor had been lonely. She missed her friendships with other young women such as Margery Fry. She was shortly, however, to meet a woman who would be a lifelong friend and companion, Elizabeth Macadam.

Elizabeth Macadam had been working at the Women's University Settlement in South London, where she had learnt the basics of social work and had run clubs and supervised cases there. There she acquired a belief in the importance of friendships and civic action across class lines. Most young women graduating from

Somerville or LMH had experience of these settlements. Elizabeth Macadam was good at working with 'the rough boys and girls' who came to the classes and her four years there gave her training, mentors and an ability to earn her own living. She heard on the grapevine that the Victoria Settlement in Liverpool was in need of a warden and, lured by the promise of £30 a year salary, decided to apply for the post.

The Victoria Settlement was a residential house for women social workers in Everton. The Settlement had been up and running since 1897 and was a centre for girls' clubs, a dispensary for women and children, for classes for disabled children, and the centre where Maude Royden had worked. Their first appeal was for a donkey and cart to bring the children to the centre. Although the work went well, there had been financial and administrative difficulties since the centre opened and a general philosophy was lacking. Settlement workers, as Maude Royden had done, collected people's contributions – a penny a week – to the District Provident Society and referred families in distress to the Poor Law Guardians but beyond that, had no clear idea of where the settlement was heading.

Macadam had ambitions for the settlement. She wanted it to be as good as the London Settlement, where she had trained. She first began to recruit some of the now 400 women students who attended the university. Among the people she interested was Eleanor Rathbone. Elizabeth Macadam and Eleanor formed an instant rapport and between them, and Emily Jones, who had accompanied Elizabeth north, they ran the centre and transformed its work. Macadam and Jones ran the relief operations while the social investigative side of the work was left to Eleanor. The Rathbone money came in useful. Eleanor from time to time helped out when money was running short, and funded the move to bigger premises. Her mother's money paid for a garden and her aunt provided money to endow a scholarship for training in social work.

Macadam and Jones had two aims: to professionalise the work undertaken by the settlement and in order to do this, to ensure women had some training in social work and secondly to foster cross-class friendships between workers and clients. To the former end, she and Eleanor lobbied friends at the university and in 1905, the School of Social Science and Training for Social Work was set up. By 1906 the school was offering a two-year course combining lectures with practical work. Lectures covered sociology, philosophy, history, civic administration, voluntary effort and the Poor Law. Macadam also insisted that students should have some experience of Friendly Societies, the Co-operative Society and the Workers' Educational Association.

Macadam built up the branches of the work that did not involve material aid and encouraged such services as the dispensary, the holiday funds, and the work with invalid children to become to some extent self-supporting. Her belief was that the idea of independence was as important to working class people as to the middle classes. She was particularly pleased when women from the surrounding streets began to take responsibility for running the programmes. An Office of Friendly Help was set up to provide advice, which dealt with 1,000 people in its first year, not giving out money, but directing people to where they might obtain the help they needed.

With so much happening it was important to collate information about what local charities could offer, and who was using them, to prevent duplication and co-ordinate responses to poverty. A Council of Voluntary Aid was set up, its main worker funded by Eleanor, and was a great success. Even so, more State aid was needed and Macadam was happy to see services, which the settlement had initiated, taken under the wing of the local authority.

The settlement was also becoming politically active. By bringing together women who had views about what their social needs were, and had knowledge of charities and local government, they were in a position to express with confidence their ideas of what needed to be done. These women now had the opportunity to stand for election for school boards and as Poor Law guardians. When women ratepayers obtained the right to stand for the city council, Eleanor decided to try her luck. She stood as an Independent and as both the Conservatives and the Liberals wanted to keep out the Labour candidate, they agreed not to put up a candidate against her. She stressed her knowledge and experience of local government, and the importance of having a woman on the council who could represent the woman's point of view, and was voted in by 1,066 against the Labour Party's 516. She held the seat until she resigned in1935.

Eleanor had to work hard at the social investigations she undertook. She had read Classics at university, which was no sort of introduction to social surveys, but she must have been aware of the work of Seebohm Rowntree in York, whose surveys of working-class life had proved a revelation. She started studying political questions and statistics, and tested theories against the information she was gathering from working-class women about their living conditions, the conditions of the dock labourers and the household budgets of casual labourers and their wives.

She viewed these surveys through feminist eyes and sought to discover how life could be improved for the women, who had no control over family finances, since a man's wage was, in many men's eyes, theirs to do with as they pleased. But Eleanor saw that married women worked as well. They were not paid for what they did when they were bearing and rearing children, keeping house, washing the family clothes, scrubbing the family floors. They were nevertheless working extremely hard. The assumption was that the man's wage would support his family but if he chose not to do so, there was little the wife could do. Power was in the hands of the husband, and his wife was dependent on him.

The solution to this problem, it seemed to Eleanor, was that families should be paid an amount of money by the State according to how many children they had. The money should be paid to the wife, who had the primary care of the children, which would redress the financial and power balance within the family and thus at a stroke, improve life for many working-class wives.

Eleanor thought that Family Endowment – what we now call Family Allowance – was the way forward. The insight she brought to the matter was slow to develop and found its full expression years later when she wrote *The Disinherited Family*. The trade unions opposed the idea, both because it undermined men's role as providers for their families and because it might well undermine any wage claims they might wish to make.

Eleanor also tackled the question of widowhood. Widows, she argued, should be treated by Poor Law Guardians differently from others. If she was caring for her children properly, then she was performing her half of the bargain of family life. Relief for widows, she argued, should be much more generous than the shilling a head allotted to a family under the Liverpool Poor Laws and the money should be administered by women officers. She spoke with feeling about the conditions many women laboured under.

It is hard for a woman to be an efficient housewife and parent while she is living under conditions of extreme poverty – obliged to live in an insanitary house because it is cheap; waging a continual war with the vermin which infests such houses; unable to spend anything on repairs and replacements of household gear unless she takes it off the weekly food money; limited in the use of soap, soda and even hot water, because of the cost of coal; with no pennies for the postage or tram rides that would keep up her own and her children's intercourse with relatives at a distance; or give a day's holiday in the parks or on the sands; or enable her to frequent the Labour Exchange to seek better work for herself or the elder boys and girls.

Eleanor knew why widows were so badly treated. 'The reason that the claim of widows for different treatment has been so long unrecognised is clearly not far to seek. All widows are women and none of them therefore are Parliamentary voters.'

Liverpool Women's Suffrage Society (LWSS)
Eleanor had been a leading light in the suffrage movement since leaving Somerville. When the Pankhursts formed the WSPU, the LWSS, along with the NUWSS, distanced itself from it because of its violent tactics. Eleanor was convinced violence did not work. LWSS did, however, change their approach to supporting the cause. They moved out from their sedate and inward looking meetings to preaching on the street corner and on the docks, where they often had a receptive audience. The West Lancashire Federation had a caravan, in which they toured outlying villages, trying to convert people to the cause. During the passage of the Conciliation Bill in 1911 and 1912, Eleanor brought a petition from Liverpool women ratepayers to the City Council and convinced the Council to pass a resolution urging the government to give the Bill parliamentary time.

Eleanor thought that legitimate authority derived from the people as a whole, not from the passing whims of politicians, which is why she sought to build public support for her ideas, so canvassing, petitions and collecting signatures were important. She acknowledged that the militants had courage but 'it requires something better than courage to resist all temptation to quicken the pace by succumbing to the dangerous doctrine that the end justifies the means,' she wrote.

In the years before the Great War, the Independent Labour Party (ILP) was affiliated to the Labour Party, which was becoming increasingly politically important. Many in the suffrage movement had changed their allegiance from the Liberals, who they felt had failed them, to the ILP and/or the Labour Party. By 1914 the ILP had begun to be anxious about how reliable the support from the NUWSS would be in the event of an election. To show their solidarity with the ILP, three delegates were sent by the NUWSS to the ILP conference. The delegates must have been carried away by the excitement generated in the meeting because they promised that even if the Liberals pledged their support for women's suffrage, the NUWSS would support the ILP in any constituency where there was a Labour candidate standing. As a member of the NUWSS committee and a Liberal, Eleanor realised that these delegates were making promises about NUWSS policy that they had no right to make. As a Liberal, she was appalled. As an NUWSS executive committee member, she was extremely angry that the policy of the NUWSS was being made without any discussion by the executive.

With her clear and logical mind, and lack of social subtlety, she tackled the matter head-on and complained, expecting the executive to be equally outraged. They were not. They supported the three delegates. Not content to leave it there, Eleanor and her Liverpool colleagues circularised other branches, asking for their support against the executive to prevent the NUWSS Election Fund being spent against the Liberal Party. Quite apart from the fact that policy had been made on the hoof, as it were, there was the question of how successful this policy would be. Eleanor's fears were justified. Between 1912 and 1914, the NUWSS Election Fighting Fund was used to support eight Labour candidates, none of whom was successful. For four of them, though, the Labour vote was large enough to damage the Liberal vote to such an extent that the Conservative candidate was elected. Eleanor and three of her supporters resigned from the executive and though Mrs Fawcett wrote that she regretted Miss Rathbone's departure, the others did not bother her in the least.

This event was a grievous blow to Eleanor. She had been very hurt by the public criticism of people she regarded as friends and she had been on the executive almost since its formation. She had been accused, she felt, of being underhand and that she had been plotting to undermine the executive's decisions. She, of course, heard of Mrs Fawcett's comments about her supporters, which again upset her.

Wartime

When war was declared, Eleanor and Elizabeth, who had been spending considerable amounts of time in London, returned to Liverpool and immediately found themselves embroiled in war work. A total of 35,000 men had volunteered to fight for their country, 13,500 of whom were to lose their lives, which meant that many families were desperate for money, since the government had yet to sort out support for soldiers' families. Food prices had shot up and many families were in desperate need.

Very soon Eleanor emerged as the head of the local Soldiers' and Sailors' Families Organisation (SSFA), charged with the task of assisting military families. All soldiers' and sailors' families would now be eligible for maintenance payments. By September half-a-million families were entitled to support but the War Office had no idea who the wives were, how many children there were, there were no agreed rates of benefit, no claim forms and virtually no staff, so they turned to voluntary groups to do their administration for them.

In Liverpool the Victoria Settlement had an extensive network of contacts and workers so could help but money was slow in coming, so Eleanor's cousin Herbert, who was Mayor of Liverpool, was asked to help and he transferred £20,000 of locally subscribed funds to Liverpool SSFA.

This in itself raised a problem for many Labour and Liberal politicians, who objected to public money being administered by volunteers. All basic allowances were graduated according to family size and were paid directly to the wives of combatants. Left-leaning politicians thought a flat rate of payment would be better than a system that meant volunteers visiting and assessing families' needs.

In November the government turned the problem over to a select committee, headed by Bonar Law and Lloyd George who, in January 1915, summoned Eleanor Rathbone to explain the Liverpool system. By this time, the Liverpool SSFA had 17,000 families on its books. Each family, visited every week by one of the 700 volunteers, drew its basic allowance through the Post Office and was given supplementary grants from the charity, when needed.

In spite of this sterling work, Eleanor had a rough ride with the committee. Unbeknown to her, she had been 'set up'. The

Conservative leader of the Liverpool council had been, perhaps understandably, outraged that Eleanor had used her connections and persuaded her cousin to draft a very large sum of money to the charity, which was now, he told Bonar Law, under the direction of suffragettes. Rathbone stood her ground. SSFA had saved the government from scandal in the early months of the war, she pointed out. Her female visitors were more sympathetic and professional than male pensions officers. The visits established a sense of community and gave combatants' wives someone to turn to in times of trouble. The government had not been fair to voluntary workers and, if new public bodies were to be set up, they should co-opt a reasonable number of women, 'by which we do not mean one woman on each committee.'

In 1915 the government divested the SSFA of its administrative role, switching administration to a new Ministry of Pensions. Eleanor, however, thought it would not be possible for the system to function without the co-operation of the SSFA and suggested to the National SSFA that they should be prepared to be absorbed into the fabric of the new administration, which is what happened. This maintenance money, though not generous, was a regular amount that working-class wives in Liverpool had often not been used to, so they had become *de facto* members of a social experiment demonstrating the benefits or otherwise of State intervention and a national endowment system.

Eleanor and her colleagues in Liverpool made one last social survey. They consulted the police, and health, housing and education authorities, who all came up with the same statement – that children were better cared for and looked healthier than in pre-war days. 'Separation allowances (i.e. family allowances) have raised the character and conditions in the homes amongst the poorest recipients', wrote Emma Mahler in *The Englishwoman* in 1917.

Meanwhile on the suffrage front, as we have already noted, several long-standing members of the executive of the NUWSS had resigned because of their support for the pacifist movement. Eleanor thought it a great pity and tried to resolve the differences, but to no avail. She rejoined the group, however. That same year Sir Edward Carson MP raised the question of what could be done about soldiers who did not qualify for the vote and pointed out that most would no longer meet the residency requirements in any forthcoming election.

The suffragists decided that if the question of the suffrage was being raised again, then they should make some kind of response. They formed a Consultative Committee to discuss the approach they should take. They needed to show that they had popular support so by 1916, had begun to hold meetings and demonstrations. In response, a committee of MPs looked into the question and, as we have seen, suggested that women over thirty or thirty-five be given the vote. In the end, the NUWSS accepted the compromise with the age fixed at thirty. So for ten years the vote was given to all men over twenty-one, (except conscientious objectors), all soldiers over eighteen, and eight million women who were over the age of thirty and themselves qualified for or were married to a man who qualified for the local franchise. Eleanor also lobbied for the franchise to be extended to local elections so women could vote for their local councillors, and this was eventually agreed.

Eleanor spent much of her time during the war in London and as time went on she realised that the war had centralised government policy-making and increased State intervention in family life. New ministries seemed to spring up overnight, though what they were all doing seemed somewhat obscure. The war had changed everything for women, and Eleanor realised there must be opportunities to extend women's influence in the political process and, in doing so, improve women's lives. Women had, after all, moved out of the home and into industry and many women had been acting heads of their households while their husbands were away or had been killed. Now was the time to push for Family Endowment, family allowance by another name. She set up the Family Endowment Committee with seven colleagues and friends, including Maude Royden and Kathleen Courtney, who believed in her idea. All except Eleanor were Labour supporters.

The main argument they put forward was that the main barrier to women's equality was her dependence on a man's wage. A married woman 'is still the uncharted servant of the future, who receives from her husband, at *his* discretion, a share in *his* wages.' They insisted this led, without consciously realising it, to a women's personality being corroded. It checked her development, and stunted her mind, even as a girl. An independent income for the woman would free not only women but men as well from these shackles. Care of children, they concluded, should be paid work.

Although only really a group of like-minded friends, the committee was asked to give evidence to the War Cabinet Committee on Women in Industry, and the National Birth Rate Commission. Nestling among the concerns about the fall in legitimate births, prevention of illegitimacy, the death rates of babies before and during birth, venereal disease not only in Britain but throughout the Dominions, and movements of population, there were the economic problems of parenthood. Giving evidence to the Commission was Maude Royden, on behalf of Eleanor's committee.

As Eleanor put it, 'the rearing of families is not a sort of masculine hobby, like tobacco smoking or pigeon flying' so why should the expense of family life be dealt with through the clumsy device of a man being paid to support his family?

The 1920s

Liverpool, like the rest of the country, was hit by recession in the 1920s and 30s. After a brief boom following the end of the war, when prices rose but wages rose more, by 1921 a slump set in that affected the whole country. Ten percent of the workforce was unemployed, with many more than the average being out of work in areas where heavy industry was concentrated. Coal mining, ship building, steel, and textiles were particularly affected so in some areas such as the north east, as much as seventy per cent of the workforce was on the dole. Liverpool tried to counter these conditions through a programme of civic building where slum housing was cleared and new houses built.

In spite of the large amounts of money she had lavished on political causes, Eleanor Rathbone had never been short of money because of the settlement her father had made on her. Her personal fortune was augmented in 1918 by the death of her half-sister Elsie, who left to Eleanor a substantial house on the edge of Liverpool, all her personal effects, and the residue of her estate, £100,000. This funded Eleanor's political career as Elsie had probably intended it to.

Elizabeth Macadam had been working at the Ministry of Munitions in London during the war but at the end of it, returned to Liverpool to take up her old post at the School of Social Work. She was no sooner settled there than she was asked to take up the joint secretaryship of a newly-constructed Joint University Council for Social Studies in London. Eleanor would probably have liked to stay in Liverpool, but realised her friend would not be as happy as she would be, and left it up to Elizabeth to decide what she really wanted to do. Eleanor would follow, wherever that led.

Elizabeth opted for London so they bought a house within easy walking distance of the Houses of Parliament, where they lived until they were bombed out in 1940. Their lives did not go as they had planned, however. Rather than Elizabeth's career taking off with the return of peace, the economic downturn put paid to her hopes of developing training courses for women, and she found herself increasingly playing a supporting role in Eleanor's multiplying fields of interests. She was, in effect, Eleanor's housekeeper.

The Post-war Suffrage Movement

As we have already seen, Eleanor had rejoined the NUWSS when the organisation had been ravaged by the secession of the pacifists in 1915. In 1918, Mrs Fawcett decided it was time for her to retire, since there had been a partial success in gaining the vote for women over thirty. The organisation re-formed and renamed itself the National Union of Societies for Equal Citizenship (NUSEC) of which Eleanor became president, with Macadam as secretary and editor of the paper.

In the 1918 election, seventeen women managed to find seats to contest, among then Christabel Pankhurst, but only one succeeded, Countess Markievitz, who stood for election as a Sinn Feinner and refused to take up her seat at Westminster. It was a sorry blow to the hopes of everyone in the suffrage movement, who really believed that now women had the vote, society would change. At the same time, in the municipal elections where many women stood as independent, most were defeated and were forced, in order to be acceptable to the electorate, to align themselves with political parties.

In response to promises made to the trade unions during the war, one of the first measures to be introduced by the newly elected Parliament was the Restoration of Pre-war Practices Act, which effectively removed women from better paid industrial work and put them firmly back in the home. By 1921 the percentage of women in industry was no higher than it had been in 1911.

In this situation, it was important to be seen to occupy the roles and opportunities in public life that still existed. When it became possible for women to become magistrates, Eleanor became a Justice of the Peace for Lancashire. She also tried to convince NUSEC that feminism should take on board the needs of married women forced back into the home and into dependence on their husbands by supporting her idea of family endowment. Many of the members of NUSEC were, at most, lukewarm in their support and when the matter came to the vote in 1921, the adoption of family endowment as a policy failed, albeit by only three votes. It has to be admitted that as a leader, though she had the rhetoric and the clear thinking necessary for leadership, she lacked charm and persuasiveness and increasingly relied on a very small number of women to run the organisation. It was perceived by outsiders as old-fashioned, cliquey and composed of ladies of leisure, not relating to the real world of women's position in society in the 1920s.

NUSEC did, however, achieve certain aims. While not organising eye-catching marches and rallies, they were quietly working on boring, painstaking methods of raising awareness. They wrote pamphlets, they lobbied members of Parliament, they drafted Bills, and when some project failed, they started again. Their ideas were rarely wholly adopted but they gradually moved matters in their direction. The decade saw an improvement in women's access to pensions, divorce, the guardianship of children, and separation and maintenance from abusive husbands.

By the mid 1920s, some members of NUSEC were wanting to extend its fighting front to cover the 'grievously oppressed' working mothers by lobbying for access to contraceptive advice and, of course, a family endowment policy. This made others of the feminist movement uneasy, notably, Viscountess Rhondda, who wrote that it was now clear that NUSEC contained several people among the leadership who were first and foremost sociologists and philanthropists, or internationalists and party politicians, and only secondarily feminists, and that feminists should be concerned primarily with equality between the sexes. This argument rumbled on, mirrored in America by the same problem of how to define feminism and therefore how to decide what their aims should be. Equalitarians, as Rhondda's supporters were named, had adopted a 'pitifully narrow definition of equality', according to Eleanor, which took no account of women's lives as lived. However, both sides agreed on the need for equal franchise, though Rhondda's faction labelled NUSEC no longer a feminist body.

Both sides united in 1928 to organise an Equal Franchise Council, which would organise a great public meeting to press for an extension of the vote for women. NUSEC's membership soared as it was realised one final push was needed and on 2 July 1928, the Equal Franchise Bill became law. Following that landmark decision, NUSEC went into steady decline, with its energies directed towards building up civic associations in towns on the lines of the Women's Institute in country areas. These were known as the Townswomen's Guilds and the NUSEC newspaper, *Woman's Leader,* became *The Townswoman.*

Westminster

While much progress had been made in opening up opportunities for women, Eleanor realised that to make more progress, there had to be an engagement with national politics. Two women had been elected to Parliament – Nancy Astor and Margaret Wintringham – with Astor taking her husband's seat of Plymouth when he was elevated to the peerage in 1919, a seat she kept until 1945; and Wintringham also taking her husband's seat at a by-election caused by his death. Margaret Wintringham was a member of the Women's Institute and said her time in that organisation had given her a very good grounding for Parliamentary life. Elected in 1921, she lost her seat in 1924, but had made good use of her time there. She worked to increase women's suffrage, for equal pay, for state scholarships for girls, and for women-only railway carriages. (This was at a time when many trains had no corridors.)

Eleanor Rathbone had no husband but she had plenty of clout in the Liverpool area – relations, money, and a family history of philanthropy. In 1922 the Liverpool Labour and Liberal parties decided not to split the vote against the Conservatives and withdrew their candidates so Eleanor could have a clear run against the Conservative sitting member. She knew she was the underdog and said, 'I am bound to say that, middle-aged woman as I am, I feel like a very inadequate David going out to do battle with Goliath'. Everyone was fairly confident she stood a good chance of winning the seat but on the eve of polling, a leaflet appeared warning that Miss Rathbone advocated a dangerous and socialist scheme that would tax single men to subsidise married men with children. As Sir Archibald Savidge, leader of the local Tory party, put it: 'What the Britisher wants is freedom, and I say a man who has earned his weekly money has a right to spend it as he thinks'. The Conservative won 15,149 votes to Eleanor's 9,984. Eleanor did not contest a Liverpool seat again.

Though not in Parliament, Eleanor did not waste the following few years. She wrote *The Disinherited Family*. She starts from the premise that the family is the most important social institution, but its claims as an economic unit have been ignored. Economists usually consider the portion of the population directly involved in paid work (usually men). The labour through which the population is produced and made productive (women) is largely ignored. So poverty is treated as largely the result of low wages. With relentless logic and the use of irrefutable statistics, she goes on to show that the family endowment scheme is the only sensible idea to solve the problem of children growing up in poverty and women's subjugation. Like slavery, marital dependence, in Rathbone's opinion, might be caused by economic factors but it was lived out in labour and pain, physical and sexual. 'A man has no right to want to keep half the world in purgatory, because he enjoys playing redeemer to his own wife,' she wrote.

Eleanor wrote the book to influence the powerful people of her day, and she succeeded. The Labour Party was requested by the ILP to place family allowances on its legislative agenda, which directly led to the setting up of the Labour Party and Trade Union Congress's Joint Committee on the Living Wage, chaired by Ellen Wilkinson. William Beveridge, at that time Director of the London School of Economics, was completely converted to Eleanor's way of thinking after reading the book. Crucially, during the Second World War, Beveridge wrote the Beveridge Report, which was instrumental in setting up the welfare state, brought in during 1945 by the Labour government. The TUC, led by Walter Citrine, was actually opposed to family allowances and sabotaged the progress Eleanor felt she was making. Neither Citrine nor his colleague Ernest Bevin had any sympathy with what they thought of as Eleanor's bullying approach. Having seen how the unions had fought to exclude women in earlier years in order to protect men's jobs and wages, Eleanor cannot have been surprised at their opposition.

The 1929 Election

This was the election when, for the first time, women had equal voting rights with men. It became known as the Flapper election and no one knew quite what would happen. In the event, there was a hung Parliament but the Labour party won most seats, though with no overall majority, so Ramsay Macdonald became Prime Minister.

Eleanor had decided it was worth trying again for election to the House of Commons. She refused to align herself with any party so would have to stand as an Independent. The older universities had had a Member of Parliament to represent their interests for many years and, because of the creation of the new universities, there were now twelve such seats. Any graduate was entitled to vote and, given the demographic of people graduating, most of those elected were Conservatives. Eleanor had been interested to note, however, that in the 1924 election, an Independent had been voted in for the University of London. The two-member constituency of Combined English Universities had been added in 1918 to give representation to places such as Birmingham, Leeds, Manchester, Bristol, Reading, Sheffield, and Durham. Being new, apart from Durham, and forward thinking, these universities were considerably less hidebound than Oxford and Cambridge, and Eleanor felt she might have a chance of success. Most people who stood for election in these seats did not canvas. Perhaps it was considered unsporting. But Eleanor wanted to win. So she travelled to the various university towns to explain what she believed in. To her great delight, she came top of the polls in every university she had visited. She could thus join the thirteen other women who had been elected to Parliament: nine Labour, three Conservative and one Liberal. Being an Independent had both a good and a bad side to it. For the good, she did not have to fit in with a party whip and vote or speak about anything in which she did not truly believe. The not so good side was that she had sometimes very little support, and little influence on party agendas.

There was a great deal of unspoken resentment and nervousness from the male Members of Parliament. Churchill, never short of a jibe or two at women's expense, is rumoured to have told Nancy Astor he felt as if she had entered his bathroom when he was undefended by so much as a sponge, to which she briskly replied, 'Nonsense, Winston, you're not attractive enough to have fears of that sort'.

Amazingly, one of the first debates to attract Eleanor's attention was what is now called Female Genital Mutilation (FMG) but was then called cliterodectomy. This was in December 1929, when the Duchess of Atholl raised the matter in the course of a debate about East African colonies. The debate was about colonial policy in relation to 'the coloured races'. They excluded India from the discussion, and discussed the situation mainly in East, Central and South Africa, where substantial numbers of whites had settled.

The Duchess and her fellow workers on the subject, among them Eleanor Rathbone, had been to see the Secretary of State to ask him to set up a Select Committee to look into the matter, but he had refused, though he promised to communicate with Governors of the Crown Colonies when she told him that some of the Kikuyu themselves would like to see the practice discontinued.

The thinking behind the debate, when it started, was about land settlement, the need to protect black men from being exploited by their employers, but it also included a phrase referring to 'due care of Native social well-being', where the speaker discussed the importance of the health and education of the native population. This made it possible for the Duchess of Atholl, a Conservative, to raise the matter of female circumcision. She revealed that a small group had been meeting and talking with missionaries and doctors who had practised most notably in Uganda, Kenya and Southern Nigeria. The Duchess of Atholl spared none of the details of how the mutilation was carried out, and the subsequent consequences to the girls – the blood poisoning, which killed many; their health in adult life, and the excruciating difficulties when giving birth, which resulted in only six out of ten first babies surviving. The practice was on the decrease in Uganda but the lack of midwives in Nigeria and among the Kikuyu in Kenya was a great bar to progress.

John Maxton, a member of the ILP and MP for a Glasgow seat, accused the Duchess of Atholl of pursuing her own interests, at which Eleanor Rathoben interrupted him, saying 'Women do not count!' The speaker ruled in the duchess' favour and the debate continued. She gave an example of a Christian girl who had resisted the mutilation to no effect, except that afterwards she had sought a ruling from the native court, which had ruled that no grievous harm had been done to the girl. She then made an appeal to the Supreme Court of Kenya, which upheld the native court's decision. The woman who performed the operation had however been fined thirty shillings.

Eleanor then spoke, supporting the Duchess but extending the discussion further by stressing that the conditions women and girls were living in in parts of Africa amounted to slavery. Girls, she said, were sold by their families as wives, having no choice over the matter. They had no autonomy, no education, no protection, and were forced to do exactly as their husbands demanded. 'It has been a terrible shock to many of us,' she said, 'that there is slavery under the British flag, not in small numbers but some millions of women, and it is tolerated so long as you can get away under the pretence that it is a domestic custom.' She asked for a small amendment to be added to the Bill. She wanted 'or sex' added so the motion would then read: 'Native self-governing institutions should be fostered and franchise and legal rights should be based upon the principle of equality for all without regard to colour or sex.'

The debate quoted above clearly demonstrates one of Eleanor's tactics. Not having the support of a political party, she used amendments to Bills already introduced to make the law more aware of women. Just the introduction of the words 'or sex' immediately included all the women in the colonies who had hitherto been virtually excluded from legislature, and raised men's awareness that women also had needs that did not necessarily coincide with those of men. This did not, of course, mean they would act on their knowledge.

She also made sure she was aware of the facts about a given subject, collecting information from witnesses who had direct experience of a particular situation. She made sure there was a group of people both inside and outside Parliament who would join her in a particular campaign, and she also made good use of Parliamentary questions, a tactic that would be used effectively in debates about child marriage in India, about housing, child welfare and other matters that concerned her.

In 1931 the Labour government, elected in 1929, was struggling with the country's finances as the recession hit ever harder. One solution being debated was the idea of cutting back on unemployment benefits. Margaret Bondfield, a shop worker before she engaged in politics, and the first woman minister in government, was Minister of Labour, a poisoned chalice at this particular time. She suggested that because of the financial situation, special regulations should be introduced limiting payments to groups reckoned to be claiming benefits while not looking for work. These were seasonal workers, short-time workers and married women. Rathbone tabled an amendment to delete the married women's clause, thus gaining the support of the ILP contingent of the Labour Party. The debate went on all night. Conservatives and Liberals went home, but the Labour members – and Eleanor Rathbone – slogged it out into the early hours. Rathbone suggested that married women were being scapegoated and Bondfield retorted that most married women supported her Bill. Rathbone's amendment was defeated, though Bondfield later agreed to exempt women whose husbands were dead or incapacitated. The Anomalies Act, as this piece of legislation became known, diminished the Labour Party in Eleanor's eyes so when Ramsay Macdonald decided to form a cross-party National Government in the summer of 1931, Eleanor Rathbone supported it. The country went to the polls in 1931 when the Labour majority was wiped out and there was a landslide victory to the Tories, who gained 76% of the seats.

The new intake of politicians – described by Eleanor as 'prosperous young men who have come almost straight from college' – didn't impress her. 'What do they know about working-class lives?' she asked. She did her best to educate them. She stopped talking about family endowment in these straitened times but used her knowledge of the housing legislation to urge local government to use subsidies to help poor families with their rents. She watched the benefits that had accrued to working wives disappear and their position regarding health insurance deteriorate.

In this Parliament, there was a great deal of cross-party collaboration and as the economic situation worsened and unemployment rates soared, fears arose about the effects of poverty, particularly on children. This fear was justified by a British Medical Association study on the level of nutrition for poor children. Eleanor was, of course, aware of this. She recruited Harold Macmillan and Robert Boothby, newly elected Conservatives, and Liberal Geoffrey Mander, into a Children's Minimum Council (CMC), which had one goal – to ensure that no child in a poor family was deprived of adequate food and necessities. She and Mander introduced an amendment to a Bill instructing the Unemployment Assistance Board to take into account the minimum requirements of healthy physical subsistence when setting rates. The amendment failed but, privately, the Minister of Labour promised the Board would indeed adhere to these principles. The CMC then bombarded the Board with literature about nutrition and sent deputations to Ramsay Macdonald, the Board of Education, and the Ministry of Health suggesting a range of measures – free milk, school meals and rent rebates for poor families – as the best way to ensure children were protected from the worst excesses of the recession. It was Eleanor and women from the Family Endowment Society who did most of the work.

The government refused to implement most of what the CMC suggested but the price of milk in schools was halved in 1934, probably because of a glut of milk and to pacify the farming lobby, and the number of children participating in the scheme more than doubled. The school meals service was also extended. By the late 1930s people such as William Beveridge and Mary Stocks on the Unemployment Insurance Statutory Committee and Violet Markham on the Unemployment Assistance Board came to agree that the only way to ensure a fair distribution of assistance was through family allowances. So while Eleanor had started her campaign for family endowment because of her feminist principles, by the time her idea was beginning to be adopted, the rationale behind the idea had changed to one of alleviating poverty.

India
Eleanor then returned to colonial matters, and particularly the position of women in the colonies, when the subject of the Indian constitution came up for discussion. In 1919 the Government of India Act had stipulated that the Indian situation should be considered every ten years. By 1927 a Commission had been established to look at that very question. It brought out its report in 1930 and was immediately subject to a barrage of criticism because there had been no Indians on the Commission. So round table discussions were set up to discuss devolution, to which Indian politicians were invited.

Eleanor, meanwhile, had read a book called *Mother India* by Katherine Mayo, which put forward the proposition that Hindus should not be allowed to govern the country because of the way they treated women, child brides being an aspect the book particularly focused on. The book was salacious and lurid and focused on the sexual aspects of Hindu culture, and was meant to sell. It did. It was very popular in Britain and America but Indians were outraged that they had been misrepresented in this way. Never having been to India, Eleanor wrote in a rather approving way about the book and organised a conference on the subject, to which she too omitted to invite any Indian women. Dhanvanthi Rama Rau, who went on to found the Family Planning Association of India, challenged Rathbone from the floor of the conference. She expressed Indian anger at the Mayo book and asked why Rathbone, who had written in support of such a tendentious and meretricious book, was chairing the conference. There were a great many educated Indian women who worked to ameliorate conditions in their own country, women who understood what they were about. The problem in India was not the fault of the people but the way the country was run, she said.

Eleanor must have been angry with herself for making such a monumental blunder and distanced herself from the subject for the time being. She did, however, take into account what Rama Rau had said. Having discovered that Indians had been the prime movers behind the Child Marriage Restraint Act in 1929, known as the Sarda Act, she tried to find out how well the Act was working. She peppered the Secretary of State for India, Willliam Wedgewood Benn, with parliamentary questions, to no avail. He either couldn't or wouldn't supply her with any information.

Having failed to obtain any useful information from the government, she tentatively began to contact Indian women for their assessment of the situation. She wrote first of all to Muthulakshmi Reddi, a doctor and former president of the Madras Legislative Council and to Radhabai Subbarayan, a moderate involved in constitutional negotiations. Both women told her that Indian women's organisations found it difficult to implement change because of government indifference and their own lack of political power. Indian women, at this time, had the same right to vote as men, but because it was based on property and few women held property in their own right, the proportion of men to women voters was twenty to one. Rathbone suggested the easiest way to even things up was to extend the vote to women whose husbands had the vote and increase the number of women in provincial and federal assemblies by reserving a quota of seats specifically for women. This would strengthen their political power and enable them to tackle the position of women in India.

Indian women, however, were opposed to these ideas. They wanted parity of voting power without being in any way dependent on men. Eleanor realised that there was no chance of this situation being granted by the British political classes and thought that this halfway house would at least ameliorate the situation. She failed to realise that Indian women were far more concerned about the independence of their country than they were about having the vote. Eleanor saw the Indian women she knew as partners, whereas they considered the British, even people who were sympathetic to their cause, as occupiers of their country. In effect, Rathbone was a problem for the Indians because the British government saw her as an expert although she was presenting not Indian women's feelings and ideas but her own.

When members of the round table talks decided to travel to India to increase their understanding of the situation, Eleanor's friends lobbied for her to be included – to no avail, however. Undeterred, Eleanor decided to go anyway. She also booked herself on the same boat as that taking the round tablers to India, hoping to be able to lobby them en route. They kept a very low profile on the journey, however, so she was unable to strike up any conversations with them.

In India she travelled widely. Talking to women in India itself, she came to realise the strength of the nationalist movement and the brutality of the British official response. She also enquired about the working of the Sarda Act concerning child brides. Wedgwood Benn had assured her that provincial governors were monitoring the workings of the Act but she found that these same men had never heard anything about it from Westminster.

She had learned a lot from her visit. In 1931 she told the Commons that independence for India was coming and that 'it is not for British women to dictate to Indian women as to how they shall use the power so entrusted to them', though it was certainly British women's responsibility to ensure that Indian women received their share of power, since the British government had failed to do so.

Palestine

Before these momentous events, however, Eleanor had her portrait painted and she and Macadam went to Palestine, part holiday and part fact-finding mission. 'I do not believe that I belong to the small class of persons who justify public portraits,' she said. It was a frivolous venture, she thought, when times were hard and, anyway, where would it hang? 'A spinster does not want to gaze on her own portrait in her own house', she said. But she reluctantly agreed and James Gunn was commissioned to paint her. It now hangs in the National Portrait Gallery.

The reason for the visit to Palestine was that at the time Eleanor was in conflict with the Colonial Office about a proposed municipal franchise bill for Palestine, which would disenfranchise women who had the vote in the Jewish areas of that country. Why was it any concern of hers? Because the Middle East, which had been part of the Ottoman Empire for four hundred years until the First World War blew it apart, had been carved up by Britain and France, with each country having areas of influence. The Sykes-Picot agreement, made in secret in 1917 and looking forward to a position after the war when the Ottoman empire might have fallen, gave to the British the responsibility of administering a strip of land between the River Jordan and the Mediterranean, Jordan, Southern Iraq and a small area on the Mediterranean coast between Haifa and Acre. In 1922 Britain obtained a mandate from the League of Nations to administer these areas until such time as they could stand on their own feet. The situation had been complicated by the Balfour Agreement, a letter sent from Foreign Secretary Balfour in 1917 to Walter Rothschild, leader of the Jewish community in Britain, affirming that the government would look kindly on the idea of the establishment of a homeland for Jewish people 'it being clearly understood that nothing shall be done which may prejudice the civic and religious rights of existing non-Jewish communities in Palestine, or the rights and political status enjoyed by Jews in any other country'.

Eleanor and Elizabeth flew to Ghaza where they hired a car and drove to Jerusalem. If only one could do that today! From there, they visited the excavations at Jericho and, Bible in hand, visited places with particular resonances for Christians: Bethlehem and Nazareth, as well as Bethesda, Hebron, Tiberias and Capernaum on the Sea of Galilee, even travelling as far as Damascus.

Rathbone liked and felt at home with the Jewish women she met – women such as Golda Meir, who later became Prime Minister of Israel; and Rosa Welt Strauss, an eye surgeon and long-time suffragist; and she found Jewish women more egalitarian than women in any other country she had visited. She was much less at ease in the Arab culture. She was prevented from eating any of the food prepared for her, and when she asked to see the women's quarters she found them squalid and dirty. She had asked for and was granted, after careful negotiations, an interview with the Grand Mufti. In her usual blunt manner, she told him she thought the Arabs took better care of their boys than of their women, which appalled the district officer who had arranged the interview.

Rathbone gave very few speeches – it was, after all, a holiday. But she did agree to speak to Rosa Strauss' Palestine Women's Equal Rights Association, where she praised the egalitarian approach to life in the Jewish settlements, but pointed out that when Arab women were still shackled by a traditional subjection, Jewish women should not be content with the situation. They should strive to emancipate Arab women.

The Rise of Fascism

Disabused of her belief that the British Empire was a force wholly for good, as the 1930s progressed Rathbone found herself and came to be seen as an independent defender of democratic ideals, increasingly important with the rise of Hitler in Germany and Mussolini in Italy.

Fascism is defined by the Oxford English Dictionary as 'an authoritarian and nationalistic right-wing system of government and social organisation'. It grew as a political movement in the first half of the twentieth century in Italy, Germany, and Spain and dominated the politics of the 1930s.

The Italian dictator Mussolini was the first to establish a fascist state. Following the end of the First World War, Mussolini tapped into the discontent of unemployed war veterans and turned them into an armed squad known as the Black Shirts. These men terrorised their opponents and by 1921, Mussolini was asked to join a coalition government. The political situation descended into chaos and in 1922, the Black Shirts marched on Rome and Mussolini presented himself as the only man who could save the situation. He was asked to form a government by King Victor Emmanuel. From then till the end of the Second World War, the Italian state was held together by strong central control and the personality cult of 'Il Duce'.

Mussolini wanted to build an empire to rival that of ancient Rome. The term 'fascism' itself refers back to the bundle of rods, the fasces, carried by lictors before a magistrate or consul as a symbol of their authority in classical times.

In 1935 Mussolini decided to invade Abyssinia, now known as Ethiopia. The country was situated between two Italian colonies, Eritrea and Somaliland, and had rich soil and an abundance of mineral resources. In addition, the country had only recently seen a change of government with the advent of King Haile Selassie.

As Mussolini massed his troops on the border, he was expecting a rapid conquest of the country. The fact that both Italy and Abyssinia belonged to the League of Nations, whose main aim was to maintain peace between member countries, held him back not one whit. His troops poisoned wells and used mustard gas against undefended villages and medical facilities so it was not surprising that Abyssinia capitulated and Haile Selassie fled the country. Britain and France were also members of the League of Nations and should have done more to support Abyssinia. They were pusillanimous in their opposition, however, refusing to close the Suez Canal to Italian shipping and continuing to supply oil to the Italians.

Eleanor stood up in Parliament and pointed out that six months before, the House had urged the government to make it clear to any aggressor that the authority of the League of Nations could not be flouted but instead Britain and France had colluded to reward Mussolini. And this was not, she added, because the Italian army had been so successful. The Abyssinians were fighting back bravely. It was to avoid war with Germany and Italy. Concessions to Italy, she argued, would embolden, not conciliate, Germany and they would frighten other vulnerable states. In the event, Mussolini's flagrant breach of the League of Nations code of conduct destroyed the organisation, as Rathbone had predicted, showing it up as the weak and ineffective association it was. She thought Britain was to blame for not enforcing sanctions against Italy and pleaded unsuccessfully for a pension for Haile Selassie. She also opposed League and government recognition of Italian rule in Abyssinia and, when the Second World War eventually forced a change of policy, worked with Philip Noel-Baker to extract a pledge to restore Ethiopia to full independence.

By the time of the Abyssinian crisis, Eleanor Rathbone had had plenty of time to sort out her ideas about fascism. Hitler had risen to power in Germany in 1933 and immediately the persecution of the Jews began. In 1934, health insurance was denied them. In 1935, Jews could no longer hold German citizenship, and so on. A gradual state-led campaign to render Jews non-persons culminated in Kristallnacht in 1938 and the removal of 20,000 Jews to concentration camps.

In April 1933, just three months after Hitler's accession to power, Eleanor spoke in a debate about Britain's attitude to the new regime in Germany, which was requesting an easing of the conditions imposed following the country after the First World War, including permission to rearm. Given Hitler's ideas and treatment of the Jews, it would be a crime to accede to their requests, she said.

Eleanor judged states by their record on civil liberties and political rights, and always placed liberty as the first requirement of any state. She had been undecided about whether to support the Labour party or the government in their dealings with international relations. At first she had favoured supporting the Labour Party because of their belief in the importance of the League of Nations but, by 1935, declared herself very much against appeasement. 'No one who has studied the evidence can doubt that Germany wants peace just until she has completed the preparations for war,' she said.

When Hitler began to remilitarise the Rhineland in 1936, Eleanor spent much of her time trying to persuade the public of the need to stand up to the Nazi menace. European security rested on it, she said. One of the problems clouding the issue, in her opinion, was the extreme dislike of many in the Conservative party of communism and their distrust of communists because it made them too prepared to comply with Germany's territorial ambitions in Eastern Europe. They hoped Germany and Russia would fight it out and leave western Europe in peace. But a European crisis was likely to start in Czechoslovakia, Eleanor said, with the German minority there being secretly stirred up by Hitler. Under the current British government it was unlikely, she thought, that either Britain or France would come to the aid of Czechoslovakia. 'If we are determined to have peace at any price, even at the price of sacrificing the world's security on the altar of our own security, let us say so,' she declared. 'But whether we shall secure peace even for ourselves permanently by a policy of continually truckling to dictators, yielding step by step, many of us doubt.' She thought Churchill's analysis of the situation accurate and was heartened that someone, albeit someone distrusted by the left of the Labour Party, could see clearly what was afoot. She got nowhere with her rhetoric, however.

In July 1936 another crisis arose, this time in Spain. An election had given power to the Popular Front, a Republican political movement. This was immediately challenged by a junta of military leaders in Morocco. Foreign powers immediately became involved. The Soviet Union supported the Republicans, while the Germans and Italians supported the Nationalists, soon to be under the command of General Franco. Their aircraft airlifted the generals and their supporters from Morocco to the mainland. A few months later, in August, the first International Brigade arrived in Spain. These brigades were mainly made up of communists and socialists from across Europe, even from Italy. The international aspect of the conflict was co-ordinated through Paris and within Spain, Albacete became their headquarters. French communists provided the uniforms. Approximately 2,300 people from Britain joined the International Brigades, among them Julian Bell, nephew of Virginia Woolf, who died at Brunete in July 1937.

The British and French governments had decided on a policy of non-intervention. Eleanor disagreed because the Spanish government had been elected by the people, and the Germans and Italians were so flagrantly interfering. She agreed to chair the Communist-inspired Committee of Inquiry into Breaches of International Law Relating to Intervention in Spain. They heard eye-witness accounts of the war and concluded that the attitudes of the British and French governments had denied arms to the Spanish government while failing to block supplies to the Nationalists. Eleanor spent the next six months castigating the government for its lack of action and pointing out how the Germans and Italians were acting, including the infamous bombing of the Basque town of Guernica, the first bombing of civilians in war.

She tried to interest the League of Nations in the matter, but they were so hamstrung by their fear of communism that they refused to act. Eleanor's Parliamentary interventions became more and more strident. In 1936–37 she asked 89 questions and in the following year, 100 in order to obtain as much embarrassing information as she could from the government. She was a voice crying in the wilderness, however.

Well, if the country could not be roused by her rhetoric and the government would not mount any opposition to the encroaches of fascism, she would do it herself. She joined forces with Katherine Stewart-Murray, Duchess of Atholl, with whom she had been corresponding since 1933. Eleanor had become fully cognisant of Hitler's ideas on politics and the state because the Duchess of Athol had read *Mein Kampf* in the original German and had been so appalled at the omissions made in the English translation that she had commissioned an unexpurgated edition with key extracts published in pamphlet form.

In 1936 after the duchess gave a speech about the need to sustain the independence of the East European states, Kitty, as Eleanor had begun to call her, was surprised to learn that it had been widely read in Romania and she was deluged with invitations to visit. The Duchess decided to go and invited Eleanor Rathbone to accompany her. In their notes back to the Foreign Office, they recorded the high level of Nazi propaganda and anti-Semitism in Romania but also a great enthusiasm for ties with Britain.

Two months later they set off again, for Spain, this time accompanied by Ellen Wilkinson, a Socialist member of Parliament, and Dame Rachel Crowdy, former director of the Social Welfare Section of the League of Nations. Atholl and Rathbone travelled as chairman and vice-chair of the National Joint Committee for Spanish Relief whose aims were to care for refugees from the conflict, oversee the evacuation of civilians from war-affected areas and to provide medical relief. Their visit was one of solidarity with the elected government so naturally their travels were restricted to the parts of the country controlled by the Republicans.

They reported that the Republic was dealing very well with the needs of children and political prisoners, but was desperately short of medical supplies and food. The National Committee was hampered to some extent by the refusal of the Catholics and the pro-Francoists to work with Communists, who were members of the committee, but they nevertheless raised £100,000 for medical and food aid. One of their most effective campaigns was the removal of 4,000 Basque children to England when the Basque Country fell to the Nationalists in 1937, and the dispatch of medical supplies and food in 1938.

Just before the city of Santander fell to the Nationalists in August 1937, Eleanor was trying to get supplies into the city and refugees out. A captain of one of the boats, who was prepared to fetch refugees, cabled her to say that the British Navy seemed more concerned to keep British ships out of Spanish territorial waters than to protect them from Nationalist shelling within the three mile limit. The night before Santander fell, more than 100,000 refugees crowded the quays trying to flee the shelling of the Nationalists. Many drowned and there was nothing Eleanor could do about it. She was incandescent with rage. The Hague Convention insisted that refugees should be rescued if their lives were in danger, she pointed out. The bombing of Guernica, the fall of Bilbao,

Santander and Gijon and the ports along the north coast of Spain; the ruthless mass executions of prisoners – none of these would have happened were it not for the policy of preventing Spain's legitimate government from arming while ignoring the continuing fascist intervention, she thundered and blamed Chamberlain, by then Prime Minister.

The Spanish civil war continued until 1939, by which time even more momentous events had happened. In February 1938 Chamberlain told the Commons that the Eastern European states should not count on the League of Nations to protect them and three weeks later, in March, Hitler invaded Austria. Rathbone was in despair.

> When freedom has been submerged all over Europe, will our freedom survive, or alternatively, at some point in that intolerable descent into the valley of humiliation, will the point be reached at which we shall fight, but – what is only too likely – fight alone, or with insufficient allies, because by reason of the selfishness of our present policy, we have been left practically alone.

Chamberlain, that most secretive of politicians, took himself off to Munich to parley with Hitler with the knowledge of very few in the government. He returned, having signed the Munich agreement with Daladier of France, Hitler and Mussolini, though not Czechoslovakia, agreeing that Hitler should occupy that part of Czechoslovakia where many Germans had settled, the Sudetenland. Chamberlain thought he had secured 'peace in our time'. Rathbone knew better. She spoke at a 2,000-strong meeting of the National Committee of Peace and Friendship with the Soviet Union, denouncing the agreement as 'peace without honour'. Eleanor did not suffer any political setback for her opposition but the Duchess of Atholl did. She was accused of disloyalty and resigned her seat, fighting it as an Independent. This by-election was seen as a commentary on the Munich agreement and was thus of prime importance to the Conservative Party. Chamberlain was delighted when Atholl lost.

Refugees
The 1930s saw huge movements of people in response to the political events of the time. Jews, of course, from Germany,

Czechoslovakia, and Austria, and later from Poland; half a million Spaniards fled to France; non-German Czechs fled east from the Sudetenland. Some Jews might be resettled in Palestine, but the sensitivities of the Arabs in Palestine had to be respected. Britain declared it would not take immigrants.

Voluntary bodies in Britain had to guarantee that immigrants would not be in need of financial support, and Germany's policy of stripping Jews of everything they possessed made this difficult. When Austria followed Germany's example and began to persecute the Jews, the resources of the voluntary bodies were stretched to breaking point.

Visas were another difficulty. The number of visas issued was very limited and they were slow to be processed in situations when speed was of the essence. After Kristallnacht, Chamberlain and Baldwin softened their attitudes somewhat but the necessity of a visa and financial support remained. Following the Czech crisis, Rathbone appealed to the Home Office for 2,000 visas but only 100 were forthcoming. A Parliamentary Committee for Refugees was formed, funded entirely out of Eleanor's own money. It combined lobbying with casework, responding to individual requests for help. Through it she kept track of regulations and policies and what was happening to individuals. It was time consuming and boring, work she was eminently suited to do. She used contacts and friendships remorselessly, far beyond the bounds of polite social intercourse. She was also involved in the Council for Civil Liberties, the League of Nations Union, the Abyssinia Association and several committees concerned with Spain. With every request for assistance and easing of the bureaucracy, she was met by stonewalling and delaying tactics. Her ability to keep on lobbying in the face of so much indifference was astonishing.

She had more success in the Spanish crisis. When the Republican towns began to finally capitulate to the Nationalists, she and an ally at the Foreign Office, Wilfrid Roberts, circumvented the official position by asking the Mexican ambassador to co-operate with a plan to hire a ship and run the blockade on their own. They got out several boatloads of refugees and persuaded the government to intercede with the French to grant landing rights to the *Stanbrook*, a packed and stinking refugee ship chartered by the Spanish. British consular officials had, however, cost several thousand lives by delaying embarkation that fortunately for the government, was not raised in the House of Commons by Eleanor though she did inform R. A. Butler at the Foreign Office.

In all these transactions we can see how Eleanor worked. She drew on her contacts who provided her with up-to-the-minute accurate information to badger officials and politicians to get her way. If officials and politicians failed her, she broadcast their failings or went behind their backs. Her great-nephew complained that she used people and she didn't mind who she bored if she got her own way. No wonder people dodged her! Immune from party discipline, she was impossible to control. But she was also responsive to suggestion. So when Butler told her it would be easier to deal with her requests for asylum for Spanish Republicans if they came from a committee, she promptly set up a committee – the British Committee for Refugees from Spain – which selected, arranged passages and guaranteed support for the few hundred the government would allow in.

In the summer of 1939, Eleanor worked via letters and articles in the newspapers to persuade the country to bring Churchill back to power. If he were in the cabinet, she thought, it would send a message to Soviet Russia that Britain finally meant business. At least Britain had guaranteed the Polish borders. If Hitler invaded Poland, there would be war. Although having predicted it for years, she would rather have been wrong.

The Second World War

War was declared on 3 September 1939 when Germany invaded Poland. Eleanor duly registered with the Ministry of Labour, saying how she could serve the country. She was good at writing reports, she said, and at running organisations. She believed she was good at directing staff and getting much work out of them without friction. She had excellent health, an exceptionally strong constitution, and could drive a car. She wasn't called on to drive a car, but her organisational skills stood her in good stead. She was asked to serve on the Advisory Committee to the Ministry of Pensions, which she duly did, but this took up very little of her time. She thought the country needed to get rid of Chamberlain as its leader, and she set about making his life uncomfortable. In the eight months remaining to Chamberlain as PM, she asked 85 questions ranging from air raid precautions to war aims, mobilisation of manpower, and provision of news to soldiers serving abroad. She was active behind the scenes, as was her wont.

The day after war was declared a circular letter went out from her house, signed by herself, Bob Boothby and Harold Nicholson, who had collaborated with her on child welfare, and Graham White, David Grenfell and Arthur Salter, who had helped with her work on refugees. The letter asked other parliamentary allies if they would like to meet regularly. This became the All Party Parliamentary Action Group. Clement Davies chaired the meeting, Bob Boothby was honorary secretary, and Eleanor was convenor. There were subgroups on foreign policy, economic warfare and home defence, and they met once a week. They immediately asked to discuss war policy with Chamberlain, who refused, so they bypassed him and called on experts themselves, asking Lloyd George to chair a meeting on war aims. Here, out of the limelight and away from the whips, they could formulate strategies and form alliances. Eleanor was a lynchpin in this organisation because she was outside party politics and had no parliamentary ambition.

As news began to filter through in April 1940 that Norway had been occupied by Germany, Rathbone rose to mount a critical attack on Chamberlain. Why had he not brought any of the younger men into his war cabinet, men who had shown independence of mind and courage? Chamberlain was too influenced by his personal likes and dislikes, she said. The country needed to use all the talent it could lay its hands on. This was no way to run a government. As the events of April ran their course, attitudes to Chamberlain hardened and in early May, the Labour Party asked for a vote of confidence in him, which he lost. Churchill took command of a coalition government, with many of the All Party Parliamentary Action Group being awarded ministerial jobs. Eleanor was delighted.

While being sometimes critical of Churchill's decisions, particularly where refugees were concerned, Eleanor's loyalty to him never wavered. She told him, that 'not only this nation but the world owes more to you that to any other British statesman who has ever lived'. In 1942, at a point when Churchill had returned to the House after a bout of illness following a long and arduous journey abroad, he was attacked by Aneurin Bevan, who questioned the Prime Minister about the regulations governing the behaviour of a serving member of Parliament (by which he meant Randolph, Winston Churchill's son) who had disclosed to the Press what had been discussed in Parliament about military matters.

Eleanor rose to her feet. She said she knew nothing at all about the letter that was reputed to have been sent, but she wanted to say something she felt needed saying. Aneurin Bevan, she said, had a malicious and virulent dislike of Mr Churchill. Considering that Mr Churchill had just returned from a long journey in the interests of the nation and had also been ill, it was an example of bad taste on Mr Bevan's part. She thought the house should not break up that day 'without someone saying, and perhaps I may say it because I am so completely outside this issue, and not a member of the Prime Minister's party, and that is with what disgust and almost loathing we watch this kind of temperament, these cattish displays of feline malice.' She was cheered loudly from both sides of the house, and went home to apologise to her cat Smuts, for having maligned the feline species.

Enthusiastic supporter of Churchill as she was, Eleanor nevertheless kept a wary eye on him, since he was no feminist. Unusually, she teamed up with Nancy Astor in 1940 to form the Women Power Committee, which paid attention to feminist issues. It pressed for an expansion of nursery places so married women could take up paid work, and eventually launched a campaign for post-war legislation on equal pay. But she soon lost interest. She now thought of equality in terms of women's equal right to sacrifice and their equal right to serve. In the 1930s she had sometimes been accused of militarism, but in tears she confessed to her nephew that if she could sacrifice her own life and save those of young men, she would. This may have been why she and Elizabeth stayed in London throughout the Blitz when their house was bombed, to share the danger not only of Londoners but also of all those young men who would lose their lives.

She favoured conscription for women. 'Equal citizenship should bring with it equal responsibilities,' she said. Women had the right to serve in dangerous places and when one MP said that women over forty-five were too deranged by the internal stresses and strains of the menopause to be able to serve, she gave him an angry retort. The only criterion for placing someone in a job, whether male or female, was whether they could do the job, she insisted. Her words fell on stony ground, however. The Ministry of Labour called up unmarried women and childless married women, while women over fifty and married women with children were never called up.

One of the first decisions of the Churchill government in May 1940 was to intern 'enemy aliens'. Not an unreasonable thing to do in wartime, one might suppose. However, the difficulty was how to recognise a dangerous enemy alien. Seventy-seven per cent of the 55,460 enemy aliens were German Jews who had fled Hitler's persecution. The Home Office categorised them into three bands, those falling in to the A and B bands were to be interned, but those in category C were to be released. Magistrates administering this system, however, played safe and over-committed people to the A and B bands, sending them to either a housing estate in Huyton or to the Isle of Man. There were two suicides, which prompted Professor Weissenberg, leader of the Huyton inmates, to send a telegramme to the Parliamentary Refugee Committee asking for an end to these arbitrary internments.

The day following Weissenberg's telegramme, Eleanor answered saying the appeal had been heard in the House and promising to visit Huyton. When she arrived she spoke to the men, asking for their patience and apologising for the situation but saying it was a difficult time for Britain as it was living in fear of invasion. Her final words were 'You are not forgotten'. She gave them hope and followed up on her commitment to them.

Eleanor had been asking questions in the House about conditions in the camps and demanding timetables for release of the internees. Her attention to the matter was given added impact by the torpedoing of the *Arandora,* a cruise ship which had been requisitioned to take Category A and B German and Austrian aliens to Australia. In July Eleanor pointed out the waste involved in locking up people with language skills and cultural knowledge, not to mention the expense. Five days after the debate, the roundups of aliens was halted and two advisory committees were appointed, one to recommend categories for release, and one, on which Eleanor served, to advise on individual cases. Three months later more than a third of the internees had been released.

The Home Office under Herbert Morrison refused to release internees en masse so each individual case had to be dealt with on its merits. The Parliamentary Committee helped families assemble the right documents and guided them through the rigmarole of applying for release. There were other groups doing this, in Oxford and Cambridge and also the German Emergency Committee of the Society of Friends. It was nevertheless a slow, painstaking process, which did not daunt Eleanor. It was what she was good at. She arranged for a colleague to ask a question in the House which resulted in the terms for release being enlarged. Artistic and scientific work was designated as 'work of national importance', thus facilitating the release of another group of internees. Rathbone also took on cases of people who had lived in Britain for a long time but had never had enough money to apply for naturalisation, she checked the situation concerning internees who had been shipped out to Australia and investigated aliens with a criminal record who had automatically been categorised as Category A internees, even if the crimes they committed had been petty pilfering.

Up to June 1940 Eleanor had paid all the office expenses herself. She could not afford to carry on subsidising without accessing her capital which, being a good Rathbone, she was not prepared to do, so her friends had a whip-round and found enough money to help keep the committee up and running. By March 1942 more than 20,000 people had been released. Of the 8,858 who remained, more than half were in Canada or Australia. The *Manchester Guardian* wrote: 'Nothing like justice has ever been done to Miss Eleanor Rathbone's work for interned refugees' and only those closest to her knew that she worked incessantly through blackouts and air raids, her work illuminated by a bicycle lamp under a blanket. Eleanor continued her work on the project until the end of the war, but clashed more and more with Herbert Morrison who turned a deaf ear to all appeals to narrow the terms under which men were interned.

Eleanor and Herbert Morrison fell out irreconcilably over the plight of the Jews in Europe. The Jews in Germany were completely beyond help, but there were groups who might have been helped if there had been the political will to do so. It was not for want of trying that Eleanor failed in her attempts to ameliorate the slaughter. She found that her usual ways of working – pulling together like-minded people to form committees, which would lobby the House; writing pamphlets; badgering politicians and civil servants, and generally kicking up a fuss, made no impact. Politicians and civil servants alike ganged up on her and as they did so, her rhetoric became more strident and emotional, as indeed the situation deserved. Who would not get emotional at the thought of men, women and children being experimented on, or marshalled into gas chambers, being forced to dig their own graves, then shot.

She helped form the National Committee for Rescue from Nazi Terror and was part of a delegation of churchmen and politicians, which included the Archbishop of Canterbury, to parley with Herbert Morrison in early 1943 about the deportation of Jews from camps in unoccupied France to Poland and certain death. Home Office policy was to admit to Britain only those people who could be useful to the country but the outcry over the removal of Jews from French camps drove Herbert Morrison to seek to admit Jewish children from the camps but the Cabinet decided to admit only those children who had parents in Britain, a very small number indeed.

Eleanor naturally thought this was niggling and parsimonious. One solution would be to facilitate the removal of Jews from unoccupied France to neutral countries such as Switzerland, with or without the permission of Laval, the prime minster of the Vichy government. She asked for 2,000 visas for threatened children and relations of men serving in the British forces. Morrison argued that letting in a great many Jews would exacerbate anti-Jewish feeling in the country. He warned individuals against acting in a private capacity. 'You should be extremely careful what you do, Miss Rathbone,' he threatened. But 10,000 people were deported and lost their lives as a result of his refusal to act.

Throughout the rest of the war, Eleanor continued to work to save the Jews, mostly to little avail. She worked with Victor Gollancz, the left-wing Jewish publisher, and Jewish Associations. At the end of 1942 the Foreign Secretary announced in Parliament that it was now obvious that Hitler intended the extermination of the Jews. The House stood in silence to honour the dead. Moving as this was, it did not solve the problem and Eleanor was concerned that politicians and the public, having acknowledged what was happening, would feel their consciences relieved of the burden of guilt. 'There is nothing more dangerous than a relieved conscience,' she wrote.

By this time, however, the end of 1942, the majority of Jews in Poland were already dead. The massacre was concentrated in the period between mid-March 1942 to mid-February 1943. But substantial numbers were still alive in the satellite countries such as Hungary, Bulgaria or Romania, and in countries occupied by Italy. Morrison thought the refugee problem should be seen as an Allied, rather than a British, problem and that no distinction should be made between Jew and non-Jew. The network people who sympathised with the Jewish cause organised debates in the House of Commons and the Lords, asking for block grants of visas in neutral countries to facilitate the migration of Jews – but to no avail.

Following this debate, Eleanor moved to outright antagonism of the government. She was aware there was nothing she could do being treated with courtesy, but kept at arm's length. She continued to write pamphlets, newspaper articles and ask questions in the House but without any effect on the political process though it kept the matter before the general public.

By this time her health, which had always been robust, began to fail. She hurt her leg when walking to the House of Commons in the blackout and the cut was slow to heal. Being absent-minded, and somewhat clumsy, she kept on damaging her leg and in 1944 had to spend several weeks in hospital and was absent from the House for three months, during which time her own house had been hit by a V2 rocket. This was not conducive to work, and interest in the Jewish problem rather lapsed while she was incapacitated.

'If ever there was a mongrel race,' said Eleanor in 1943, 'it was ours.' When the war was over, she thought, Britain should admit many more immigrants, because immigration enriched the pool of talent, and should admit many more Jews, who had much to add to the cultural heritage of the country.

After the War

The Family Allowances Act was put through Parliament during Churchill's caretaker government in 1945. It had been one of the ideas contained in the Beveridge Report of 1942 and consisted of a payment of five shillings a week for every child in a family other than the eldest. It was seen by journalists, politicians and civil servants as Eleanor Rathbone's achievement, and it was passed because of the cross-party insistence of backbench MPs against the lethargy of the Cabinet. Eleanor was the one, however, who absolutely insisted that the money be paid to the mother. In 1942 she had said, 'We want our children and their mothers to be recognised not as dependents hung around the necks of their fathers and husbands, but as human beings with their own feet on God's earth and their heads in the sunshine – and more sunshine than is allowed now to trickle through the windows of their dingy and overcrowded homes.' The officials drafting the Bill ignored all requests for it to be paid to the mother, however, and when the Bill was brought before Parliament in February 1945 it stipulated that the allowance should be paid to the husband.

Eleanor Rathbone led the charge against this. The Cabinet, being composed of men, could not understand how strongly women felt on the issue, she said. By its thoughtless actions, the government was allowing sex antagonism to rear its ugly head and if they had to, the women's societies would make sure every woman knew how her representative had voted on the Bill. If it were not amended, she herself would vote against it. Eleanor attended the third reading of the Bill in a wheelchair. She sat there 'flustered and surprised' as the tributes and cheers rang round the chamber at her success.

Eleanor had one final project: the starving children and old people who were flooding into Berlin to escape the Russians, people who had had nothing to do with the Holocaust, and who needed the pity of the victors. They needed feeding. The government, however, was not to be moved. The British people themselves might not be starving but they were tired of eating spam! What food there was should go to the people of Britain, who had struggled so long against the Oppressor. Save Europe Now, a charity established in 1944 and run by the Society of Friends, aimed at sending food parcels to countries ravaged by the war. Eleanor was a keen supporter but her support was to be brutally severed. After a morning spent writing an article for Save Europe Now and an afternoon at the dentist, on the evening of January 2, 1946, Eleanor had a stroke and died.

Throughout her life, her biographer Pedersen points out, she kept faith with politics. Purposeful, collective action in a democratic state could improve life, she thought, and prevent the selfishness, hatred or apathy which inhibited man's humanity to man. She knew it was only ever partially successful, but could see no alternative.

7

Ellen Wilkinson (1891–1947) and Socialist Politics

Ellen Wilkinson came into the suffrage movement from a rather different background from Eleanor Rathbone and Maude Royden. All three were northerners, and from a dissenting background, but while Rathbone and Royden came from wealthy families in Liverpool, Ellen Wilkinson was born into a working-class family in Chorlton-on-Medlock, a suburb just south of the Manchester city centre. In the nineteenth century, it was an area of spacious middle class housing but at the end of the century, had become a working class area.

Ellen lived as a child in a two-bedroomed back-to-back with an outside lavatory, and no doubt with a tin bath hanging on the wall, ready to be unhooked on a Friday or Saturday for the weekly family bath. There were a number of cotton mills in the area, which may have contributed to the lung diseases Ellen suffered from the whole of her life and which ultimately killed her. She shared the house with her parents, and her two brothers and one sister, all older than her. While the family was poor by Rathbone standards, they were not the poorest of the poor. Her father was an insurance agent, going from house to house collecting money from people saving for their burial fund, so he wore a suit, not overalls, and must have had clean hands, no mill grease under his fingernails. So taking into consideration working-class sensibilities, the Wilkinson family may well have been a cut above some of their neighbours. Her father was a staunch trade unionist and Liberal Unionist and, unlike the adult Ellen, was unsympathetic to the problems of the very poor. He had dragged himself up out of the gutter, so why couldn't they?

Both Ellen's father and uncle were Methodist preachers and, following in the family tradition, her brother Richard became one too. As a child Ellen would go to chapel, then return to her grandmother and repeat for her what the preacher had said. She was thus gaining experience of analysing the structure of the spoken word and training her memory to follow the thread of an argument, invaluable experience when she turned to politics. Her Methodism was not just about religion but had a political edge, since preachers used political situations to illustrate their points. So through religion, she came to know about Belgium's King Leopold II and his terrible exploitation of the natives in the rubber plantations of the Congo Free State. She also learned about the colonisation of Ireland and India, and sweated labour at home, all this presented as an outrage against humanity and an abuse of power by those in authority – no wonder she became embroiled in left-wing politics. With her red hair and tiny frame, as an adult she became known as 'Red Ellen'.

She did not thrive in the secondary schools she attended. She hated the 'educational sausage factory' and the sadism of some of the teachers. Fortunately, her father was self-taught and took his daughter along to lectures and encouraged her to read widely.

From her early experiences in the chapel, she learned to be comfortable on the stage. She took part in missionary meetings, where the stories of missionary work were acted out, and she recited poems at the Band of Hope, the organisation formed to encourage working class children to steer clear of the demon drink.

What to do when she left school presented something of a problem. She was a clever, self-confident girl and not destined for the cotton mills in the nearby streets. By the time she left school at fourteen, her older siblings would be bringing in a wage, which must have helped the family finances, and it was decided that Ellen would be a teacher, notwithstanding her unfortunate experiences to date. There were three ways to qualify – a degree course at university, a two-year course at a training college or, for the less well-off, a combination of pupil teaching and training college. This third alternative was the only one available, given the family finances, and Ellen enrolled at the Manchester Pupil Teachers' Centre. She flourished here. She was encouraged to write stories and articles for the school magazine and to speak in public on political issues of the day. Her real political education, she said, dated from this period when she was asked to stand as a socialist candidate in a mock election. She read Robert Blatchford's *Britain for the British* and *Merry England*, which made her a socialist.

Ellen decided she wanted to find out more about politics and, dressing up in her Sunday best, travelled to the Free Trade Hall where the speaker was Katherine Glasier, a prominent member of the ILP. This was a turning point in her life. Not much taller than Ellen, and dressed in a plain blue woollen dress, Katherine Glasier showed Ellen what might be possible. 'To stand on the platform of the Free Trade Hall, to be able to sway a great crowd as she swayed it, to be able to make people work to make life better, to remove slums and underfeeding and misery ... that seemed the highest destiny any woman could ever hope for,' she said.

She could, however, see no way of doing it. Parliament was for men and the Labour Party existed to get working men into Parliament. 'They won't even let me vote for it!' she said. Nevertheless, in spite of her misgivings, in 1907 at the age of sixteen and the year after the ILP affiliated to the Labour Party, she joined the ILP and remained a member until it disaffiliated in 1932.

Her course at the college was not going too well. She loved the learning but loathed the teaching practice, not because of the children but because they were treated so brutally by the staff. Luckily, when she was nineteen, she won a history scholarship to Manchester University and here she flourished. All the things she had ever wanted – books galore, friends, interesting lectures, and the stimulus of teamwork. She learned to think analytically, to research, to write clearly and factually. What she did not like was the fact that the history was all about high politics, war and diplomacy. What about how ordinary men and women lived? Social history, in fact.

She turned to politics, honing her speaking skills and refining her political ideas. She was a founder member of the University Socialist Federation, becoming its vice-chair. She organised meetings through which she met the radical trade unionist and feminist, Mary McArthur. And in 1912 Ellen joined the Manchester Society for Women's Suffrage. (MSWS) and ran the local branch of the Fabian Society, a left-wing forum for discussing political ideas founded in 1884. In 1913, the year of her graduation, she joined the Women's Labour League.

She landed her first job with the MSWS as an assistant organiser in training at a salary of two guineas – £2-2s-0d – a week. This was a respectable amount of money and she and her family must surely have been pleased that 'our Ellen's' talents had been thus acknowledged. She was just in time to help organise the Manchester group taking part in the Suffrage Pilgrimage. This march had several streams, converging on London. The Manchester contingent joined north-western branches, which had begun their journey in Carlisle. It moved south via Oxford, before turning eastward towards London. The Pilgrimage was in part a demonstration against the militant suffragettes, who suffragists thought were damaging the cause. The Pilgrimage, therefore, was highly organised, peaceful and showed both how many women supported the suffrage movement and how competently they could organise. Ellen toured the area around Manchester, advertising the march and drumming up support and when the group left Manchester, there was a crowd of 600 to cheer them on their way.

While Ellen's temperament might have inclined her towards the more militant actions of the suffragettes, the suffragette movement had no structure and could not support a paid worker. Ellen needed a job that paid a reasonable wage and in 1912 the Labour Party had promised to throw its support behind the suffrage movement.

Following this exciting debut, Ellen set up a Suffrage and Labour Club in Ancoats, an industrial suburb of northern Manchester. The MSWS thought setting up these clubs was a distinctive feature of their work and brought the question of votes for women before a wider audience than hitherto. Ellen spoke in the streets to anyone who would listen and became used to handling hecklers.

The First World War

In 1914, Ellen was very much against the war with Germany. She thought it was an imperialist war being fought over territorial rights, particularly in Africa. War meant that millions of men would die defending the rights of their bosses. It was a very unpopular thing to say in 1914. The NUWSS was riven with dissent about the matter. Ellen joined Maude Royden, Kathleen Courtney, and other pacifists in the movement, and resigned when Millicent Fawcett declared that it was a just war. Most of them transferred their allegiance to the Women's International League for Peace and Freedom (WILPF), as did Ellen. The MWSS agreed to stop any activity about suffrage so they could support people suffering from the disruption caused by the war. This might have been a disaster for Ellen, as she needed the money. Fortunately, the MWSS decided to keep on its staff and deployed Ellen to Stockport, helping to organise voluntary help for the relief of distress. The two staple trades of Stockport, cotton cloth production and knitting, had collapsed when war broke out, so Ellen set up a sewing room. She found a large room, borrowed machines and tables, and appealed in the newspapers for material and second-hand clothing. The sewing room was soon employing 150 women.

Ellen soon found another job that suited her down to the ground. She became a national organiser for the Amalgamated Union of Co-operative Employees (AUCE), with special responsibility for shop assistants and factory workers. Here she would gain the experience and network of colleagues that would be important for her political career. The generous salary was also very welcome – £25 a month and expenses was not to be sneezed at. 'She'll organise the angels when she gets to heaven,' wrote one commentator.

Like Eleanor Rathbone and many others in the suffrage movement, Ellen was angry that women were paid less than men for the same work. Being in direct contact with employees and employer, she was able to make a direct impact on the situation, which Rathbone had not been able to do. By 1916 Ellen negotiated male rates of pay for women in 57 different co-operative societies across Britain. She spent a great deal of time and energy on the working conditions of laundry workers. They were difficult to organise into unions because they were split into small, often home-based, groups. Working conditions were poor with women often suffering from burns, the atmosphere was steamy and gas filled, and the floors swimming in water. In 1909 the government had passed the Trades Board Act, which set up Boards to fix minimum wage rates. Initially there were only four boards created, but Ellen set up the Joint Laundry Board and together, gradually and piecemeal, they improved working conditions and wages. After a while she managed to set up a national programme of wages and conditions of labour for all the laundries affiliated to the Co-op.

Ellen was also embroiled in difficulties with craft unions. The Co-op employed quite a lot of craftspeople across the country, but there were only a few in a given place of work. Because of the small numbers in each workplace, the craft unions had never tried to recruit them and they now started joining the AUCE. Some of the craft unions objected and 1916 saw the first confrontation. Plymouth Co-operative Society had refused to increase the pay of its workers. Ellen took her holiday in Plymouth so that, if called upon, she could negotiate with the Co-op. The Co-op employees organised a strike, which was going so well it looked as if they might win, until the craft unions encouraged their workers to stay at work, to blackleg. The conflict attracted the attention of the sitting MP, Waldorf Astor, and his wife Nancy, who were sympathetic to the workers' need for more money. Eleven weeks later, the AUCE admitted defeat and the workers were forced to negotiate. As a consequence, the Plymouth branch of the AUCE lost over a third of its members.

These disputes between the AUCE and the Craft Unions continued until 1918 when a strike began in a printing works in Longsight and looked as if it would follow the same pattern as Plymouth. The government intervened, censuring the AUCE, and insisting the workers return to work. Just after the end of the war, Ellen was told she had lost her job, largely because of her perceived mismanagement of the Longsight dispute. There were so many objections to this decision from branches, groups and individuals, including a Special Delegate meeting which challenged the right of the Executive Council to dismiss her, that after an apology by Ellen for past mistakes, the Executive Council reinstated her.

The Post-war Period
After the war Ellen was a member of various left-wing movements: the Labour Party, the Communist Party, founded in 1920 from various Marxist groups, and the Fabians. Politics were more fluid than at any time since then, so it was quite possible for people to belong to more than one group, and many on the political left did so.

In 1919 Ellen changed jobs. Though still within the AUCE, she became part of a team of advisors, investigators, and negotiators at central office who were called upon to give evidence to commissions, arbitrations and Trade Board enquiries. In June 1919, Ellen successfully negotiated a 48-hour week for laundry workers and an improved minimum wage. After a couple of years' prosperity following the war, the economy entered a downward curve and it was no longer possible to negotiate higher wages. Ellen spent the next few years fighting to maintain the advance that had been made in working conditions and wages. With the return from the war of men who once again resumed the jobs they had been doing before, women were out of work, and the number of members of the AUCE plummeted. In an attempt to keep the number of members buoyant, the AUCE amalgamated with the National Union of Distributive and Allied Workers (NUDAW).

Ellen gave evidence to the Cave Select Committee, which was examining wages in the Distributive and Laundry trades, an important achievement, but to counter this, in 1923 she was involved in a long-drawn-out strike when the Co-op directors imposed a wage cut on their employees. She was in her element, rushing round the country addressing groups of employees but, unfortunately, when the matter went to arbitration, the male trade unionists comprising the majority of the panel upheld the wage cuts. Ellen blamed the trade unionists for their chauvinism and thought women did not join trade unions because of the sexism they found there. Men, she believed, were fighting for fair wages for men but didn't give a toss about the women.

As a member of the Communist Party, Ellen was asked to take part in a special commission of five members to formulate a Programme of Action. The Communist Party also tried to affiliate to the Labour Party, who would have none of it. The Labour Party executive said the Communist Party wanted a 'Dictatorship of the Proletariat' brought about by revolution and the Labour Party supported the democratic gradualist approach to changing society.

This posed a problem for Ellen, as she belonged to both parties. She attended the Congress of the Red Trade Union International in Moscow, her first-class travel paid for by the Russian Communist Party. She met Trotsky, with whom she kept in touch after the Conference. Ellen also helped form the Red International of Labour Unions in 1921, helped by the Soviets' representative, Grigory Zinoviev. The aim of this organisation was to create a revolutionary Labour Union to wage class war and ensure the triumph of the working class. Direct action was the way forward, she thought, using not just strikes but street demonstrations, and violent opposition to the conveyance of goods to or from blackleg enterprises. She and her colleagues, she said, had but one aim – to overthrow world capitalism. And the battle had to be carried on throughout the world. 'It is no more possible to have a Communist Russia in a capitalist world than to have a Communist Manchester in a Capitalist Britain,' she said.

She very much admired the position of women in Russia. They had the right to vote for and fill any office, the right to equal pay and equal rations, and the right to seek an abortion. Illegitimate children were not stigmatised as they were in Britain. Compared with Britain, she thought Russia had made enormous progress in women's rights. When compared with the situation in Russia, in Britain 'what has really happened is that a few rich women have used their working class sisters to get rid of bonds that were irksome to the ladies, who, with the spoil of victory, then retired into the ranks of capitalism'.

In spite of these combative and unfair words, in 1921 Ellen joined the Six Point Group, a pressure group founded by Lady Rhonda, and in 1923 joined Nancy Astor, Millicent Fawcett and Eleanor Rathbone, not exactly members of the working class, on the platform at a rally in Central Hall, Westminster, to work towards votes for women over twenty-one, equal pay, equal moral standards, and equality in industry and the professions.

As we have seen, Ellen was a great joiner. She had joined the Women's International League of Peace and Freedom (WILPF) in 1915. At their first post-war meeting in 1919, tensions arose between the pacifists who believed war was wrong, and the anti-imperialists, who condemned armed force used by capitalists but supported armed struggle to promote socialism. Naturally, Ellen was in the second category and so vociferous that one fellow member of the Labour Party asked her to tone down her rhetoric.

The following year she joined nine other representatives of the Manchester branch to investigate the horrors of the Black and Tans in Ireland. The Black and Tans were a force of British Army veterans, recruited to support the Royal Irish Constabulary in maintaining peace in their fight against the IRA. It was Winston Churchill's idea and they were meant to perform such supporting duties as guarding barracks. They were paid 10 shillings a day on top of their keep. Unfortunately, they were extremely undisciplined and reacted with violence against the civilian population of Ireland, burning and sacking a string of small towns and blockading the town of Tralee for a week, closing all the shops and preventing any food from entering. They had alienated many of the civilian population, who covertly began to support the IRA. In March 1921, Ellen was asked to give evidence to the American Commission on Ireland, a body set up to try to help solve the problems of the civil war then raging there. A partial solution to the civil war led, in 1922, to the island of Ireland being divided into the Irish Free State in the south and the six counties of Ulster in the north.

Ellen also had decided views on Iraq, which was at this time a British mandate. Both Shia and Sunni Muslims united in their opposition to the British, as they feared they would become part of the British Empire. They raised troops to challenge the British Army so Winston Churchill sent aircraft to crush the rebellion. Six thousand Iraqis and 500 British and Indian troops died in the encounter. Ellen put it down to the need for oil and 'the Tory Imperialists who are pouring out millions that are desperately needed at home for education, housing, and for employment'. These new lands, she said, 'have to be held down against the wishes of the vast majority of the inhabitants and may involve us in war with the whole Mohammedan world.'

The government was very concerned about the possible growth of communism and kept a wary eye on Ellen and her comrades. It was particularly concerned about the possibility of the infiltration of the Labour Party, though they need not have worried as the Communist Party was close to bankruptcy by 1922. In the run up to the 1924 election, in which Ellen had been selected as one of the Parliamentary candidates by NUDAW, though she failed to win the ballot, the Labour Party decided that no one who was a member of the Communist Party could also be a member of the Labour Party. As a result, in March 1924, Ellen resigned her membership of the Communist Party and devoted her energies and abilities to Labour.

She had not long to wait for another attempt at election. Ramsay MacDonald, leader of the minority Labour government, dissolved Parliament and announced another election for 29 October 1924, the third in three years. This time Ellen stood as a candidate for Middlesbrough, a town on Teesside whose livelihood depended on the iron and steel industry, and ship building. A few days before the election, what became known as the Zinoviev letter was made public. This purported to be a letter written by Grigory Zinoviev, now an important figure in the Soviet Union, calling for increased communist agitation in England. It was a forgery put about by the Conservative Party but it affected the outcome of the election, which went decisively against the Labour Party. Ellen Wilkinson, though, won the Middlesbrough seat. What a triumph for a girl from the back streets of Manchester!

Into Parliament, 1924

As one of only four women in the House, and the only woman on the opposition benches, Ellen stood out. Amid a sea of dark and sober grey, her flaming red hair and fashionable clothes were noticeable – she was a firebrand waiting to set the House and the world on fire! She was tiny and sat like a little girl with her feet dangling, unable to reach the ground. She soon learned, however, to rest her feet on her dispatch case full of letters from her constituents.

Her presence in Parliament got a mixed response from the Press. Her union journal reported that, 'Miss Wilkinson has pluck, she has charm and she has wit – a welcome change after the stodginess of the Labour intellectuals'. The Women's Freedom League was, of course, delighted to see her there. They had helped canvas for her and helped towards the narrow victory – 927 votes – over her opponent. The *Yorkshire Post* commented that 'Miss Wilkinson's manner was decidedly and provocatively pugnacious' but I don't suppose the right-leaning *Yorkshire Post*'s opinion mattered too much to Red Ellen.

On the second day of the Parliamentary session, she made her maiden speech. The House was packed with members who had come to see this phenomenon – a working-class woman. She began her speech. Noting that it was customary for members to wait seven years to make their debut in the House, she said: 'I didn't think that Middlesbrough had sent me to the House of Commons to wait seven years'. She started as she meant to go on. She put forward the need for votes for women, increased welfare benefits, better insurance and factory law reform. Not a bad beginning! Her time spent in the suffrage movement, dealing with hecklers and repartee, stood her in good stead in the sometimes raucous atmosphere of the Commons. She was in her element. She had no intention of modifying her clothes to blend in with the blacks and greys of the men who surrounded her, until Nancy Astor took her on one side and advised her that her appearance was diverting attention away from what she said to what she looked like. She toned down her appearance but not her rhetoric.

The room allotted to the women was the small room set aside for Nancy Astor when she was the only woman in Parliament. It now had to accommodate four, Astor, Wilkinson, the Duchess of Atholl, and Margaret Bondfield, and would go on to squash in eight, then ten. There was a washstand, a tin basin, a jug of cold water and a bucket. And no mirror! While Nancy Astor accepted the situation, Ellen did not. She protested. She protested about women being excluded from the Strangers' dining room and in 1928, persuaded the Speaker to allow women to eat dinner there, though he would not allow them to eat lunch.

Her day as an MP began at six in the morning. For the next three hours, she wrote articles, then from nine o'clock she answered letters: 1,394 letters and telegrams in her first few weeks as MP. The rest of the day was taken up with party meetings, committee work, and interviewing delegations and constituents.

In her constituency, she held weekly surgeries, spoke at meetings, visited local schools, factories and businesses, and attended functions. As a woman MP, she received a great many letters from women, not just from all over Britain, but from abroad as well. In 1926 she travelled 2,000 miles and spoke at 41 mass meetings. No surprise, then, that she suffered from throat and lung infections, aggravated by smoking.

Surprisingly, given their different backgrounds, Ellen and Nancy Astor formed a close working relationship. They worked together to promote women's interests both in the House and with outside agencies such as the Women's Freedom League and the National Union of Societies for Equal Citizenship (NUSEC) under the leadership of Eleanor Rathbone, the successor to the NUWSS. She asked questions in Parliament about giving women the vote and when the suffrage movement organised its last march in July 1926, she was there. When the Prime Minister, Stanley Baldwin, announced in April 1927 that women over twenty-one would get the vote, she carried on reminding him of his promise, and eventually, on 12 March 1928, yet another Representation of the People Act gave women voting parity with men.

Three years before, in 1925, Ellen had introduced her first Bill, backed by Nancy Astor. It was to permit more women to join the police forces. Ellen believed that if there were more women police, parks and public places would be safer for women and children. She and Nancy Astor sponsored the Bill recommending equal treatment of the sexes in prostitution laws, elimination of the term 'common' prostitute, and making children born out of wedlock legitimate if their parents later married. Only the treatment of the sexes in prostitution laws failed to get onto the statute book. That had to wait until attitudes had changed, until 2009, in fact.

They also campaigned for pensions for widows with young children but in 1925 when the Old Age Contributory Pensions Act was introduced, Ellen thought it had not been drafted carefully enough. She found several anomalies and the House supported her. Even the *Yorkshire Post* was won over by her attention to detail and her careful assembly of the facts.

In 1929 Astor and Wilkinson, supported by newly elected women MPs, put forward a motion to amend the nationality laws. As the law stood, any foreign woman who married a British man was automatically given British nationality. Conversely, a British woman who married a foreigner lost her British citizenship and assumed the citizenship of the man whom she had married. This Bill made it possible for a British woman to keep her British nationality on marrying an alien, while denying British Nationality to a foreign woman who had married a British man. The Bill failed and it was not till 1933 that this amendment was adopted.

A hot topic in the 1920s was the question of contraception. At the time it was illegal to sell contraceptives or give advice on the subject. Maude Royden had argued persuasively about the need for women to limit the number of children they had, pointing out the sheer wastefulness and mental and physical distress of bearing large numbers of children, many of whom died. Marie Stopes had dived into the argument in 1919 with her book *Married Love,* while Isabel Emslie Hutton had published *The Hygiene of Marriage* in 1925, outlining the different kinds of contraception available.

The year before Hutton's book was published, in 1924 Ellen chaired a meeting of Labour Women when one member wanted the party to campaign to make it legal for doctors to give advice to married people about contraception. It took all Ellen's political skills to keep order in the hall. Miss Quinn, a Catholic, who represented thousands of working women in the clothing trade, spoke in outrage saying that working mothers did not want instructions in impure and unchaste matters. Birth control was a device against God and humanity. They were not going to allow such filth! Ellen re-established order in the room, told Miss Quinn she had been given ample opportunity to express her views and that others had a right to have their say. When the motion was put to the meeting, only six voted against contraceptive advice. Miss Quinn had lost her battle.

Ellen was ambivalent in her attitude to the discussion of contraception. As she pointed out to Dora Russell, wife of the philosopher Bertrand Russell, and leader of the birth-control lobby, as a single woman she had to be careful what she supported as she could not risk being accused of immorality. The idea of birth control had been taken up by members of the eugenics movement who thought the working classes produced large numbers of unintelligent and physically underdeveloped children and it would be better for the country if there were many fewer of them. Ellen could not agree with that. From a political point of view, there were large numbers of Catholics in Middlesbrough whose vote could well be lost if she came out in favour of making contraception easily available. Contraception was a private matter, she maintained. Unofficially though, she did not oppose the idea. In 1930 the Minister of Health agreed that local authorities, if they wished, could provide birth control clinics and information to mothers where further pregnancy would be detrimental to their health.

Another area where she had to tread carefully was in the field of protective legislation in the workplace. Some women thought legislation that protected women worked against equality. Ellen thought women needed all the protection they could get. In 1926 Ellen introduced a Factory Bill giving women and young people a forty-eight-hour working week, safer machinery, better lighting, sanitation and ventilation. The Bill received praise from everyone but then went on to be defeated by the Conservatives. Gaining improvements for any member of society was not easy but struggling against the male bias of Parliament was very hard work indeed.

On Monday, 3 May 1926, the TUC called a general strike, precipitated by the reduction in wages of the coal miners, who had seen their weekly pay reduced from a high of £6 a week to £3.90. The strike lasted nine days, during which time Ellen toured the Midlands, speaking at meetings to stiffen the resolve of strikers. She also wrote an inflammatory piece in *Labour Weekly* entitled 'Cheaper than horseflesh' where she described the work of 1,500 men and boys in the mines at Radstock. They worked, she said, stark naked, on all fours, with a rope round their waist and a chain between their legs hitched on to a wagon, to transport the coal from the coalface. The rope rubbed the skin raw, dirt got in, and septic sores resulted. The pit ponies had legislation to protect them, she said, but not the men. Many people thought she was exaggerating and trying to stir up trouble, which of course she was, though with some justification. In the debate on the strike, Ellen proved her point by holding up a harness. The last time this harness was worn, she insisted, was not sixty years ago but the end of April 1926.

The following year the Conservative government pushed through the Trades Disputes Act, which limited workers' rights even further. It made sympathetic strikes illegal, banned civil servants from joining unions affiliated to the TUC, protected blacklegs, and made picketing almost impossible. It also made the political levy, which was part of a union member's subscription, voluntary rather than mandatory. People had to opt in to the levy rather than opt out, which naturally affected a union's income. 'People who denounce the Conservative Party as stupid make me tired,'. was Ellen's response. 'In things they care about, the Tory leaders are clear-sighted and determined men.' As a result of this legislation when the next general election became due in 1929, NUDAW could only provide seventy-five per cent of the money she needed for election expenses.

In recognition of her growing political reputation, in 1927 Ellen was elected onto the National Executive of the Labour Party (NEC). At this time, the NEC was responsible for forming the policy of the party and communicating it to party members. Included in her work for the NEC was the responsibility for producing all the leaflets, posters, speakers' notes and lantern slides. She wanted the Labour message to the electorate to be short and pithy, but was overruled, which resulted in a muddled manifesto. In spite of that, Labour was returned to power but with no overall majority. Ramsay Macdonald again became Prime Minister alongside fourteen women – the first time women over twenty-one had had the vote. Ellen increased her majority by 3,199, which delighted her. Two women were appointed to the Cabinet – Margaret Bondfield, who became Minister of Labour; and Susan Lawrence, Parliamentary Secretary to the Ministry of Health. Ellen was made Susan Lawrence's Parliamentary Private Secretary. She was thought by some to be far more efficient and popular than either of the other two women. In 1929 Ellen lost her place on the NEC but was appointed to the Donoughmore Commission, a Royal Commission set up to investigate the powers of civil servants and ministers, an appointment that marked the growing confidence of the Labour Party in her seriousness as a politician.

Susan Lawrence asked Ellen to work on the improvement of conditions for mothers and babies in hospitals and to help steer the Mental Health Bill through Parliament. This Bill proposed that people with mental health problems could be treated in hospital without being certified as lunatics. She supported Arthur Greenwood's 1930 Housing Act, which provided subsidies from central government to local councils for clearing slum housing and building new homes to rent. She commented acidly that: 'Londoners strike one as having an infinite capacity for being uncomfortable... Their forebears must have belonged to the Antiquated Society of Sardine Packers'. She knew about slums. She had visited houses in the north east where the floors were rotten, the roofs leaked, wallpaper hung off the walls and babies got bitten by rats. 'I came away amazed at the heroism of the working-class woman in trying to make the best of the worst possible conditions,' Ellen said.

Unlike her women colleagues, Ellen often spoke in debates about economics. The financial situation in the 1920s and 30s was desperate, particularly in the heavy industrial areas such as the north and Wales. The pound was strong against the dollar, which affected exports, and industries such as coal mining, shipbuilding and the cotton and woollen industries were suffering. Ellen blamed the bankers. She said it was they who were controlling economic policy and that Parliament just did as they asked. The bankers' interests ran counter to those of the workers, she maintained, and there was a choice to be made between the sham democracy controlled by international finance and the real democracy controlled by the people. *Plus ca change!*

In 1929 the Wall Street crash precipitated a worldwide crash known as the Great Depression. In Britain unemployment, which had been high in the 1920s, became even worse – seventy per cent in some areas of the north. For the government, there were two alternative ways of dealing with the situation: cut expenditure, or spend its way out of recession. Ellen, with a great many other people, thought Britain should abandon the gold standard, which would devalue the currency, thus making exports cheaper. She also wanted the government to introduce a living wage, offer cheap credit to the working class and thereby spend their way out of the mire they found themselves in. The Chancellor of the Exchequer, Philip Snowden, thought otherwise. He believed in balanced budgets, so decided to put up taxes, and reduce government spending. The Bank of England supported the Chancellor. 'Nationalise the Bank of England' was Ellen's response. The Chancellor's austerity programme hit the poor the hardest and Ellen thought a more positive way of dealing with the crisis would be to spend money on employment opportunities and invest in distressed areas to generate jobs. In Ellen's view, the bankers were to blame:

> We are told that the budget does not balance, that there are terrible things going to happen unless you are prepared to make cuts – cuts everywhere except in the dividend of the bankers! The sooner we increase the buying power of the poorer classes, the sooner we will get out of this depression.

It is astonishing to read that her attitudes and analysis of the economic situation can so closely mirror the events and comments on the economic situation in the twenty-first century.

At the end of 1931, the government set up the May Committee to examine the question of unemployment and the funding of it, and recommended there should be an increase in unemployment insurance contributions and a twenty per cent reduction in benefits. Ellen suggested trying to increase exports to Russia: forty-two power stations were needed, new motor units for Leningrad, blast furnaces for Ukraine. She thought the only way out of the impasse was to nationalise the means of production. But even Ellen agreed it was well-nigh impossible to put into place the half-hearted attempts at public works that the government had suggested.

What the government did was pass the Anomalies Act, put forward by Margaret Bondfield, the Minister of Labour. This was aimed at eliminating abuses of the benefits system. It united Ellen in a very strange alliance between herself, Eleanor Rathbone, the Labour MP; Jennie Lee, wife of Aneurin Bevan; and, a very strange bedfellow indeed, Lady Cynthia Mosley, the first wife of Oswald Mosley and at first, like her husband, a Conservative, though they were soon both to become Fascists. These women were all opposed to the inclusion of married women in this Act. Married women, it was decided, would be disqualified from claiming benefit because they were married and therefore could be classed as not seeking work. It affected 180,000 women. The Labour government collapsed shortly after since only eleven out of twenty Ministers voted in favour.

Ramsay Macdonald resigned and became leader of a National government and was promptly expelled from the Labour Party, along with Philip Snowden. Ellen despised Macdonald from then on. She confronted him in debate about a reduction of ten per cent in the wages of all public employees and again when the Family Means Test was introduced on anyone unemployed for more than six months. Macdonald's reply was that he could not afford over so large an issue to be sentimental. She had scornful words for the type of politician who thinks that safeguarding the poor against the abyss of destitution and unemployment is sentimental. Macdonald called another general election in October 1931.

Out of Parliament, 1931

Election meetings in Middlesbrough could become very heated at times. Ellen had fireworks thrown at her, and on another occasion had to be escorted from the hall by policemen to protect her from a crowd of Liberals. When she was alone in the street, she was attacked by a group of fur-coated women wearing Liberal colours, who broke a window of her car, bashing the headlamps and hammering her with their steel-framed handbags.

The National government won a landslide victory at the expense of Labour, which won only fifty-two seats. Not one of the Labour women was re-elected, including Ellen.

Unleashed from the restraints of a Parliamentary position, Ellen's rhetoric became more left-wing as she wrote a series of articles for the Press. Although she had lost her Parliamentary work, and her position on the NEC, there was plenty for her to agitate about – the rise of fascism, for instance. But she also had a living to earn. Fortunately, she was able to resume her work with NUDAW and what time was left over from that, she used for writing – a detective novel as well as political treatises about fascism. She also wrote regularly for several papers, among them the *Clarion, Daily Herald, John Bull, Daily Express, Daily Mail.* In 1933 she was very pleased to be taken on as one of the correspondents for *Time and Tide.* This was the organ of the Six Point Group, founded in 1921 by Lady Rhonda, the equalitarian feminist who had disagreed so strongly with Eleanor Rathbone. The original six points were:

Satisfactory legislation on child assault
Satisfactory legislation for widowed mothers
Satisfactory legislation for the unmarried mother and her child
Satisfactory legislation on the rights of guardianship for married parents
Equal pay for teachers
Equal pay for men and women in the Civil Service.

While admirably specific in some ways, defining six clear ideas that would improve the lives of particular groups of women, the phrase 'satisfactory legislation' was much less so but allowed for different interpretations of the idea while highlighting the area of specific need. By 1933 the writers involved with *Time and Tide* were people of the highest literary reputations: Vera Brittain, Winifred Holtby, Virginia Woolf, Storm Jameson, Rebecca West and D. H. Lawrence, so Ellen was right to feel her writing was of a high standard.

In her view, men had made a mess of the world and the only women men valued were those who 'thought like a man'. This, of course, was an epithet that had been applied to Eleanor Rathbone, of whom Ellen thought very highly. She was, she said, worth ten ordinary men MPs. Women, she thought, did not have the abnormal respect for vested interests that male politicians showed. No woman would 'stand flabbily around and let the experts prove that though there is plenty of everything we must all scrimp and suffer because of economic laws.' This, of course, was feminist rhetoric disproved by the actions of Margaret Bondfield, who had brought in the Anomalies Act.

Ellen highlighted the dangers of married life – more women died from childbirth than from workplace accidents, and conditions in the home, which was the married woman's workplace, were not regulated in any way. 'For every class of woman worker the law lays down regulations for air space, ventilation, lighting and heating, weekend rest, hours of work, but the married woman enjoys no such protection'. She also considered it a dreadful waste of talent that on marriage, women should have to give up work. She also felt outraged that women's personal incomes were added to those of their husbands for tax purposes, that women found it difficult to get credit, and almost impossible to do business.

Fascism: Germany

The rise of fascism in Europe was a worry to everyone. Ellen was so concerned that with Edward Conze, a German socialist writer, she co-wrote a book to try to define what fascism was and why it had arisen. Of course she applied a Marxist analysis to the situation. 'When economic breakdown becomes a terrifying reality, when to the hunger and despair of the workers is added the ruin of the middle classes,' they wrote, 'fascism rears its head.' Fascism automatically led to war because its leaders wanted to take land and resources from other countries. Fascism was as much a failure of the left to provide leadership as of the right who provided a different model of how to run a state. 'In Germany, as in Italy, Poland, Hungary and elsewhere, dictatorship has usurped the place of democracy. Persecution and terror have overthrown freedom of speech and freedom of the Press. Religious and racial intolerance in its vilest form has reappeared,' she wrote.

Ellen was a favourite of the German left. In July 1932 she was asked to go to Germany to help the socialists in the coming election. She was told: 'Hitler is a travelling showman with a booming voice and inwardly so paralysed by dark fears and apprehensions that he is totally incapacitated except when he can boom away. His booming has filled his hearers with a pretentious bravura that carries him and them into a drunken ecstasy of sadistic revivalism'.

She was told socialists might well be beaten up, which made her very keen to go! She spent three months learning German so she could speak at rallies then embarked for the Continent. In Germany, socialism failed to persuade the masses that it was a viable way forward and the Nazi Party grew stronger. In 1933 Hitler became Chancellor and called for new elections. Six days before they took place, the Reichstag was set on fire. A former communist, Van der Lubbe, was found on the premises. He was accused by the Nazis of burning down the building, at which the Nazi Party announced that a real terror would begin when every socialist, every communist, every Jew and every left-leaning intellectual would be hunted down.

Ellen reported all this in the *Daily Herald*. She recorded the arrest of leading socialists, such as the Deputy-leader of the Reichstag and the ex-Minister of the Interior who had had their houses broken into and everything within smashed to pieces. The men themselves had been imprisoned and every imaginable humiliation heaped upon them. Berlin, she reported, was a city where everyone was afraid.

Four leading communists were arrested for supposedly burning down the Reichstag. In London, Ellen immediately invited a number of anti-fascists to her small flat and together they planned a Legal Commission of Enquiry into the burning of the Reichstag, a mock trial to highlight the evidence for or against the events in Germany. The commission had no legal standing but to give it more legal authority, Ellen hired the Law Society Court Room. The German government complained and tried to prevent the 'trial' taking place. The ambassador, Prince Bismarck, called at the Foreign Office to complain that the event was a flagrant intervention in Germany's internal affairs and asked for the government to stop it. If they did not do so, it would damage Anglo-German relations. The Foreign Office told him there was nothing they could do, though privately they tried to pressurise Ellen and the rest of the anti-Fascist group and asked the Law Society to cancel the booking. The Law Society refused to do so, so the Foreign Office was driven to sending undercover agents to monitor what was going on.

Aware that it was important to play by the book and that any infringement of the rules might well give the Foreign Office reason to close the enquiry, the proceedings were kept formal, rigorous and legalistic. Several German refugee writers and intellectuals gave evidence. The former President of Police in Berlin, who had been responsible for security at the Reichstag, testified that the Nazis must have helped the fire get started. Having heard all the evidence, the judges decided that Van der Lubbe was not a communist but an opponent of it; that he could not have acted alone; and that the Reichstag was set alight by Nazi leaders.

The report by the Commission was given a great deal of publicity in the Press, which roused anti-Fascist feeling in the country, which had been Ellen's aim. It also provoked anger in Germany and led to Nazi newspapers demanding the death penalty for anyone who had given evidence for the accused. Surprisingly, the German courts found four of the defendants not guilty but Van der Lubbe was found guilty and executed in January 1934. Shortly after, Hitler declared that any further treason trials would take place in a new

Nazi-dominated People's Court. Historians are still arguing about the rights and wrongs of Van der Lubbe's trial and execution, but whatever the truth of the matter, it marked the end of the German system of legal justice and the beginning of the domination of the law courts by Nazi rule.

The Labour Party was keen to distance itself from the Communist Party so although they were certainly well aware of the threat posed by Fascism, they insisted that any members who were also members of the League Against Fascism should renounce their membership of the latter, as they believed it was a communist-fronted organisation, which it was. Ellen, who predictably was a member, since she joined every conceivable political left-wing organisation, had to give up her membership, though she continued to help with its campaigns. Foremost among the Labour Party was Herbert Morrison, who would eventually become Home Secretary in the Attlee government. It was rumoured that Morrison and Wilkinson, though they clashed in public about policy, were secretly conducting an illicit love affair. Morrison's marriage was an unhappy one, and Wilkinson was free enough of conventional ideas on the sanctity of marriage to embark on an affair. Whether this was the case or not, neither of them minced their words when speaking about the other. Ellen blamed the Labour Party and Herbert Morrison for not taking an official stance on Nazism, leaving it up to a voluntary body such as the Reichstag Investigation, while Morrison lambasted Ellen for setting up ad hoc committees and not working through official channels.

A number of would-be refugees from Nazi Germany turned to Ellen for help. She gave the money she earned from journalism to help their cause, and often put people up in her own flat. She also publicised their plight. She was concerned about the casual anti-Semitism she heard in the streets and criticised the government for allowing in so few refugees She did, however, manage to persuade the government to allow in the remaining communist members of the Reichstag, although this did not mean they were necessarily safe from Nazi assassination. Ellen also organised humanitarian relief in the Saar, a German region bordering on France and governed jointly by Britain and France under a League of Nations mandate until 1935, when it voted to be reunited with Germany. Ellen helped refugees with food and clothing, and helped set up a children's home for children who had been orphaned by the Nazis. She even managed to persuade the Home Secretary to allow German refugee children into the country and guaranteed funding for them.

Through her refugee contacts, Ellen had access to information about continuing atrocities in Germany and she continued to publicise them in the articles she wrote for the newspapers. One piece she wrote described how Einstein's house and books had been vandalised. He was one of the lucky ones, she wrote. He had not been beaten to a pulp, or tortured. 'The contempt for civil order, for personal rights, for constitutional methods of change is slowly engulfing Europe like a thick black wave of despair,' she wrote. The Nazis had no time for women outside the home, she pointed out in *Time and Tide*. Women were being dismissed from their posts in universities and law practices, from hospitals and public services. Nazi officers strode round university examination rooms checking there were no Jews or socialists there. She noted that in this instance Jewish women were given parity with Jewish men; they were persecuted to the same extent. Ellen became known in Germany as a 'Jew of the Jews' and when Goering was invited to visit Britain by the German ambassador he refused, saying that 'all those Ellen Wilkinsons will throw carrots at me'.

In February 1936, Ellen undertook one of the most daring and dangerous escapades of her life so far. She flew from Hendon aerodrome as a reporter for the *Sunday Referee* to find out what was really happening in Germany, rather than what was churned out by Goebbels' propaganda. She had, by this time, been banned from the country and was in danger certainly of arrest, possible worse, if she were detected. She telephoned her report back to England from under a pile of bedclothes so as not to be heard in the hotel. She found that Goering's secret police had tightened their grip even more. Everyone in Berlin was talking of war. She discovered by talking to a minister that the Germans had a plan to move their troops into the Rhineland, which would frighten the French who would not dare do anything without the help of the British. 'And I don't think the British will do anything about the Germans moving German troops within their own country,' he said. As soon as she had reported that, she packed her bag and got out of the country as fast as possible. She was the first correspondent to write about it, on 16 February 1936, and the Germans re-militarised the

Rhineland in 7 March, thus breaking the Treaty of Locarno, which they had signed in 1925.

Ellen severely criticised British foreign policy. It was all decided at dinner parties of the upper classes, she said, but saved her most savage and vitriolic language for Neville Chamberlain, whom she accused of putting the narrow interest of class before the national interest. Later, in 1938, when Chamberlain signed the Munich agreement with Hitler to allow Germany to annexe the Sudetenland, in her address to a crowd of nearly 40,000 people in Trafalgar Square at a Save Peace demonstration, she addressed Chamberlain directly, saying 'We don't trust you. We believe you went to Germany to fix up a sale of the liberties of Czechoslovakia,' and when Hitler's troops marched into the rest of Czechoslovakia six months later she called it a rape.

Fascism: Spain

Unsurprisingly, Ellen was as involved with the situation in Spain as in Germany. When Franco's troops were airlifted from Morocco into Spain to fight the elected government and suppress the miners of Oviedo in the north of Spain, who had formed a socialist republic, Ellen made an appearance. She and Lord Listowel went as representatives of the Committee for Victims of Fascism. When they arrived in Oviedo, they found that the city was in the control of Franco's troops. The miners had fled to the hills and those that remained had been suppressed by the Nationalist army, fortified by troops from Morocco, Nazi Germany and Fascist Italy. Ellen reported that the soldiers had been drunk and had rampaged round the town, doing things no regular Spanish soldier would dare do. The Spanish government promptly started arresting journalists and Ellen and Listowel, who had been booed and hissed by a group they were attempting to address, were hustled into a car and driven for seventeen hours to the border. The Spanish government maintained they had been removed for their own safety. Ellen said she had faced enough hostile crowds in her time as a campaigner for the suffrage to know when she was in danger. She said they had been kidnapped. Their visit incurred a great deal of criticism from a variety of sources.

When the Spanish civil war broke out in July 1936, Ellen believed that Britain should support the democratically-elected government. Chamberlain, unsurprisingly, thought otherwise, and the Labour Party and the TUC followed his lead. Herbert Morrison, perhaps influenced by Ellen, agreed with her although he did not follow her lead in joining campaigns mounted by the communists.

As she did to assist the German Jews, Ellen contributed a great deal of help to the humanitarian side of the war in Spain. She had helped set up the Spanish Medical Aid Committee, as well as a Parliamentary committee to help with food and clothing, and was a founder member of the National Joint Committee for Spanish Relief. As we have already seen, she joined Eleanor Rathbone, the Duchess of Atholl and Dame Rachel Crowdy on a fact-finding mission, and returned to alert the British government to the fact that the German and Italian airforces were assisting Franco. Ellen persuaded NUDAW to instigate a levy on its members to fund bringing 4,000 Basque children to Britain – and she broke down and sobbed in the House of Commons when Guernica had been bombed and the British government refused to do anything about it. The bombing did, however, change the minds of the Labour Party hierarchy, who accepted Ellen's analysis of the situation and, reversing its policy, decided to support the idea of sending arms to the elected government of Spain. The NEC set up a committee to organise an intensive publicity campaign, with their first meeting in the Free Trade Hall and with Ellen Wilkinson as the main attraction. Did she remember her first visit to the hall all those years ago when she had heard Kathleen Glasier speak and thought it must be the most rewarding thing anyone could do? How happy she must have been that she was able to follow in her footsteps.

In December 1937 the NEC sent Ellen and Clement Attlee to Spain to encourage the troops fighting for the government. Starvation was the main problem faced by the Spanish government so back in Britain she organised the Milk for Spain fund and persuaded NUDAW and the Co-operative Union to back it. Ellen made many speeches and worked tirelessly to get the British government to change its policy on Spain. In the interests of international peace, Franco should not be allowed to win the civil war, she said. If fascism triumphed over democracy, Europe would be destroyed. The British government ignored her and when the Republicans conceded defeat and Franco won the war, they acknowledged the new Spanish regime almost immediately.

Jarrow

In 1932 Ellen had been selected as Labour candidate for Jarrow. Here was a cause to fight for. The Jarrow shipyard had been taken over by a consortium backed by the Bank of England, which had promptly shut it down and demolished it. In 1934 Ellen organised a deputation of about 400 men and fifty women to meet Ramsay Macdonald in his constituency of Seaham, a few miles south of Jarrow. The publicity for the event put Jarrow in the news and brought hope to the people of the town that something might be done to alleviate their plight. In 1934 the government passed the Special Areas Act, which nominated certain areas, including Jarrow, to receive government money to help stimulate local businesses. Employers were offered cheap land, subsidised factories, new roads, having to paid no local taxes and their income tax was reduced. The year 1934 had seen the creation of the British Iron and Steel Federation by Ramsay Macdonald's government, set up to control steel production throughout Britain, and which was believed to have impeded the building of a new steelworks in Jarrow rather than facilitating it.

By 1935, Jarrow was ready to vote for Ellen. She turned a Conservative majority of 3,192 into a Labour victory of 2,350. Once again Ellen was the only Labour woman elected, though the Conservatives had six, the Liberals one, and Eleanor Rathbone the Independent. Ramsay Macdonald lost his seat, which must have delighted Ellen, and the Conservative Stanley Baldwin became Prime Minister. In her election manifesto, Ellen had promised to fight for the abolition of the means test. She made an impassioned plea to the government in 1936, pointing out the difference in health and longevity in places such as Jarrow compared with more prosperous communities.

> I remember one women speaking to me and saying that because of the means test, she had gone to live with her married son and daughter, who already had four small children. She said, 'You know, I do not want to be a burden on them, so I slip out at meal times and say that I have had a bite to eat at my neighbour's.' I remember that well, because the woman died. There was cardiac disease on the certificate but it was obvious the woman was more than half-starved.

Ellen drew people's attention to the fact that deaths in Jarrow from tuberculosis were substantially higher than in richer communities and the £15 million a year saved through the Means Test was at the expense of the lives of mothers and babies. Poor nutrition led to more maternal mortality, and a higher death rate among babies – two hundred out of 1,000 babies died in Jarrow, compared with the national average of fifty-five. People in Jarrow died earlier and consumed less milk than the average. She could at least do something about that – she persuaded the local authority to subsidise school milk in her constituency.

In July 1936, the Chairman of the Council came up with the idea of a march of unemployed Jarrow men to London. Ellen had helped plan hunger marches before, although they were usually led by communists. Ellen realised that if they were to march, it was important for them not to be used by the Communist party for their political ends. The Labour Party and the TUC must not be allowed to dismiss it as red propaganda, though they did not, as she had hoped, provide any support. The march was kept strictly non-political, and known communists were barred from the march. Ellen kept a low profile and the march was organised ostensibly from the town hall, supervised by the town clerk, blessed by the local Church and supported by the mayor. Banners were white and blue and all the political parties agreed to work together in the best interests of the town. The men were encouraged to be as smart as they could manage, carefully shaved, broken boots repaired and polished, coats brushed and mended. Led by the mayor in suit and bowler hat, they looked extremely respectable. Ellen had helped raise money for basics such as waterproof capes, which the men carried rolled up on their shoulders, pocket money, two stamps a week so they could write home, medical attention, hair-cutting, and shoe and boot repairs along the way. She found overnight accommodation for them in drill halls, schools, church and town halls, and used her union connections to ensure the men received a rousing welcome wherever they went.

Two hundred men were selected and vetted by the medical officer to ensure they were fit enough to march. They set off on 5 October aiming to reach London as the new session of Parliament was opening. Their aim was to present a petition signed by 12,000 Jarrow residents to the House of Commons. Ellen described how they all rose at 6.30am, often from the bare boards of wherever they had been sleeping. Ellen joined them most mornings and they marched for fifty minutes, rested for ten, then marched again. At noon they ate lunch, sometimes stew, tinned fruit and tea, and in fine weather took a nap on the grass. If it was raining they stood in their capes, eating sandwiches. Each night there was a meeting at which Ellen usually spoke. In spite of her poor health – her bronchitis, her asthma and other lung impairments – she walked further than any other official, taking time off only for official business relating to Jarrow. She was often in a state of collapse at the end of the day. She did take time off to attend the Labour Party national conference, where she gave one of the most electrifying speeches of her life.

'You cannot expect men, trapped in these distressed areas to stay there and starve because it is not convenient to have them coming to London,' she declared. 'What has the National Council done? It has disapproved of it. What has gone out from General Council? Letters saying in the politest language, "Do not help these men"... I tell the executive that they are missing the most marvellous opportunity of a generation... I say to the Party: put yourself at the head of a great movement of moral indignation in this country ... and say, "Our people shall not be starved"... If we cannot do this, what use are we as a Labour Party?'

Ironically the marchers received more support from Conservatives in many of the places they visited, and the Tory Press was astonishingly supportive. Ordinary people, too, were sympathetic to the men's plight. In Leicester, the Co-op boot repairers stayed up all night to repair the marchers' boots, for nothing. In Leeds, a newspaper proprietor gave them a free meal and beer; in Barnsley, the public baths were opened specially for them; in Bedford, they were given cigarettes and tobacco by the Rotary Club and sausages by the local butcher. In Edgeware, the White Hart Hotel made ready a room for them and served them a meal of tomato soup, steak and kidney pudding, and apple pie, paid for by the mayor and Rotary Club.

On 31 October, a month after leaving Jarrow, having walked 290 miles, they arrived in London in driving rain. On 4 November they tried to present their petition to the Prime Minister, Stanley Baldwin, but he refused to see them. The men were all for staging a sit-in, but settled for their leaders and their MP seeing politicians from all parties.

On their return to Jarrow, Ellen was nearly smothered by the kisses and hugs of her constituents. The march did not affect the work situation at the time. In fact, it appeared that the situation would be made worse when the government suggested the men should have their benefits withdraw as they were not available for work. But Ellen wrote a book, *The Town that was Murdered,* and the recognition of the plight of the town was assured. In fact it became the symbol of the hungry 1930s in popular perception. There was also practical help from the Society of Friends, who sold cheap seeds, tools and fertiliser for the men's allotments. Money was also raised to build a park, the work undertaken by the unemployed, and a sports stadium. Paint and wallpaper were provided so people could re-decorate their homes. No substitute for real work, but at least an acknowledgement of what the Jarrow families were going through. Eventually in 1937, after constant lobbying by their MPs, a new steelworks was built.

The Second World War

As one might expect, Ellen had hated Chamberlain's policy of appeasement and, consummate politician that she was, she joined others who were manoeuvring to ensure his resignation. War was declared on 3 September 1939 but what was called the phoney war ensued for several months. The country had to stand up against fascism and Chamberlain was not the man to do it, said Ellen. Everyone on Labour's NEC agreed that the government needed reconstructing to deal with the war. At the beginning of May 1940, Chamberlain was coming under increasing pressure to resign. 'Will the old man cling to power?' was Ellen's question in *Tribune.* On 10 May Attlee phoned Chamberlain to tell him that the Labour Party would join the government but only under a new Prime Minister. Later that same day, Churchill became Prime Minister – much to Ellen's delight.

Churchill asked Attlee to select Labour MPs for government posts and Ellen was among those chosen. Churchill was pleased. He liked her and she reciprocated, which surprised some people, given Churchill's history towards the suffrage movement and the Irish. It was, after all, his gung-ho approach that had suggested the formation of the Black and Tans. When questioned about her attitude to him, Ellen replied that he was the man for the hour. 'The ranks of labour have no cause to love him, but he has been consistently anti-fascist'. That was good enough for her.

To begin with, she was put in charge of hardship tribunals, which was a job after her own heart, but in October 1940, she became joint

Parliamentary Private Secretary to Herbert Morrison at the Home Office. She was given special responsibility for air raid shelters and the care of the homeless, which again suited her down to the ground. The Blitz began on 7 September 1940 and continued till May 1941, resulting in 20,000 dead and about 70,000 wounded. Part of her responsibility at this time was to see that a million Londoners had somewhere to sleep away from their homes. Most nights she was out in the blackout, visiting shelters, talking to people and listening to their stories. To start with, the provision of shelters was inadequate. The better-off took themselves out of the cities to the country. Many people had built Anderson shelters in their gardens, if there was room, but they were badly built and very damp. Within a week, Ellen had organised a new kind of shelter that soon became known as the Morrison, which could be used indoors and looked somewhat like a chicken coop. It was accompanied by a booklet describing how to make your house safer from bombs.

When the heavy bombing started, however, people needed somewhere safer and quieter where they could get some sleep. Many took to the Underground stations, which the government initially discouraged and instructed London Transport to ban people from using them. People ignored the instructions, however, so the government was forced to change its mind. By the end of September 1940, nearly 200,000 people were sheltering there. That same month a group of East Enders broke into the Savoy so they could use the basement reserved for wealthy guests. Ellen promptly requisitioned 500 private cellars for Londoners.

Ellen promised people 'safety, sanitation and sleep' and chivvied local authorities. Manchester Corporation's provision was poor but with Ellen behind them, they found the money to renovate shelters, build new ones, provide bunk beds, canteens and sanitation. By the spring of 1941, Londoners had reasonable accommodation underground. There was a ticket system for regular users of the shelters, where 200,000 bunks were provided, there were canteen facilities to feed people and chemical toilets. In some shelters, there were night classes, films and other activities to keep morale from plummeting. Ellen spent much of her time visiting people in these shelters. Her own home was bombed, so people knew she had sympathy for their plight.

When Coventry was flattened in 1940, hundreds of people were killed and hundreds more injured. Herbert Morrison and the king visited but Ellen was not considered important enough. It was not till the following year that she went to see Coventry for herself. She found that Anderson shelters had not been built because of a lack of material, surface shelters were falling down because they had been so shoddily built. At night there were only 2,352 bunks for 150,000 people. Ellen told the Coventry National Emergency Committee that they had been talking too much and acting too little. They had not used the money the government had made available to them and not ordered enough shelters.

Ellen visited many of the cities and large towns that were targets for enemy bombing: Plymouth, where she stayed with the Astors; and Liverpool, one of the most heavily bombed cities outside London. Between the first and second of May 1941, 680 bombers dropped 870 tonnes of bombs and over 112,000 fire bombs over the city. Half the docks were put out of action, more than seventy water mains fractured, gas and electricity supplies were severely disrupted and 500 roads closed to traffic. The fire service was stretched to capacity, dealing with as many as 400 fires a night.

After May 1941 the pressure eased off somewhat as the Germans turned their attention to Russia but in June 1944, the destruction began anew. This time it was V1s, flying bombs known as doodlebugs. At the peak of the attacks, over a hundred of these buzz bombs were being launched every day at the South East of England.

In April 1941, Herbert Morrison restructured the fire service. Before the war, the fire services had been made up of professionals and volunteers under the control of local authorities. There was too much inefficiency built in for this to work in wartime and they were merged under the new Fire Service Council when 1,400 local fire brigades were amalgamated to make thirty-two. It was Ellen's job to put these alterations into practice. In January 1941, Morrison brought in compulsory fire-watching and Ellen was put in charge. The unions were upset. NUDAW was particularly obstreperous and Morrison had to go to the conference to persuade them to co-operate. They agreed to fire-watch houses and municipal buildings, but not businesses. Even the Labour Party was reluctant to fire-watch and was only persuaded to do it when they were threatened with dismissal if they did not. MPs too were reluctant. The Houses of Parliament were hit fourteen times and damaged because MPs were too busy or reluctant to fire-watch. There was still a serious shortage of fire-fighters, so fire-watching was made compulsory for women as well. Many women refused to register and Ellen had to take the blame at the NUDAW conference for the decision to enrol women in the fire service. Her experiences with the unions had now convinced her that they were not a force for radical change. This was quite a change in attitude from when she had first set out on her political journey in the First World War, when she had been foremost among those pressing for strikes to show management that workers had rights.

The government passed the Emergency Powers and Defence Regulations Act, which prohibited strikes and lockouts and Ellen found herself in the odd situation of standing up before 2,000 men who wanted to strike and telling them they could not. She told them roundly that it was illegal at the present time to strike. 'If you want to fight, fight Hitler,' she said. She also found herself supporting Herbert Morrison when he banned the communist *Daily Worker* for a series of inflammatory articles, which might distract attention from the primary aim, to defeat Hitler.

When Russia entered the war, it changed the perceptions of British communists about the conflict and they now saw it as a fight against fascism but Ellen found herself out of sympathy with them, as she now thought them irresponsible. Communists and trade unionists found her change of attitude difficult. Where was the Red Ellen they had known and loved? The woman who articulated their anger and expressed their frustration? Ellen had changed partly because she was now in government and had to deal with the situation as it was, and not as it might be in an ideal world. The fight against fascism was her main focus, as it had to be for everyone at that time. Because of her closeness, both politically and personally to Herbert Morrison, she must have been influenced to some extent by his anti-communism. She was also in poor health. She was prescribed tranquilisers to combat the asthma, which often prevented her from sleeping at night. They were addictive and often over-prescribed.

Being part of the political establishment, she was invited to stand for election as vice-chair of the NEC, which at first she refused but later accepted. This gave her access to all the sub-committees but she focused on those concerned with the election, policy and organisation. In 1945 the Chairman of the NEC died suddenly and Ellen took his place and, in the January Honours List, was made a Privy Counsellor.

In spite of her deteriorating health, which entailed several protracted periods in hospital, she accompanied Clement Attlee, Anthony Eden and Lord Halifax to San Francisco to help set up the United Nations to replace the discredited League of Nations and while they were there, the war in Europe ended.

The end of the war meant that the Coalition government of the war years was replaced by a Conservative caretaker government until such times as an election could be organised. This occurred almost immediately in July 1945.

By now Ellen had a very influential position in the Labour party. So what did she believe in? She still believed in state control of important elements of the economy, but now she sought it through Parliamentary rather than revolutionary means. In preparation for the forthcoming election, the Labour Party NEC printed 100,000 copies of a booklet entitled *Let us Face the Future*. It had been compiled by Ellen, the sociologist Michael Young, Herbert Morrison, and Patrick Gordon-Walker. After stressing that the Labour Party stood for freedom – freedom of worship, freedom of speech, freedom of the Press – the manifesto went on to say that there were some freedoms the Labour Party would not support – freedom to exploit others, freedom to pay poor wages, freedom to push up prices for selfish profit; freedom to deprive people of the means of living full, happy, healthy lives. They pledged a great programme of modernisation, which would give full employment and affirmed that the Labour Party was a Socialist party and proud of it.

In May 1945, Ellen presided over the largest Labour Party conference they had ever had. She gave the speech of a lifetime and closed with the rousing words: 'Fight clean, fight hard, and come back with a solid majority for a Labour government'. NUDAW was proud of her. 'No one will ever forget the nerve, the verve, the wit, the confidence and the joyful challenge with which she led the Conference from its brilliant opening to its triumphant close', wrote a colleague and Ellen herself said: 'This is the proudest moment of my life.'

She then began a campaign to replace Clement Attlee as leader of the party with Herbert Morrison, who she described as a superb political organiser. Her intrigues and political manoeuvring came to nothing, however, and the NEC passed a vote of confidence in Attlee. The Labour Party won a resounding victory, with an overall majority of 146. Labour took 393 seats, Conservatives 213 and

Liberals 12. Twenty-one women Labour MPs were elected and for the first time, Labour was in power with a majority that would allow them to follow their election manifesto.

Ellen was given the post of Minister of Education. The main part of her work was, ironically, to implement the Conservative Party's Education Act of 1944, which divided secondary education into grammar, technical and modern schools, with pupils separated into the three categories by the eleven plus examination. The exam results came through to schools in three stages and there were many tears when a child's name failed to appear on the first list, the grammar school list. Only twenty per cent of pupils achieved a place at a grammar school but education there was free, for the first time in the country's history, and resulted in social mobility for clever working-class children on a scale not seen before.

Ellen also raised the school-leaving age to fifteen from fourteen and persuaded Parliament to pass the School Milk Act, which gave free milk to schoolchildren. She reduced the number of direct-grant schools and brought in university scholarships for those who could not afford to pay.

Finding buildings for this new system of education was not easy. Many of the pre-war schools had been destroyed by bombing and materials were in very short supply. Ellen had to find 5,000 new classrooms and train 13,000 new teachers. She faced opposition in Cabinet and in the end threatened that if they did not support her, she would use her union connections and public platforms to press for what she needed. The Cabinet gave in. Because of the lack of building materials, Ellen ordered pre-fabricated huts – some of which lasted well into the twenty-first century. They were not pretty but they were functional: easy to clean, easy to heat, and waterproof, unlike some of the picturesque remnants from pre-war days. The shortage of teachers she dealt with by setting up an emergency one-year training scheme and generous grants were given to ex-service personnel aged between twenty-five and thirty.

Ellen was also sent by Attlee to Germany to report on the conditions there. She wrote a secret memorandum outlining the problems. Like Helena Deneke, she found there were shortages of food and fuel, and serious health issues. Typhoid and typhus were under control but diphtheria was bad in some places, and tuberculosis was rife, as was venereal disease. In the British Zone alone there were 2.25 million displaced persons and 9,000 refugees from the east entering West Germany every day. Over two-million German troops were living in the fields. The Russians were stripping as much material and plant as they could carry, and taking it back to Russia. In education, her own area of expertise, she noted that teachers were being vetted for Nazi sympathies and that there was a shortage of suitable books. The only ones available were full of Nazi propaganda.

Towards the end of 1945, Ellen chaired a conference that aimed to establish an educational and cultural organisation of the United Nations: UNESCO. The S represents 'Science', included because Ellen felt it was important that science, which had developed the atom bomb, should be closely linked to culture so that scientists were kept aware of the social implications of their research.

Ellen's health, which had always been precarious, now became a severe problem. She smoked heavily, which did not help her asthma and bronchitis, and the winter of 1945–46 was exceptionally harsh. In February 1947, she died following an overdose of barbiturates. The coroner recorded her death as accidental. She had emphysema, acute bronchitis and bronchial pneumonia, which had put enormous strain on her heart. Her good friend Lady Rhondda thought she had died of exhaustion. She was buried in Penn Street, near Amersham, and most of the great and good attended her funeral, though not Herbert Morrison, who was seriously ill himself with thrombosis. The BBC agreed to delay the news of Ellen's death because Morrison's friends feared the shock might kill him.

8

Isabel Emslie Hutton (1887–1960) and the Medical Profession

Isabel Emslie was in sympathy with the suffrage movement but as a medical student was not allowed to take part in demonstrations or any overt support for the movement, though she underlined her medical notes in violet and green, suffrage colours. The very fact of undertaking medical training showed her commitment to equal opportunities and joining the suffragist-funded Scottish Women's Hospitals during the First World War shows her belief in the suffrage movement.

Life as a Medical Student

In 1905, when seventeen years old, Isabel Emslie enrolled for the Women's Medical School in Edinburgh; she put up her hair and lengthened her skirt to look older and taller. Most of her fellow students in the medical school were intending to be missionaries, so did not have to worry about finding a medical post when they graduated. They would go out to the furthest reaches of the Empire, most likely India, Africa, or beyond, but for Isabel, who had no such ambitions, there would eventually be the difficulty of obtaining a post. Medical posts for women were few and far between. However, that was the future. At seventeen, she was not at all worried about that. There were many bridges to cross before she was qualified.

The first lectures were in zoology and botany, which gave them not only an insight into the theory of evolution, but plenty of practice dissecting first crayfish, then worms, rabbits, pigeons, until finally they graduated to people. Isabel loved it all. When dissecting bodies, the men and the women did this separately in different dissecting rooms, both presided over by Mrs Meikle, who laid out the specimens and ensured that all body parts of the same body were gathered together at the end of the dissection ready for the Day of Resurrection. The students entered the dissecting rooms smelling strongly of carbolic and iodoform, and left it reeking of formalin, since the washing facilities there were minimal – one cold tap for the whole of the group. But, as Isabel cheerily comments, the winds of Edinburgh soon got rid of the smell.

They learnt about all the basic drugs and were taught how to make pills, fold papers, write prescriptions in Latin, and were given severe warning about the use of abortifacients. As Isabel had little idea what abortion was, this rather went over her head.

After they had passed their first exams, the students moved into the Royal Infirmary for two years of practical experience of surgery and examining patients in the wards. Some of the operations were carried out in the operating theatre used by Joseph Lister, the pioneer of antiseptic surgery. Before Lister's work, people had thought wound infection was caused by bad air. Lister swabbed wounds and instruments with carbolic acid, thus cutting down on gangrene and ensuring the survival of many more patients. Joseph Lister was still alive at this point, though he had given up medical practice after the death of his wife, who had worked closely with him on his discoveries. He died in 1912.

In spite of his work, asepsis was far from absolute. Isabel would watch in horror as Mr Francis Caird, the surgeon, peered into the abdomen of some poor patient on the operating table, his pointed moustache apt to come into contact with the patient's intestines. In some of the operating theatres, surgeons were still operating without gloves; but before Isabel's final year, masks, gloves and overalls were obligatory. Metal adjustable tables had replaced the old wooden trolleys covered with faded brown American cloth to which patients were strapped and wheeled into the operating theatre by porters wearing their outdoor uniforms.

After a short time in the operating theatres watching and hopefully learning surgical techniques, students had to take turns being chloroform clerks. Chloroform was the standard anaesthetic and was kept in a round, dark blue, twelve-ounce bottle with the stab end of a safety pin pushed into its neck, which kept the bottle partly open and allowed the fluid to run in a steady stream onto a folded linen face towel covering the face of the patient. It had to be done with one hand because the other was holding the face cloth over the patient's face and, if your hands were small, as Isabel's were, it was difficult to hold the bottle firmly and keep your forefinger tightly on the stopper. Students were encouraged to give too much anaesthetic rather than too little because the shock of waking during the operation might well be fatal. Occasionally the cry would go up: 'The patient's stopped breathing!' At this, several students would raise the foot of the table, others would administer artificial respiration while the anaesthetist would transfix the patient's tongue with the forceps clipped to his or her overalls expressly for such an emergency. In spite of this ramshackle approach, only one patient died on the operating table while Isabel was a student, and that was someone with an aortic aneurism who could have died at any time. The anaesthetist's head had to be so close to the patient's that they were in danger of anaesthetizing themselves but by the time Isabel reached her final year, the new gauze-covered light metal masks with the small drop chloroform bottle were beginning to make their appearance, which made it possible to observe the face of the patient.

Sometimes students had to do casualty duty on a Saturday night. Saturday was payday and there were a great many fights, men with men, women with women, and men beating up their wives. Faces and scalps needed stitching but this was easy. 'Most of us were good needlewomen', said Isabel airily 'and the women were voted more skilled than the men'.

The fourth and fifth years of training were on the medical wards, where life less hectic than the surgical wards. Being a small group, the women medics could gather round the patient's bed, unlike the men, whose numbers were so great they stood in serried ranks and were often not able to see the patient at all.

Generally speaking, the men students disliked the women medics, a dislike shared by many of the tutors. They tolerated the ones destined for missionary work, and left alone the drab, but the attractive ones, and judging by her photograph Isabel was one of these, were criticised, patronised, or were the butt of rude remarks.

Much of her fourth year of training was taken up with obstetrics and gynaecology. The Edinburgh midwifery cases were reserved for the men and the women medics had to go to either Dublin or Glasgow. The teaching was perfunctory and the impression

Isabel received was that gynaecology was a secondary subject. The teaching about the 'change of life' was limited to one page of notes and sterility half a page. Nowhere was there any mention that the cause of a women's inability to conceive might lie with the man rather than the woman.

Isabel was sent to Glasgow, where she first saw the birth of a baby. Neither sedatives not anaesthetics were given unless there were serious complications, and in the case of a lovechild nothing was given to ease the mother's suffering, however intense, since she had sinned and needed to be taught a lesson she would not forget. Fortunately, the repentance stools and sanctimonious public admonitions had disappeared from the Protestant churches by now but the attitude to young women who had become pregnant out of wedlock was still punitive.

After witnessing a number of births in hospital, the students were unleashed into the community where they had to deliver twenty babies. They went out in couples to the miserable hovels where many families lived. Often these consisted of just one room with a solitary tallow candle for lighting and without a water tap or sink. The double bed might well take up most of the room and if the bed were in an alcove or a box-bed, then the students would have to climb into the bed to deliver the baby resulting in disturbing of fleas and body lice. There were few clothes or hippens (nappies) for the baby and there were many difficult births because the women had suffered from rickets as children, which led to deformities of the pelvic bones. Sometimes the babies suffered from hereditary syphilis, which in the hospital antenatal clinics could be detected by the Wasserman blood test invented in 1906 but which could not be used in these home births. The students were legally bound to take preventative measures against gonorrheal infection by cleansing the eyes of newborns who otherwise might have suffered from infection-borne disease that made them blind in later life.

The students were lodged in a hostel converted from a tenement block in Anderston, a tough part of Glasgow. The person on duty slept in a cell-like room next to the telephone so that when the Maternity Hospital called them for some special case, they could dress and rush round there.

Dressing was not easy. Isabel, like all the women students, wore a cotton chemise with a scratchy woollen vest beneath, strapped in by busked and boned stays; navy bloomers, fixed at the knee and waist with innumerable buttons; with a lawn or woollen camisole; black woollen stockings held up by garters, and at least one petticoat, which varied in thickness according to the season. On top of all that was the costume – a skirt and jacket, with a shirt blouse with a stiff collar with studs, tie and safety pin; the whole ensemble finished off with a stiff belt and buckle around the waist. Not easy to don in the middle of the night! Sometimes a woman's husband or small boy would arrive at the door asking for them to hurry. There was no means of transport and students were desperate to get to the right house before the baby was born otherwise it would not count towards their twenty births.

There were several dispensaries in Edinburgh and working there for several months was part of the curriculum. Isabel was full of admiration for Alice Hutchison, who ran the St John Street Dispensary, because of her gentleness with patients, particularly children. During the First World War, Dr Hutchison joined the Scottish Women's Hospitals and went to Serbia, as did Isabel Emslie. As part of their work with the dispensaries, students visited the homes of patients and so acquired practical experience of caring for people in the community. Here Isabel experienced the death of patients in their own homes, which she found far more upsetting than in hospital because they were surrounded by their grieving families. On one occasion when visiting a man who was said to be dying, she was asked to say prayers over the patient. Unable to think of anything appropriate to say, she recited two psalms, *The Lord is my shepherd* and, *I will lift up my eyes to the hills,* a favourite of her father's. No sooner had she finished than the patient said, 'I'm a bittie better noo, Jeanie'. The neighbours and his wife were impressed. 'The doctor's prayer has been answered real quick,' and 'It's gey like a miracle,' they murmured. It did her reputation no harm at all.

From this work in the community she learned the importance of listening to patients and the healing power of unburdening oneself of worries and fears. When the women put their fingers to their lips and led her into a corner to tell her something, she knew they were about to disclose some problem of their married life. There was nothing in the medical curriculum about the sex life of a healthy married couple and nothing written in any book that she was aware of. They would often ask for advice about abortion, about which of course she could say nothing except to warn against trying by mechanical means to get rid of the foetus. She might then be asked about contraception about which, again, she could tell them nothing.

A problem the students came across regularly when working in the clinics was the effects of syphilis. The cure for this was mercury, taken for two years before the disease was cured. Unfortunately mercury itself is a poison and the effects of taking it more often than not outweighed the benefits. Small wonder, then, that patients gave up the cure as soon as their symptoms had been mitigated, though the disease would return and sometimes led to madness and paralysis known as General Paralysis of the Insane (GPI). Surgeons at the hospital disliked the work.

There was a flourishing Edinburgh University Women's Suffrage Society and the lady medics hoped to gain the University vote, then denied them. In the final year classes in jurisprudence, they learnt about giving evidence in court, about sudden deaths, murders, and suicides but when it came to rape, students were asked to read the notes at home.

The lecturer on infectious diseases, which was becoming a specialism, had much to say on diphtheria and whooping cough but nothing at all about typhus and cholera, which he said were rare. This was unfortunate since they were very common in Serbia and Macedonia where Isabel ended up in 1918.

The final specialism they were to encounter was mental illness, much feared by the general population and, if it occurred in a family, a taboo subject. Isabel learned not to fear mental illness and thought that on the whole people suffering from such illnesses were likely to be sad and timid rather than dangerous. The patients at the mental hospital she spent time at were nursed as if they suffered from a physical illness. There were no locked wards, no padded rooms or shackles. Case notes had to be prepared about each patient, which meant that Isabel got to know them very well. There was no prejudice against women doctors, which Isabel found a relief. The food was excellent and there was time to play games and read in the evenings.

When she returned for her final year of study, all the women on the course felt pressure to succeed because they were women in a man's world. At the end were the exams. Isabel sailed through the written papers but the orals still loomed. Her surgical examiner looked exhausted. 'Yours is the best paper

I've seen so far,' he drawled. 'You'd better demonstrate these instruments to me and save me the trouble of questioning you'. She worked her way through the array of surgical instruments, explaining what they were used for. When she turned round at the end of the row, she found her examiner asleep. She kept very still so as not to wake him and was finally told, 'Thank you; that will do'. Her gynaecology examiner was rather more awake. When she entered the room, he peered down at her and muttered to himself, before even starting to question her, 'D'ye know, I think you'll make a fine little doctor'. The relief was so great Isabel almost burst into tears.

There were few vacancies for women doctors, but Isabel was lucky in that she had already been invited to join the staff of the Stirling District Asylum at Larbert, where she had spent one summer working. She had not yet decided that she would specialise in mental health, a field wide open to women and therefore with plenty of opportunities for advancement in her chosen profession. The thought of a job where she could live in, have her board and laundry paid for, and a salary of £100 a year was very appealing, particularly in view of the fact that her parents still had her three brothers to educate.

The Beginning of Her Career

The Stirling lunatic asylum had a new manager. Gone were the carefree days when you ordered without a qualm any equipment you might need. Every penny was accounted for and had to be justified. Nevertheless, the living conditions were good, though for medical staff they were hedged about with restrictions. Medical staff had no off-duty time, and were not allowed to be absent at the weekend or overnight. Travel on the train had to be first class to avoid contact with the nursing staff, and the matron and Isabel had to take a cab to the station so they were not seen to walk there on foot. When board members visited, presumably to inspect the running of the establishment, they were kept apart from the medical staff, and contact with the locals was severely discouraged. Few medical staff stayed for more than a year because on top of all the restrictions, promotion was slow and getting married was an impossibility because there were no married quarters. Many people who would have made good psychiatrists left that particular branch of medicine for good.

Even so, the food was good and plentiful, which helped patients' recovery and the wards were cheerful places full of flowers, which lifted the spirit. The women particularly benefitted from asylum life because, probably for the first time in their lives, they were being cared for and had no responsibilities. They flourished but when they went home, they went with no advice on contraception, which no one talked about. There was no outpatients' department where people could be seen before their mental state deteriorated. It was all or nothing. So the women who had been nursed back to health embarked on the treadmill of more babies, more mouths to feed, and more worry.

Isabel, being Isabel, could not just sit back and enjoy the work. She wanted to obtain a higher degree and decided to write her thesis on the Wasserman technique, an antibody test for syphilis developed in 1906, and its effect on General Paralysis of the Insane (GPI). For this she needed a ready supply of guinea pigs and rabbits, and someone to take care of them. The Superintendent was not going to fund such a project, so Isabel found a patient who said he would like to do the work. 'Leave it to me,' he said and proceeded to build cages for the animals, which multiplied rapidly under his care. 'We could make a few baubees if we sold them to other people,' he said. So the hospital became a supplier of guinea pigs and rabbits to pathologists all over Scotland.

Isabel obtained her MD and went for a discussion with the superintendent of the asylum about her career. Would she get any promotion? No. Could she become a superintendent of an asylum? The superintendent's eyebrows shot up. 'If you were appointed superintendent there would be consternation in all the asylums in the country and all the doctors would revolt.' Isabel begged to differ. The Superintendent turned on his heel and walked away, signalling for her to open the door for him.

Having been three years in her post at Larbert, she applied for a post at the Hospital for Sick Children in Edinburgh, not expecting to get it, but to her astonishment was appointed to the post. There was no salary but she had saved enough from her time at the Lunatic Asylum to tide her over for the present.

Here she found that children responded spectacularly well to treatment. They came in badly fed, poorly clothed and smelly. They often suffered from rickets, osteomyelitis (inflammation of the bone or bone marrow caused by streptococcus infection), gastro-enteritis, rheumatic fever or pneumonia. While the majority made a full recovery, in some the disease was too well established to respond to treatment, and the child died. If that was the case, the mother always appeared clutching an insurance certificate that would pay for the funeral, and a bunch of Mrs Simpkins carnations, a scent Isabel was to associate for the rest of her life with those grieving mothers.

As the end of her time at the children's hospital approached, she was asked by Dr Charles Mayo of Rochester, New York, who ran the Mayo clinic with his brother, if she would like to join them. Isabel went around in a daze for several days, not only because of the fame of the clinic but also because the idea of a trip to America was alluring. As she was thinking this proposition over, the supervisor of the Royal Mental Hospital in Edinburgh offered her the post of physician in charge of the women's section of the hospital. While sorely tempted by the Mayo Clinic offer, in the end she opted for the Edinburgh post and with it a career in psychiatry.

Patients at the hospital were a mix of those funded by a payment of £50 from the parish, private patients who had the means to pay out of their own pockets, and people paid for out a Samaritan fund. The hospital was not set up to make a profit so any money that accumulated was ploughed back into whatever the hospital was thought to need. By this time the work of Freud, Jung and Adler was becoming known. Medical students had never before been taught anything about mental processes so the thinking of these psychologists gave the Edinburgh doctors a new insight into their patients.

Then the Archduke Ferdinand was shot.

The First World War

As soon as war was declared, hospitals had to be reorganised to accommodate wounded soldiers, and many of the staff resigned from the mental hospital so they could nurse them. Isabel would have liked to do the same, but all her seniors stressed how indispensable she was. However, as she saw how retired nurses and doctors were coming out of retirement to fill the gaps, she became more determined to play her part. She went along to the Scottish Nurses Hospital Office, funded entirely by the suffrage movement, and offered her services. Her mother was upset as she now had all four of her children serving in the forces, though luckily they all survived.

Isabel was sent to France to begin with, which was a relief to her mother, but something of a disappointment to Isabel who had hoped to go to Serbia. It was not only a desire to serve her country that motivated her. She wanted adventure, and the experience of wartime surgery and medicine in different lands. It also solved a personal problem for her since she had fallen in love but had no wish to marry as that would see the end of her medical career because married women had to resign their posts on marriage.

In grey and Gordon tartan, the staff of the Scottish Women's Hospitals were easily recognised as they embarked for France and the city of Troyes, the medical centre for the French casualties in the Champagne area. There were 250 beds in tents, where patients at first felt they were risking their lives in the breezes that blew through the tents. Isabel was put in charge of pathology but soon found that in wartime, you turn your hand to whatever is needed.

A colleague in charge of the X-ray department was Edith Stoney, who went on to establish stereoscopy to localise bullets and shrapnel, and introduced the use of X-rays to diagnose gas gangrene. Miss Stoney was 'a mere wraith of a woman' with infinite physical endurance. She could carry heavy loads and work tirelessly on a near starvation diet.

After several months, the SWH unit at Troyes was moved. They were not told where to, though rumour had it they were going to Salonika, in Greece. The first step on the journey was a train journey down to Marseilles. Here they visited the hospital and saw first-hand the large numbers of severe head wounds, some of which caused blindness. However, the introduction of tin hats, first introduced in rudimentary form by the French, lessened the prevalence of severe head wounds. In 1915 they were superseded among the British by the Brodie helmet.

They sailed from Marseilles, along with a ship full of French soldiers and a hold full of ammunition, to Malta and from there to Piraeus, landing in Salonika in November 1915. The automobiles the French had brought with them were the first the Macedonians had ever seen and they fled from them in terror. One of the first things Isabel did as head of the SWH unit was to cut her waist-length hair and to order all her staff to do the same in a bid to defeat the head lice.

The situation in Salonika was somewhat volatile. The Greeks had not yet become embroiled in the war, and there were 30,000 enemy

Turks in the city. However, the Scottish nurses were not staying in Salonika but travelling a further 50 miles north to the Serbian border, to a town called Ghevgeli. Three French divisions had gone further north to help stem the tide of Austrian and Bulgarian troops who were threatening to overwhelm the Serbs. The 10th British Division went to Ghevgeli with the nurses, regaling them with hot sweet tea. They had come straight from the Dardanelles, still dressed in cotton shirts and shorts. Ghevgeli was full of Serb reservists, dressed in brown homespun suits braided in black, with traditional sandals or opanke on their feet, sheepskin caps and fancy socks with knitted tops of red roses and yellow trees, or pink roses and forget-me-nots. The conditions at the army barracks were grim. Isabel describes the scene:

> Wounded and dysenteric patients were huddled together on the floor in excrement. The surgeons operated by the light of thin tallow candles and without anaesthetics; the suffering was past telling and was only equalled by the boundless courage of the patients.

This spurred the SWH to establish a hospital as fast as possible. They took over a large silkworm factory. On the ground floor they established the X-ray department, the laboratory and the dispensary. On the first floor were the bales of equipment, which the senior staff slept among and on the second floor, thirty members of the unit slept. There was no heating but the splendid Miss Stoney had climbed along the rafters to install lighting throughout the building and had finished her work by dusk. Meals were taken in the open. The wards were the large tents they had brought with them from Troyes, but there was a delay putting them up because the Greeks had stolen the tent poles. The French soldiers however cut down trees as substitutes, which worked well.

At the beginning of December the 'Vardar', a bitterly cold wind from the north, began to blow, which especially affected the French colonial troops who suffered from frostbite, with some of them dying at their posts, their rifles still in their hands. The nights were the worst as the wind whistled through the cracks in the shuttered windows of the factory and the jackals howled.

On 4 December the order was given to abandon Ghevgeli. The Serbs had been overrun by the combined forces of Austria and

Bulgaria, and Serbia now belonged to the enemy. The thoughts of the small group of medical personnel were with their colleagues in Serbia, some of whom had been captured by the Austrians, among them Alice Hutchinson, who opted to stay with their patients rather than join the terrible trek across the mountains by defeated Serbs and SWH personnel to Albania and safety.

The Ghevgeli group and their equipment were evacuated by train, the cooks even bringing away the bricks and fire-bars, as well as firewood, so as to be ready for the next camp. They arrived at Salonika nine hours later, having slept on the floor of the train, and immediately started to unpack and set up their hospital near the sea. A consignment of small green tents had arrived for them so the staff were able to have a tent apiece. Luxury indeed! Miss Stoney again rigged up lighting – she had brought her own Lister generator from England – the French engineers established a water supply, and Isabel herself was responsible for the sanitary arrangements. They took turns to dig sewage pits and by 17 December, the hospital was up and running.

For the next two or three months life proceeded fairly predictably but in April, as the weather got warmer, the flies became an absolute scourge. Among the natives there was no sanitation so dysentery spread by the flies was rife. Ants too were a nuisance since, although they did not spread disease, they bit, and where they had bitten they left large, irritating swellings.

But the deadliest scourge was mosquitoes. Before the war, Salonika had been free of malaria – but many of the villages further north were not. As mosquitoes can only fly a short distance and villagers did not travel far either, much of Macedonia had remained free of malaria. But now there was a constant movement of troops, numbers of them affected by malaria, so the disease gradually spread to the whole of the country. It became unbearably hot as the summer progressed. The nursing was exhausting because both malarial and dysenteric patients needed intensive nursing. There was no ice to cool down the patients, and all the water had to be boiled because chlorination was not strong enough to kill all the bacteria. Sandfly fever was also a problem, not life-threatening but those people bitten by the fly were laid low with a three-day fever that left them debilitated and unable to work. Then infective jaundice struck. Many people had to be sent home while those who replaced them often succumbed within a short time, so life was difficult.

But the French and British troops were gradually advancing and gaining ground from the Austrian and Bulgarian armies. In May 1916 the remains of the Serbian army – 120,000 men – also joined the advancing forces. The Serbs suffered with dysentery and malaria but also scurvy, which puzzled the medical staff because they had exactly the same provisions as the rest of the troops. There were also Russian and Italian troops and the autumn of that year saw the arrival of the hospital unit funded entirely by the American suffrage movement. They were sent up to Ostrovo to support the advancing army, who finally captured Monastir from the enemy. The Serbs wanted to press on but winter was fast approaching and it was impossible to fight in winter.

1917 was an eventful year: the Greeks opted to join the Allies; following the October revolution, the Russians left Macedonia; and in August, there was a huge fire that swept through Salonika. It started in a small way behind the bazaar but fanned by the north wind, the varda, it spread rapidly and gobbled up house after house, street after street. The hospital was outside the town but great fireballs were blown across from the town. The nursing staff climbed on the ridgepoles of their tents with brooms and beat out the fireballs as they landed. By midnight the wind had changed and the fire swept south away from the town towards the port area. Inshore boats were set alight and as they tried to sail away from the fire, they spread it to others. However, by the morning the fire had died down. It had left the Turkish quarter unharmed, and many of those people whose houses had been destroyed were insured with Lloyds of London, who, much to everyone's astonishment, paid up without a quibble. Considering there were no fire precautions or fire brigade, they had been very generous.

Both the British and the French did a great deal of pioneering work on malaria at that time. Sir Ronald Ross, who had discovered that malaria was carried by the anopheles mosquitoes, came to give expert advice and, since fighting could only be pursued in spring and autumn, in the winter and summer there was time to do lab work. The SWH had the best research lab in the country and much useful work was done on tropical and semi-tropical diseases by the French and the British. Isabel carried out the cerebrospinal fluid examinations for the consultant physician to the British army, Colonel Purves Stewart. Many of the malarial marshes were drained and those that could not be so treated were spread with petrol to prevent the development of the mosquito larvae.

One of the consequences of the malaria problem was the number of personnel who succumbed to the disease. Two of the commanding officers of the American SWH had fallen ill with malaria and had had to be sent home to recuperate. Isabel was therefore asked, in the summer of 1918, if she would take over leadership of the American unit now stationed 90 miles west of Salonika in Ostrovo overlooking Lake Ostrovo. The place looked idyllic with its green hillsides starred with cyclamen and lilies, the waters of the lake reflecting the towering mountain Kaimakchalan. But it was malarial and Isabel was determined to move the hospital to a healthier site.

In the autumn the Serbs advanced northwards into Serbia by 120 km, taking many German and Bulgar prisoners on the way. Those Serb patients who had two legs danced the *kolo*, their national dance and, one by one, the nursing sisters joined in. The Serb army outstripped their supply lines but sent message back saying 'Don't send us food, send us shells'. On 30 September news came that Bulgaria had capitulated.

The medical situation was catastrophic as the retreating Austrians and Bulgars had taken everything, and destroyed the railway, which meant that medical supplies would be stranded in Salonika. Isabel travelled down to Salonika in a SWH vehicle and met the Serbian Director of Medical Supplies, who was in despair. He wanted the SWH hospital to advance to Vranja but could get no transport. Isabel went to see General Long, the chief of the British Transport Service and told him of their requirements, and he arranged the transport there and then.

On her return to Ostrovo she called all the staff together and told them of the plan to advance to Vranja, which would be both dangerous and arduous, and gave them the opportunity to resign if they felt it would be more than they could cope with. No one did. On 23 October a convoy of nine automobiles set off on the five-day trek to Vranja. The road was crowded with Serbian troops and Bulgar prisoners. Dead horses and donkeys littered the roadside, with blue jays pecking at the carcasses. All the bridges had been destroyed but the water was low at this time of year and they splashed through unimpeded. The Babuna Pass, which they traversed on the second day, had thirty-four hairpin bends but the drivers were up to the challenge and nothing untoward occurred.

As they approached Vranja, they could see a huge white building dominating the skyline. It was the regimental barracks, which would house the hospital but which was now acting as both barracks and dressing station.

As they clattered into the parade ground sleet began to fall. It was bitterly cold but no preparation had been made for them since the army doctors and nurses of the Second Drina Dressing Station had been swamped by the 1,500 patients they were trying to deal with. They had no equipment and only as many field dressings as their pack mules could carry. Priests were ministering to some of the dying, but many of them just died unnoticed.

The operating room was a ghastly sight. The floor was swimming in blood. There were pails filled to overflowing with amputated limbs, covered in flies. The surgeons operated without anaesthetics, their uniforms covered by waterproof aprons, while patients kept up a constant wail. There was no lighting – the town had run out of candles. Delirious patients were wandering about the corridors moaning for water and, amid this scene from hell, white haired old guards, their job to guard prisoners, marched aimlessly about.

The SWH staff cleared two rooms and each sister unfolded her camp bed, opened wide the windows, letting in the snow but letting out some of the stench, and tried to sleep. At daybreak the Second Drina Dressing Station marched out leaving Isabel responsible for the patients in the hospital, the population of Vranja and outlying villages for 50 miles around, as well as the supply and transport service. 'Everyone was in good health and heart and eager to tackle whatever had to be done, it would be accomplished somehow – and it was!' wrote Isabel.

For many weeks all but the most seriously ill were turned out to fend for themselves as they made their way home to their villages. That first morning as Isabel surveyed the scene, she saw patients lying in their torn and blood-stained uniforms, their wounds not dressed since their application on the battle field; their clothing crawling with bugs and maggots and their bodies with lice. Many had pneumonia, because the Spanish influenza pandemic had reached the country. In the ceremonial hall of the barracks about a hundred Bulgar prisoners were dying of dysentery and the hall and adjoining grass court were foul with excrement. How to tackle this?

By noon the sisters had done a surface clean with brooms improvised from twigs. They had burnt the rubbish accumulated from heaven knows how long. Fifty of the old guards had been detailed to work outside and began to brush and whitewash, but they kept stopping to watch the Voluntary Aid Detachment (VAD) who were washing the woodwork with paraffin to kill the bugs. The theatre sister and the dispenser were instructed to get on with their work, which they duly did. The sanitary inspector, Miss Barker, shovel in hand, galvanised the old guards into action and set about improvising a system for disposing of waste and purifying the wells.

In the afternoon the first of the lorries carrying their equipment arrived. The last vehicle to arrive parked on the lid of the cesspit, which promptly gave way and it sank into the depths. The drivers were fed by their indomitable cook Selina Tubb who had, by this time, prepared invalid food for the patients and an Irish stew for everyone else. Having eaten, the drivers stretched out beside the kitchen stove and fell asleep. Late that night Isabel walked through the building and felt a certain satisfaction. Some progress had been made. The patients were warm in bed, the worst being tended by sisters with lamps in their hand, just as Florence Nightingale had so many years before, the stoves were blazing, the old guards had stacked their rifles in a corner and were helping the sisters stoke the heating stoves and fetching and carrying without complaint.

After a while when the first euphoria of conquest had dissipated among the Serbs and they returned to their villages to find them ravaged, their farms stripped of animals and grain, their wives and children either dead or disappeared, many of them descended into deep despair and vowed to wreak their revenge on any Bulgar they could find. Morale plummeted and the will to work to improve living conditions in the barracks went with it. The old men could no longer be chivvied into cleaning and maintaining the place, and began to resent the SWH women, these interlopers. 'Patience, brothers,' one was heard to say. 'We suffered four hundred years of the Turk. Stick it out. These Scottish women, too, will soon depart and leave us in peace.' But even this phase of despair passed.

Armistice Day came and went without anyone realising what it meant. Isabel chiefly remembered it for one thing. A large convoy of Bulgar prisoners was waiting in the outpatients department for treatment when one of the VADs crossed the yard with a pail full of scraps for her chickens. The pail was snatched from her and upended, and the prisoners grovelled on the ground to eat the potato peelings, the bones and the garbage meant for the hens.

One of Isabel's responsibilities outside the hospital was to examine army recruits. The Commandant instructed her to pass them all unless they were blind, deaf, dumb or legless. She sat on a platform while the hall filled with young men naked but for their sheepskin caps. 'Remove your caps,' bawled the Commandant and, to a man, they doffed their caps, saluted and were pronounced fit.

The outpatients department dealt with people from the town and the surrounding villages, and while the doctors dealt with the wounds of the four hundred or so soldiers, the sisters stitched, dressed or lanced the wounds of the civilian population. There were gunshot wounds, because Serb celebrations usually involved shooting guns into the air. There were burns and bites from wild dogs and wolves, which were sometimes difficult to clean because the family often stuffed the wound with wet tobacco leaves and wrapped a newly-drawn rabbit skin around it.

When the weather became colder and it started to snow they had their first case of typhus. Being in good working order, the hospital was ready to cope with an epidemic. They opened a typhus ward immediately, knowing this would be the first case of many. Typhus is passed on by fleas and lice so if these can be eliminated before a patient even enters the hospital proper, there is no risk to contacts. A bathroom was arranged at the entrance to the hospital where patients' clothes were fumigated. Patients were then shaved of every hair on their bodies. Nurses on bathroom duty were quite likely to be bitten in spite of their all-encompassing suits, long boots and rubber gloves. There was much light-hearted chat at mealtimes as people recounted how many lice they had caught. It was routine to count the number of days from the catch to be able to calculate the length of incubation of the disease.

Patients were nursed in wards with wide-open windows and a blazing stove. By the fifth day of the first symptom, they were usually delirious and completely lost control of their bodily functions so they needed constant changing and careful nursing. They were fed every hour on a mixture of brandy, sugar and egg, and were able to eat this without really coming back to full consciousness. The medication (we are not told what this was) was given by hypodermic syringe every four hours, and every hour as the disease reached its crisis on the fifteenth day. The patient's high temperature then dropped so low that the patient appeared dead, which may account for the Serbian tales of people crawling out of the mass graves dug for typhus victims.

When spring came the typhus epidemic disappeared, Serbian depression lifted, the women took out their distaffs and again walked along spinning, the potters sat at their wheels, and the fur workers cured the skins of fox and wolves they had caught in the winter. The wards, cleared of typhus patients, could be used for civilian operations. Isabel operated from eight in the morning until late afternoon in a room that now looked like a hospital theatre not an abattoir, ably assisted by young doctors straight from medical school who were able to update her on methods. She undertook operations she would never have had the opportunity to perform at home. Much of the work was plastic surgery: removal of scar tissue, removal of non-malignant tumours and repairs to harelips.

On 7 June peace was signed and the Bulgar POWs could go back over the border, which was an immense relief. As summer passed into autumn, there were many invitations to weddings, christenings and betrothals. At all of them everyone danced the *kolo*. They would then ask for a demonstration of the *skotski kolo,* which the Scottish women would be happy to provide, finishing with the singing of *Auld Lang Syne*, which was the only way to persuade everyone to go home.

It was time to close the hospital but before she did, Isabel set up a fifty-bed hospital run by a local committee. She moved to Belgrade and in March 1920, the SWH in Serbia was wound up and all the equipment given to the Serbian people.

Peace at Last, of a Sort

Isabel intended to go straight to Vienna, before departing for Scotland, but doctors were needed at the Lady Mabel Paget's Mission for Children in the Crimea. The Crimea, at this time, was packed with refugees from Russian cities further north, fleeing the revolution. They were supporters of the Tsar and were known as White Russians, as opposed to the Reds, who had fought for the Revolution.

To get there Isabel had to pass through Constantinople and decided to have a few days' holiday in the city. One of the events she attended was a polo match between a British Army team and a

Navy team. Rather to her surprise, she discovered she knew most of the players, having met them during the war. Among them was the Military Secretary Major T. J. Hutton, who very kindly offered to show her the sights of Constantinople. One day as they viewed the Mosque of Suleimani, he asked her to marry him. Isabel was astonished and disconcerted. They had enjoyed a blissful few days together but marriage was not on her agenda. She felt wedded to her career, which she found completely satisfying. She prevaricated. 'I'm going to the Crimea,' she thought. 'He'll have forgotten me by the time I get back.'

She set sail for the Crimea and tried to forget him. The ship she sailed in was crammed with Russian men and women wounded in battles with the Bolsheviks. Now restored to health, they were keen to return to the battlefield and continue their fight against the Reds. At Sebastopol the quay was crowded with British soldiers of the Military Mission, which had been supporting the White Army of the Tsarists under General Wrangel, but had now been withdrawn. This was because Wrangel, leader of the White Army in Southern Russia, had been instructed to keep his troops within the confines of the Crimea, which he had failed to do. In such an event, the British, they had told him, would have no alternative but to withdraw their support. But Wrangel himself had had no alternative but to send his troops further north, since there was insufficient food in the Crimea for his army.

Lady Muriel Paget's Mission had been in Sebastopol for several weeks, but had no proper accommodation and little equipment. With the departure of the British soldiery, one of their messes was taken over as a nurse's hostel and a school building was handed over to them to form the hospital, which became the nucleus of child welfare work in the Crimea.

The cultural life of the Crimea at this time was extraordinarily rich because of the influx of people fleeing the Bolsheviks. Tolstoy's youngest son Sasha, a fine singer of gypsy songs; the aforementioned Baron Wrangel and his wife, who worked for the Red Cross; most of the members of what had been the Imperial Opera, apart from Chaliapin; many members of the Imperial Ballet including their ballet master, who was keen to learn the Scottish men's dances. 'I can show you,' said Isabel. 'I've been dancing them since I was a child,' and proceeded so to do. The opera singers formed the choir of the cathedral where the priests strongly believed the Church could regain the support of the people from the Bolsheviks. They duly sent out a band of priests, with an icon at their head, which passed through the White Army lines and was never seen again.

As the winter of 1920 approached, the medical fraternity looked with dread to the expected outbreak of typhus and the extreme cold. Isabel writes in one of her reports:

> No lice, no typhus. But there are no disinfection plants and no changes of clothes for the troops. The Russian D.M.S (the Director of Medical Services) calculates there will be seventeen thousand beds needed for typhus patients. There will be little food, less wood and no coal and many cases of pneumonia, frost-bite and deaths from exposure. The children are all underfed and many have no warm garments and neither blanket nor boots.

Consequently Isabel set off for Constantinople to collect winter supplies. She decided to approach the Navy for help, as she had often done in Salonika. She was given permission to buy coal, which she duly did. In November, General Wrangel admitted that the Crimea would be in a state of siege all winter from the Red Army and anyone who wished to go over to the Bolsheviks should do so straight away. By 10 November Wrangel had conceded defeat and asked for ships of any kind to evacuate the Crimea, saying he would re-form his forces and attack the Bolsheviks from the Ukraine in the spring.

The following day, the women at the Mission were told to leave Sebastopol. Isabel objected because there were orphans there who needed their care. The answer was that if there was the slightest resistance, they were to be taken 'in irons if necessary'. Isabel accepted the inevitable. The nurses packed their bags but took the orphans with them and when they reached Constantinople they were found accommodation. But what of the White Russians who had packed onto every available boat to escape from Sebastopol? Lloyd George, the British Prime Minister, had given orders that no help was to be given by the British, though the French had officially recognised them as refugees. With the fall of Sebastopol having been so sudden and unexpected, nothing had been done to accommodate them in Constantinople and there was no food.

Unofficially the British set up a committee in the neutral ground of the Embassy church vestry to raise funds and immediately spent

£300 on provisions, the first instalment – rice, milk and bread – was taken out to one of the 120 ships, crowded with refugees, which had not been given permission to dock. The British Refugee Committee continued working until 25 November, by which time the French had made arrangements to feed and house the White Russians. That same day they learned that Winston Churchill had insisted the government make money available and £20,000 had been voted through to help them. A camp for 2,000 people was soon established. The bathing and delousing of the women and children was undertaken by the Refugee Committee, with Isabel's nurses carrying out the work, and the British Army raising money to feed the people at the disinfection station.

Homeward Bound

Finally Isabel decided that she would head for home. Her old job was waiting for her in Edinburgh and she looked forward to taking up her position. She had performed so many operations in Serbia that she no longer hankered after a career in surgery. Mental illness still appealed.

She retraced her steps: Salonika, Belgrade, where she was interested to see that the Russian emigres were settling into posts left vacant by the slaughter of so many during the war. In Vienna, where she intended to spend a short time, the streets were full of frightened people, and Communist demonstrations were a daily occurrence. The psychiatric clinic she visited was poverty-stricken, the bedding threadbare, and the food coarse. There were many suicides among the general public and obvious despair on the faces of the people. Such was the hunger that when she reached London, the children appeared rosy and fat to Isabel compared with the children in Vienna.

She was welcomed by her parents after five long and dangerous years away and scolded by her mother for looking so thin, weather-beaten and shabby. She took up her post at the Royal Mental Hospital, where few staff from before the war remained. But before many months had passed, Major Thomas. J. Hutton, who had not forgotten her, persuaded her to marry and took her south, away from Scotland where she was never to live again.

Married Life

Being now a married woman she was no longer eligible to apply for any salaried public health and hospital posts and the change in her circumstances was difficult to bear. From being the bringer of succour to the helpless, an organiser in the midst of chaos, an expert relied on by other experts, suddenly she was nothing – a housewife whose work was supposed to centre round the needs of one house and one husband. How was she going to bear it? She wasn't.

She started looking for ways around this unacceptable situation. Her husband considered her career more important than his own. He was now based in Camberley, Surrey, at Sandhurst, the college for army officer training, where he was now a student. They lived in an army house and Isabel wondered how she could possibly survive without going mad. Soon, however, their house was needed for one of the staff and it was made known that students would benefit from living in college where they would meet their fellow students at mealtimes and in the evenings.

Meanwhile Isabel had been looking around Harley Street in London and had spotted a small unfurnished maisonette available for a modest rent. It was decided Thomas would live in college during the week and come up to London at weekends while Isabel would study at the Royal Society of Medicine because she intended to become a Fellow as soon as she could find someone to sponsor her.

Finding Work

A post-graduate course was just about to begin at the Maudsley Hospital. This was, and still is, the largest mental health training institution in the British Isles. It had started in 1907 by a gift to the London County Council (LCC) of £30,000 given by Henry Maudsley who wanted to establish a mental hospital that would take early and acute cases, would have an out-patients department, and would provide teaching and research. During the war it had been requisitioned by the Military but returned to the LCC in 1923, when an Act of Parliament was passed so that people could become voluntary patients without being certified as insane. Sir Frederic Mott, founder of the hospital but still working there as director of the laboratory, approached Isabel and asked if she would consider undertaking a year's research on adrenal glands in his laboratory for a fee of £100. She started work the following day.

Given that the Maudsley was supposed to be a modern and forward-thinking hospital, Isabel was astonished to find that there were locked doors and padded rooms. Doctors were incredulous when she said that Scottish hospitals had had no such thing for a century. One day Dr Mapother, the Medical Superintendent, asked her if she would be willing to join the staff as third medical officer. It would be a full-time post without the need to live in, so it seemed like the offer of a lifetime. Her old Larbert chief, Professor Robertson, advised her to refuse the job because it was not good enough for someone of her experience and suggested she should build up her private practice.

Her job application was not even looked at, however, because she was married. Shortly after, another post became available, that of Junior Commissioner in Lunacy, Isabel being the only woman with the relevant experience to do the job. She called for a chat with the secretary of the Board of Control. He was interested and encouraging, until she said she was married. His manner changed, becoming one of frigid politeness. Isabel was furious. 'What a pity I told you I had committed the heinous sin of marrying,' she flashed. 'If I had concealed my marriage no one would have been any the wiser. Better still, if I'd lived in sin any post would have been open to me.' He opened the door and, his face set in extreme disapproval, ushered her out, closing the door behind her immediately. A man was appointed.

Isabel was bitterly disappointed but determined to find a way round all the difficulties. She decided to follow the advice of her old chief at Larbert and concentrate on building up her private practice.

The Hygiene of Marriage

She had been turning over in her mind for some time the difficulties people had confided in her when she was a student to which she had been unable to provide answers. Now she was a married woman with experience of sex, she thought it time to write a book of practical explanations in straightforward English about the problems couples might face before and during marriage. She aimed to cover every aspect of married life. She was not the first person to write a book about contraception, since Marie Stopes' book, *Married Love,* had been published as early as 1918. It had reached its sixth imprint within a fortnight and ran to nineteen editions by 1931. Isabel's book, however, was written by a medical doctor and covered every aspect of courtship and marriage.

To type up her notes, she employed a demure elderly lady called Miss Florence Jasper, whose sight was not of the best. She had to peer through think lenses at the script and made no comment about the content of the book until it was finished, when she wrote what she had not been able to say. She wrote that it had been a privilege to help in the production of the book, she felt it would be extremely helpful to at least one young couple she knew and that she wished the book well. This gave Isabel confidence that she had hit the right tone and level of detail, and she approached Professor Robertson for his advice on publication. He strongly advised her not to. It was a book that should have been written many years ago but it would damage her career.

The second person she consulted was Dr Mapother of the Maudsley. He was quite old by this time and said married couples had got by perfectly well without all this knowledge. He thought people could know too much and advised her to put it to one side. The third person, Dr Sydney Mann, a well-known biochemist, said: "Do you feel it is essential that the public should have this information?' Isabel said, 'Of course, otherwise I wouldn't have written it.' 'Well then....,' said Dr Mann.

She found a publisher in Heinemann's Medical Publications. Although the book was reviewed in the medical journals – the British Medical Journal (BMJ) said 'The language is quiet, but explicit, the taste and tone are unexceptionable and the information is in accordance with scientific knowledge' – it received no publicity whatsoever and for some years it had only a small circulation. It did, however, stay in print from 1923 to 1947, and ran to eight editions, with the eighth being reprinted four times. It covered everything you might need to know about sex and, of course assumes, the reader is married or about to be. Its eight chapters cover sexual diseases and how to deal with them, courtship and the honeymoon, consummation, detailed descriptions of techniques and body parts, when to have sex and when not, menstruation and the menopause – she is very brisk on these topics – childlessness, including the possibility that the man may be sterile, birth control and contraceptives. Altogether it was a book that many girls would have given their eyeteeth for when their only knowledge of sexual matters was the anatomy of a rabbit and the stories that circulated at the back of the sewing class.

Mental Health

In the same year Isabel's book was published, the Maudsley opened an out-patients clinic. The department had no official staff but Isabel worked there for three half-days a week and stayed for more than seven years. An outpatients department was something Isabel had felt was needed in the mental health field because problems could be picked up early and might never reach the acute stage necessitating admittance to hospital.

In 1925 she obtained the kind of post she had wanted since she returned to Britain. It was as honorary consultant psychiatrist at the British Hospital for Mental and Nervous Disorders, a post she served in for thirty years. She would have her own clinic and be able to carry out treatment on her own lines.

The British Hospital was very short of funds and was administered for less than a thousand pounds a year. It seemed the general public did not like to contribute funds to a mental hospital although collecting boxes in pubs brought in a small amount.

The committee that ran the hospital eventually decided to give up the idea of having inpatients and to concentrate on outpatients, and this was certainly a wise decision. There were some five hundred new cases every year, with six thousand attending per year. There were people suffering from depression, anxiety, from neuroses that took the form of phobias or fears and obsessions.

This small, shabby hospital with its informality and gentleness of approach became very much appreciated by the many patients who passed through its portals. The hospital survived the Second World War, continuing its work throughout that time. After the war, the National Health Service came into being. The hospital could have carried on outside the NHS, but there was the possibility that psychiatrists who would come in the future might not be prepared to work in an honorary capacity – so control of the hospital was ceded to the NHS. It carried on exactly as before, except that now the psychiatrists were paid a handsome salary. The drawback was that there was a statutory retirement age, which people could not work beyond, and a further disadvantage was that voluntary work at the hospital did not count towards a pension – you had to have worked for ten years to qualify.

Albania

One of the sons of Elizabeth, Countess of Caernarvon, the Hon. Aubrey Herbert, had been keenly interested in Albania and had used diplomatic means to further the aims of Albanian independence. After his early death in 1923, his mother very much wanted to help Albania in some practical way as a memorial to her son. In 1925 the League of Nations had published a report on Albania showing the devastating effect malaria was having on the country. The Countess decided that a suitable way to commemorate her son would be to establish an anti-malarial mission there. Consequently, there had been an advertisement in the British Medical Journal (BMJ) for a doctor to spend twelve months in Albania fighting malaria. While Isabel could not spare a full year, she thought she might very well manage three months, and got in touch with Lady Elizabeth.

Her offer was accepted, providing she could find a driver for the ambulance they would need. There was no problem with that. Vera Holme, ex-suffragette and ex-driver for the SWH, was more than willing to take on the adventure.

The two women set off with very little personal luggage but large supplies of quinine and other medicaments, along with a precious case of tinned food that Vera insisted on. They established themselves in an unfinished barracks in Valona. They had two rooms each, with a camp bed, without mosquito net, and no facilities for cooking. The Anglo-Persian Oil Company took pity on them and allowed them to join their mess until they left the area, and after that they lived on the tinned food they had brought. After a few days they found an aged crone to fetch water from the well for them and wash their clothes. 'She was a good laundress,' writes Isabel, 'and damped down the clothes before ironing by squirting water through a hole in her front teeth'.

Isabel and Vera decided to concentrate their efforts on a prison, and the schools that were only for the better-off, to try to establish a centre for treatment and demonstration purpose. They examined the children in school and found a high incidence of malarial infection. It was similar in the two prisons, where wells and gullies swarmed with mosquito larvae. They were very insanitary places so Isabel called for twigs and broomsticks and showed them how to sweep out the gullies and dispose of the filth. She also showed them how to whitewash the prison, bit by bit. They were keen to do this and to show her the progress they were making and it became a pleasure to visit them.

Establishing village centres was more problematic. Vera kept careful records but people were illiterate and, worse, sometimes had no idea of their own names or ages, so they gave any name that came into their heads. Undressing was also complicated. Villagers rarely took their clothes off, day or night, and the children were sewn into theirs. The women were in purdah and had separate quarters, which they rarely left. Most Albanians thought malarial fever was caused by the warm wind or sleeping too close to the ground.

Isabel and Vera took every opportunity for propaganda and Isabel was asked to write a weekly article for a newspaper, which she was pleased to do. They also had large posters of a mosquito made and distributed. These were very popular as it was the only picture many of the villagers were ever likely to possess.

Lady Caernarvon came out to Albania to see how work was progressing and was very pleased, but felt everything was going rather slowly. After a short time she left to go to Tirana to see the president and ask for the dismissal of the head of the medical services, the establishment of a quinine factory, and for the use of an aeroplane to spray the marshes. Lady Caernarvon kept on pestering the government with charm combined with a steely tenacity, which got her ideas accepted, and eventually achieved what she wanted.

After three hectic months, their time in Albania came to an end. There was one hitch. The money they had been expecting by diplomatic bag failed to arrive and Vera had to obtain cash from the shopkeepers in Valona against a cheque she had written out. The main part of the money was two one-thousand lire notes. One of these was used to pay the purser, who could not change it so an obliging passenger did so. On arrival in Brindisi, they went sightseeing and were arrested for passing false currency. The courteous passenger had taken the note to the bank, where they saw at once it was false. 'The Consul advised us not to breathe our names as we should be written up in every European newspaper as financial crooks,' Isabel writes. After much gesticulating and shouting they were acquitted but the judge tore up the offending note and they had to surrender their other bill, leaving them with no money. The Consul refused to advance them any money, saying that although they seemed respectable, there was no guarantee that they were. So they scraped together what little cash they had and travelled third class in the train to Santa Margherita to meet Lady Caernarvon, unable to buy anything to eat. By the time they reached Santa Margherita, the small bowl of pasta Lady Caernarvon gave them was very welcome.

Lady Caernarvon's persistence and advertising of the problems in Albania was rewarded several years later when in 1930 the Rockefeller Foundation put money into the anti-malaria campaign in the Balkans and, working on a grand scale, were obviously able to achieve more than Isabel Emslie Hutton had achieved in her very short term there. She had, however, blazed a trail that others who were better funded were able to follow.

The International 'B' Pilot's Certificate for Women

Although they were able to obtain authorisation to fly non-commercial planes, women had been barred from flying commercial aircraft by the International Air Conference of 1923. The reasoning was that tests were carried out every six months to ensure that pilots were at the peak of physical perfection. Women menstruated, and got pregnant, so if this were the case, they would not be able to fly, thus costing the airline money as they would be grounded.

In 1926 the Medical Women's Federation, to which most women doctors, including Isabel, belonged, was approached for help by a woman wishing to obtain the 'B' pilot's certificate, which would give women the right to fly commercial aircraft. The Federation set up a sub-committee comprising a gynaecologist, a surgeon, a physician, a physiologist and Isabel, a psychiatrist, to write a report about the matter for the next conference in three months' time. It would also be useful to the British Air Ministry as they had before them for the first time a woman applicant, Mrs Elliott-Lynn, who wanted to fly commercial aircraft. There was very little written in any context about the effects of flying on women's physiology. There was an account of a Miss Stocks, who had ascended in a balloon with a naval officer in 1824. The balloon had come down very quickly and crashed. The naval officer died, but Miss Stocks merely swooned and lived to go up in a balloon again. The committee report strongly supported women's ability to pilot commercial aircraft. Their only concession was to agree that women should perhaps be examined every three months, rather than six, to ascertain they were not pregnant. Mrs Elliott-Lynn went on to become the first woman to 'loop the loop', and the first person to fly from South Africa to Britain. She set up a new height record for light aeroplanes by reaching 23,000 feet, and made spectacular parachute jumps from a great height.

The Psycho-analysis Committee of the British Medical Association

In the aftermath of the First World War, psycho-analysis was a topic for considerable debate. The general public knew very little about it and the medical profession was not much better informed. The first translation of Freud's work was not published until 1913 and, at that time, there were other things on people's minds. However, when the troops returned home, some of them suffering from shell shock, mental health assumed a greater significance.

The British Medical Journal now decided to take action and resolved to appoint a special committee to investigate psycho-analysis and report on it. The committee was set up in 1927. It included general practitioners, school medical officers, psychiatrists – some who were against the whole idea – and Isabel Emslie Hutton, representing the Medical Women's Federation. There were three speakers who would expound on Freud, Jung, and Adler. The atmosphere was oppressively serious; there was not a single joke in the whole time the committee was sitting. What provoked most opposition to Freudian theories was his idea that infant sexuality played an important part in a person's psychological development. The idea of infants and sexuality, put together in this way, repelled many people. Freud believed that sexuality did not begin at puberty but was present in the first year of a child's life and thought the Oedipus complex was the basis of every neurosis. At the start of their investigation there was much opposition to Freud's ideas but by the end, the committee had been converted. They could not, however, give a collective opinion about psycho-analysis since they could not follow a case from beginning to conclusion, but the report was called by many people 'the Psycho-analysis Charter.'

The Ellen Terry Home

In 1926 Isabel was approached by Sir John Carswell, a well-known Scottish psychiatrist. Recently retired from his post as Commissioner in Lunacy, he had come south to be near his son and daughter-in-law, who were writers.

He asked Isabel how she was succeeding in her work. She told him it had been a struggle but she now had plenty to do. Her private practice was growing and she was working at three hospitals: the Maudsley, the West End and the British. Dr Carswell knew the British Hospital well and was so impressed with their outpatient clinic that he had adapted the idea in Glasgow and had begun to treat early mental patients in the wards of a general hospital.

The main reason he had come to see Isabel was that the Ellen Terry Home for Blind Defective Children at Reigate needed a psychology specialist to take over the medical side of the home. Isabel had never been interested in disabled children up to this point but Sir John was so pressing that she agreed to do it, and thought she might hold the appointment for a short time. In the event, it was fourteen years.

The home had been opened in 1925 but following the opening, Dame Ellen had never visited again, being too ill. She died in 1928. Much of the support for the home came from Theosophists, a quasi-religious sect who believed in the Brotherhood of Man, the need to investigate the study of comparative religion, philosophy and science, and the unexplained laws of nature and the powers latent in man. They were vegetarian, and any medical treatment was given by chiropractors. Orthodox medicine played little part, so they were against vaccination and injections. The Board of Control who inspected the home soon felt there should be regular supervision by a psychiatrist, who would be responsible for the medical care and training of the children.

Between them, Isabel, the matron Miss E. M. Cooke, and Miss Browning, a woman who had previous experience of teaching blind children, but not blind and mentally disabled, devised a routine that was flexible enough to accommodate the needs of individual children but could be applied to all the children.

Children often arrived at the home unable to walk, feed themselves or talk. Some were so frail they could not stand and had to have their muscles massaged until they were strong enough to attempt to walk. Potty training was begun as soon as the child arrived and sometimes took a great deal of time to establish. Children were taught to feed themselves, to wash, and brush their teeth. Learning to walk is more difficult for a blind child because it takes longer before a sense of balance is acquired. By schoolroom standards some of these children achieved very little, but they improved and developed in other ways. Handwork improved their dexterity, singing and dancing enthralled them. Their sense of touch was developed by Montessori equipment, modelling and handwork. On balance, Isabel felt the children gained a great deal at the home, being given experiences and skilled attention they might not have received at home. Each child was funded by their local authority, but this money did not fully cover the expenses incurred so the home relied on the founders and their friends to bridge the gap. In the early days, some children sent by the local authorities were not suitable cases so Isabel started interviewing both children and parents in London beforehand. The age range of the children at the home had originally been from two to twelve but as they gained more experience, the home realised that taking children younger than two meant they could start their training programme sooner, and when they found that children could continue to improve after the age of twelve, they could stay on at the home. Isabel expresses no anxiety about removing children younger than two years' old from their parents. While this would probably raise eyebrows nowadays, she perhaps felt that on balance the children would learn to cope better under professional care, where they would be stimulated and encouraged to learn, than at home.

The Second World War
Early in 1938, Thomas Hutton, who has not featured very much in this account of Isabel Emslie Hutton's life, was promoted to Major-General and appointed to the Western Independent District of India. This is Balochistan, now a part of Pakistan but at that time, before the independence of the Indian sub-continent and the dividing up of the land, part of India. A Major-General in a high administrative position needs a wife to organise a social life and to get to know the women and children. Isabel was rather looking forward to taking six months out of her busy life to accompany Thomas to India. They would be based in Quetta, the capital of Balochistan, where a new house was being built for them, one that was proof against earthquakes, as the last one had been totally destroyed in 1935 in a quake which had killed 25,000 people.

In Quetta, as elsewhere in India, the English kept to their compounds and rarely met any Indians. There was an English church, an English hospital, and English nursing sisters.

Engrossed in her new life in India, Isabel gave little thought to the political situation back home. Just before she had sailed, Prime Minister Neville Chamberlain had returned from Munich waving a piece of paper from Hitler and declaring 'Peace in Our Time'. The letters she was receiving from an ex-colleague in Albania, with whom she had worked in 1925, were giving her pause for thought. Thinking she was in London, he beseeched her to seek influential advice on the possibility of his country being invaded by the Italians, which they duly did on Good Friday 1939. There was nothing Isabel could do, however, and the matter was certainly never discussed in Quetta.

After a short time, she and Thomas moved to Simla, high in the Himalayas at 8,000 feet, where the air is cool. The news that greeted them from Europe was sad. Holland had surrendered to the Germans and the Queen of the Netherlands was in London. There had been heavy fighting in France, and Belgium had capitulated.

In Simla the only kind of wheeled vehicle allowed was the rickshaw pulled by coolies. No handcarts were allowed during daylight hours and all the heavy lifting and carrying was done by job porters. The coolies, two thousand of them, and the same number of job porters lived in appalling conditions, with their working life reckoned at only six years. But the situation was beginning to change.

'I don't know what Simla is coming to,' sniffed one lady. 'I told my rickshaw men to hurry and one of them said, "Lady Sahiba, we are but human". Did you ever hear such insolence? It's all the fault of that governess who is trying to make the coolies as good as we are, teaching them reading and writing.' Isabel asked who the governess was. 'Miss Jennie Copeland' spat the lady. Isabel determined to look her up but had no need as Miss Jennie Copeland turned up on her doorstep one day. She asked if Isabel would help with the Coolies' Welfare Society. In winter Miss Copeland helped the sweeper class, untouchables, in old Delhi, teaching them leatherwork so they could earn a living. Isabel asked if she could run clinics to deal with the minor ailments that afflicted the coolies, wounded feet being a prime one. It was decided two clinics a week would be run, one at each end of the town, at lunchtime so the coolies would lose no fares. Their feet were carefully cleaned, bathed, treated and a string sandal evolved, which kept the dressings in place. Their coughs and colds, eye and skin complaints, were treated, especially scabies. They were given instructions on how to deal with this but they also suffered with toothache. The resourceful Miss Copeland tracked down an Indian dentist and persuaded him to work for nothing. Someone drew a poster showing a downtrodden coolie and advertising the clinics. This brought in lots of money as people realised what a good service they offered. A welfare officer was appointed to make sure coolies didn't carry a heavier weight than was allowed. Blankets, cloth, waterproofs and cooking pots were bought in bulk and sold at cost price; their money was banked for them and free soap was doled out each week. All this was achieved through the enterprise of one woman doing God's work, as she saw it.

In September 1940, Isabel and her husband learned that their London home had been bombed. Fortunately the couple looking after the property had escaped with their lives, although their neighbours had been killed. Isabel and her husband were determined not to grieve over worldly goods when so many people were losing their lives, but were pleased to hear that the builders who had done some alterations for them at the London house had taken it upon themselves to salvage what they could of the furniture and pictures and had put them into storage.

Isabel felt isolated from the action in the rest of the world. She asked the head of the medical services if he could make use of her skills as a psychiatrist but at that time, as in England, married women were not employed and it was not till two years later that the situation changed. When Thomas and Isobel moved from Simla to Delhi, she decided to implement a scheme she had thought of when they were in the mountains, something she thought would be a money-spinner for war charities: a thrift shop, what we would now call a charity shop. She had seen how much moving around there was and how much equipment was bought, then left, and bought again at the new place the family had settled. It was particularly the case when there were young children. When a family moved out, the *kabari wallah* moved in and disposed of the goods for a paltry sum. And this was going on all over India. What if the equipment could be bought and sold in a shop where the profit went to a war charity? She canvassed this idea but no one was prepared to take it on until she met three young women in the English Club who were interested in doing some war work. Isabel found the premises and the women made posters and handbills to advertise the service. It was in a central position in Delhi and soon became popular. Isabel wrote about it in the *Statesman* newspaper and the idea spread throughout the country, a small contribution, she felt, to the war effort.

The war effort was late starting in India. The Red Cross and the Order of St John, which had been long established, worked closely together. The Women's Army Corps (India) and the Women's Voluntary Services were started and were highly praised for their work during the Burma campaign. Isabel was involved with neither of these, but she chaired the meetings of the Ladies' Advisory Committee of the Auxiliary Nursing Service (ANS) and was director of the Indian Red Cross Welfare Service. The committee of the ANS met regularly to ensure the aims of the organisation were being met. The aim was to produce, as quickly as possible, a large number of partially-trained nurses capable of rendering assistance under supervision in either civil or military hospitals. Eventually 3,400 women were enrolled.

To begin with there were few war wounded, mostly from the Middle East, and these could be dealt with by voluntary bodies. With the development of fighting in Burma, the number of casualties increased and it was felt necessary to provide a comprehensive service throughout the country. It was known as the Indian Red Cross Welfare Service, and Isabel was asked to become director soon after its foundation. There were special problems because of the caste system, and it was established from the beginning that members of all races and creeds should be eligible. The aim was to establish one welfare worker for every 250 hospital beds. Their duties would include organisation of a hospital library, and entertainments, letter-writing for patients, shopping and postal services – nothing to do with the physical care of patients but a great deal to do with the mental health and welfare of the wounded. Another important aspect of the work was to research details of the wounded and missing. The Japanese never provided a list of prisoners of war or the dead, so this work became of increasing importance as the Burma campaign developed. One of the most rewarding aspects of the work was getting Indian, Anglo-Indian and British women to work together.

Isabel's husband Thomas was put in charge of the campaigns in Burma, but the general opinion was that he was better at managing an army in peacetime than organising campaigns. The couple returned to Britain in 1946, repaired their London home and lived there peacefully, until their deaths, Isabel dying in 1960 while her husband survived until 1981, dying at the age of ninety.

Conclusion

It is clear from Isabel's writing that the First World War was a liberation for her and the women she worked with. Physically they freed themselves from long hair, some wore trousers rather than skirts; they were fit and strong. Mentally, too, they dealt with extremely unpleasant events. They took responsibility not only for their own lives but for those of their patients. Their competence was recognised by the men they met. To return, therefore, to the stuffy confines of the English social system must have been very difficult. But Isabel showed that as a psychiatrist she could make a living and that, since she and Thomas had no children, there was no need to follow the traditional pattern of married life. She worked with like-minded women to break down the petty barriers erected to prevent their advancement in their working lives, all achieved because of her unfailing belief in her own judgement.

9

Virginia Woolf (1882–1941) and the Literary Scene

To the general public Virginia Woolf's name is synonymous with the group of artists and writers known as the Bloomsbury Group. They might also know that Virginia suffered from time to time from mental health problems and that she committed suicide by walking into a river with her pockets full of stones. Before that, she wrote rather odd, wispy novels that are difficult to get to grips with. Rather an unkind synopsis of what many, even quite well educated, people might think. Leonard Woolf describes his wife as 'the least political animal that has lived since Aristotle invented the definition.' So why is she included in a volume about suffragists and what they did after they had the vote? Here's why.

Having dismissed his wife's lack of interest in politics, Leonard Woolf goes on to say, 'she was not the frail, invalidish lady living in an ivory tower' that literary critics have painted. She was intensely interested in things, people, and events and highly sensitive to atmosphere, so could not ignore the political menaces threatening in the 1920s and 30s. To quote a recent academic, Virginia Woolf had 'a consistent and intense concern with the political foundations of the social order'. She showed this in a host of book reviews and two books she wrote setting out her feminist philosophy: *A Room of one's Own* and *Three Guineas*. Her life and her writing all show how these attitudes were acquired and developed.

Virginia Woolf was born Virginia Stephen, her father Leslie being a writer and a political radical. He was a friend of Henry Fawcett and a follower of John Stuart Mill. As a writer, he created the *Dictionary of National Biography*, which continues today and, once he had escaped the clutches of Cambridge University where celibacy for dons was still the order of the day, he married twice, thus creating one of those complicated families so common in Victorian times.

His first wife, Harriet Marion, Minny for short, was the daughter of W.M. Thackeray. This marriage produced one daughter, Laura, who Virginia's biographer Quentin Bell labels unceremoniously 'insane'. After Minny's death, Leslie married Julia Duckworth, a widow with three children of her first marriage, George, Stella and Gerald. Between them they then produced four more children: Vanessa, Thoby, Virginia and Adrian.

Socially Quentin Bell's biography of Virginia places the Stephen family precisely in 'the lower division of the upper middle class.' As such, they kept seven maidservants but no manservant, kept no carriage but travelled sometimes by car. If they went by train, they travelled third class – but they expected their boys to be educated at public school, then Cambridge University, while the girls would 'become accomplished and then marry'.

The family all agreed that Virginia was clever. Before she was seven, her mother tried to teach her Latin but was too impatient to be a good teacher. Her father tried to teach her mathematics, but kept losing his temper, and Virginia, for the rest of her life, counted on her fingers. Fortunately Leslie and Julia managed to get something right. Leslie was a brilliant storyteller and a very good artist, so could draw pictures to illustrate his tales and Julia was kind and a loving mother who cosseted her husband and kept the household calm. The girls had access to tales about ancient Greece and Rome from Thoby, who on his return from school would regale them with stories of the Trojan Wars and the wooden horse, the travels of the wily Odysseus and his journey back to his faithful wife Penelope who was still sitting there weaving.

Vanessa and Virginia were inculcated into the supposed delights of music, which they did not enjoy. Piano lessons were a nightmare and with their singing teacher, Virginia soon found that the woman was profoundly religious and when asked the meaning of Christmas, Virginia, knowing full well what Christmas celebrated, said it was to commemorate the Crucifixion, then was overtaken by such gales of laughter that she had to be removed from the room. Dancing was taught by a woman with a glass eye who wore black satin and carried a stick. The girls hid in the lavatory as much as they dared. Holidays were spent at St Ives and passed in a haze of rock pools, sea and surf, where the children were completely happy.

But there were shadows. Mad, unpredictable Laura was still there and cousin James, a brilliant young man, who was struck on the head, appeared to recover completely but thereafter slid slowly into madness, at one time rushing upstairs to the nursery at the Stephen household clutching the blade from a sword stick. Fortunately he only stuck it in a loaf of bread, but the incident must have been disturbing, to say the least.

In 1895, at the age of thirty-eight, Julia died, leaving her sixty-three year old husband bereft. Vanessa was by now fifteen and Virginia thirteen. At the age of twenty-six, their half-sister Stella had to carry the burden of a grieving stepfather. He was not a man who could see the grief of the rest of the family and he became totally focused on his own distress. 'At meal times he sat miserable and bewildered, too unhappy and too deaf to know what was being said,' writes Quentin Bell, 'until at length ... he broke down utterly and, while his embarrassed children sat in awkward silence, groaned, wept and wished that he were dead'.

It was at this time that George's kindness to his grieving half-sisters overstepped the mark and 'there were fondlings and fumblings in public when Virginia was at her lessons' and excursions into the night nursery when there was no one to see or restrain what went on. The girls had no one to tell about this, and it was many years before the truth emerged. Bell says, 'Virginia felt that George had spoilt her life before it had fairly begun. Naturally shy in sexual matters, she was from this time terrified back into a posture of frozen and defensive panic'.

Small wonder that in the summer of 1895, at the age of thirteen, Virginia had her first episode of madness, a malady that was to recur throughout her life, when she heard voices and experienced periods of frenzied excitability and deep melancholia. The family doctor ordered four hours a day outdoors, walking or taking bus rides, and no mental exertion, so lessons were banned. The outdoor sessions were organised and supervised by Stella, who was organising and supervising everything else that went on in the household.

Stella then married Jack Mills and set up house just along the road from the Stephen family. Virginia, meanwhile, had been allowed to resume her lessons to some small extent, while

Vanessa, being interested in art, prepared for entrance to the Royal Academy. However this period of relative calm was short-lived, for Stella contracted peritonitis, failed to make a complete recovery and finally, in July 1897, died. Her husband was, of course, devastated, but her stepfather, though saddened, was not. He had found another woman to prop him up: Vanessa. At seventeen she took on responsibility for running the household and above all, keeping the household accounts. Leslie Stephen was always chronically worried about money, and once a week Vanessa had to appear before him and present the accounts, proving that they were within budget, which was not always easy as the cook was not a penny pincher. Most weeks, therefore, there would be a row, when Leslie, groaning and sighing, would complain that they would have to move from Hyde Park Gate and go and live in Wimbledon. Vanessa, meanwhile, would stand and listen to him without speaking until he signed a cheque for the requisite amount. Virginia was a witness to these dramas, and was angry that he screamed and bellowed at the womenfolk but his behaviour was quiet, gentlemanly and rational with men. He had different expectations of women: from them he expected kindness and sympathy but got neither from Vanessa. A complete and self-effacing devotion was what he expected but she did what she considered her duty and no more.

Thoby was by this time at Cambridge and making friends with young men such as Lytton Strachey, Clive Bell and Lionel Woolf. Virginia was aware of the mental stimulation that Cambridge provided and, while she was herself learning to read Greek and reading history in the mornings, she had to spend the afternoons in ladylike pursuits such as entertaining friends, presiding over the tea table and making polite conversation. She knew that compared with these young men she was badly educated because she was a woman and that realisation was to stay with her for the rest of her life.

Meanwhile Vanessa and Jack Mills, Stella's bereaved husband, were falling in love. This was illegal at the time as a man could not marry his deceased wife's sister, a situation not changed until 1907. Half-brother George was trying to make his mark in high society and a scandal that might be caused if Vanessa and Jack's relationship became known would be socially extremely disadvantageous to him so he brought pressure to bear on Vanessa and Jack and the relationship ceased.

From time to time, he persuaded one or other of the sisters to accompany him to a party or other social gathering. They both failed miserably at these events. Virginia wrote: 'Really, we cant shine in Society. I don't know how it's done. We ain't popular – we sit in corners and look like mutes who are longing for a funeral. However, there are more important things in this life – from all I hear I shan't be asked to dance in the next.' (One of the topics she failed to absorb from her education seems to have been the use of the apostrophe!)

She attended King's College from 1897 to 1899, where she studied Latin and Greek. It must be from this period that Lady Tweedsmuir, John Buchan's wife Susan, records dinner parties held at the Stephens' house. 'I was impressed by the dark, shadowy house with its high rooms and tall pictures, and by the two completely silent girls who moved about in it,' she writes. 'Vanessa showed my mother some of her drawings while Virginia and I tried to talk to each other. I thought her good looking but dowdy and I have no doubt that she thought me empty-headed.' Her one invitation to dinner was an ordeal. She sat next to Leslie Stephen. 'He handed me one end of a snake-like attachment to his ear trumpet. I was naturally diffident about my conversational powers and I was stricken into horrified silence when I realised that I was expected to converse into an ear trumpet before a critical and speechless company which included Vanessa and Virginia.'

In 1904, Leslie Stephen died. This was a great relief and release for Vanessa, who could now do what she liked, where she liked, with no one to naysay her. Virginia, however, was struck by grief, which precipitated another bout of madness. The main task of caring for her fell to Vanessa, but a friend, Violet Dickinson, also shouldered some of the burden. Three nurses were employed to restrain her when needed. She heard voices urging her to do destructive things and, thinking that hearing the voices was caused by what she ate, decided not to eat. Violet took her to her house in Burnham Wood, where she heard the birds singing in Greek and Edward VII hiding in the azaleas, shouting obscenities. She threw herself out of an upstairs window, in an attempt to kill herself, but the window was not high enough, and she survived.

By the autumn, she was recovering, though still weak, and went to stay with a cousin who was head of Giggleswick School in Yorkshire. While there she visited Haworth Parsonage, which stimulated her to write an article on the subject. She sent it to the *Guardian*, a London weekly newspaper catering for clerics. This was her first written work to be published and she continued to write articles from time to time for the *Guardian*, though she was an agnostic.

Early in 1906, she returned to London to the newly-established household in Gordon Square, Bloomsbury where Vanessa had set up house because it was rather a long way from their relatives and the rents were cheap. It was also near to the Slade, which Vanessa was hoping to attend. Vanessa, Thoby and Adrian were ensconced there by the time Virginia returned to London. This formed the basis of the group that became known as the Bloomsbury Set. They were not, in fact, very unconventional, at least at first, though having no mature adult to supervise the girls and no chaperone was decidedly unusual.

Gradually Thoby's friends from Cambridge began to visit, which enlarged the family circle somewhat. Clive Bell, Lytton Strachey, Leonard Woolf were intellectuals and their discussions were an eye-opener for Virginia. This was what she had missed by not going to Cambridge, she realised. They none of them dressed well, the men stayed talking till the early hours, and their manners were less than exquisite. George, with his elegant, upper-class bride on his arm, was shocked. Only Clive Bell met with any approval from George because he was better dressed and had a good seat on a horse.

Meanwhile Virginia had been approached by Mary Sheepshanks, principal of Morley College, to talk about pictures and books to some of her students. Morley College had begun life as a series of 'penny lectures' backstage at the Royal Victoria Hall, the 'Old Vic'. By 1889 the lectures had expanded as the music hall acts had declined, and Morley College for Working Men and Women was established in 1889, named after its benefactor, Samuel Morley. One important aspect of the college was that women were admitted on equal terms with men.

Mary Sheepshanks fell in love with Virginia, as women were apt to do, but Virginia was dismissive of her attentions, although she accepted the challenge to teach at the college. It was not pictures and books she talked about so much as history, one of her passions. Central themes of her teaching were the role of women in the process of history, often not immediately apparent even today! She also covered such aspects as the opportunities denied to women in the past, the institution of marriage, the inadequacies of histories as they were traditionally written and the necessity of seeing history in terms of individuals. She wanted to empower her students to think for themselves as part of history. She encouraged them to write about their own lives from a historical perspective. This was a far cry from the traditional teaching of history as a succession of rulers, wars and peace treaties. It was, in fact, social history.

She worked hard preparing these talks and was upset when they were suddenly curtailed to make way for a series of lectures on the French Revolution by the famous historian G. M. Trevelyan, grandson of Macauley and a Cambridge man. If she were alive today she might be pleased to know that his high reputation barely survived his death in 1962 and he has been described by Roy Jenkins as ' among the great unread,' and referred to as a 'pontificating old windbag'.

In 1906 the Stephen family decided to visit Greece. This was a big romantic adventure. A month before their sisters, Thoby and Adrian set off on horseback for Trieste, Montenegro and Albania, while Vanessa and Virginia took the train to Brindisi and then went on by boat to Patras. Once in Greece, their adventure turned to disaster. Vanessa fell ill, then Thoby succumbed to some unnamed disease. They managed to get home where Vanessa's health improved but Thoby's condition deteriorated. His doctor had diagnosed malaria, but the nurse thought it was typhoid. The nurse was right and he died. In her grief Vanessa turned for comfort to Clive Bell, who asked her to marry him and she accepted.

Virginia was unhappy at the alliance with a family she thought not good enough for her beloved sister, but Vanessa was extravagantly happy. Virginia and Adrian moved into a house in Fitzroy Square, not too near the Bells in Gordon Square. But though fond of one another, Virginia and Adrian had terrible arguments that sometimes ended with them throwing the pats of butter which Sophy the cook had so laboriously fashioned. The walls were spattered with them. The family decided that Adrian would benefit from looking after himself but Virginia was in need of someone to take care of her now

Vanessa was married. Virginia needed a husband. The problem was most of the young men she knew from Cambridge were gay.

Virginia gradually re-established the Thursday evening meetings that Thoby had instigated and to one of these came Lady Ottoline Morrell, society hostess and patron of the arts, brought by the artist Augustus John. In the next two or three years, from time to time Lady Ottoline brought with her various of her friends: her lover Bertram Russell, her husband Philip Morrell, who was a member of Parliament; Winston Churchill, described by Virginia as 'very rubicund all gold lace and medals on his way to Buckingham Palace'; Raymond Asquith, barrister son of the Prime Minister; Vanessa and Clive Bell, with their friend Duncan Grant, the artist.

In 1910 Virginia Stephen's life was further enlivened by an event that became known as the *Dreadnought* Hoax. Several of the Cambridge group led by an ex-Cambridge friend of her brothers, Horace Cole, and including Adrian Stephen, set out to hoodwink the Admiralty by pretending to be the Emperor of Abyssinia and his entourage. A telegramme was sent from the Home Office by one of their contacts saying that the Emperor would like a guided tour of the navy flagship, the *Dreadnought*. This was duly arranged and Virginia, dressed as an Abyssinian prince complete with blackened face, whiskers and a beard, set off from Paddington as part of the entourage. They were received with ceremony in Weymouth and taken aboard the *Dreadnought* where they were escorted around the gun deck, the sick room, and the wireless room. They refused any refreshments, which they thought might dislodge their whiskers, were escorted back to Weymouth and took the train to Paddington without being detected. The event would never have been revealed if Horace Cole, an inveterate self-publicist, had not mentioned to a journalist what they had done.

Shortly afterwards Virginia was again confined to a nursing home because of the severe headaches she was experiencing, which were usually the forerunner of madness. By dint of resting in a darkened room with little stimulation, and being forced to eat more than she wanted, a period of real madness was avoided.

The Bells' marriage was beginning to disintegrate and as that happened the Bloomsbury group began to acquire a reputation for licentiousness provoked by Vanessa's behaviour. In 1911 she fell in love with the artist Roger Fry and for two years they carried on an affair. At the end of that time, however, Vanessa turned her attentions to Duncan Grant, one-time lover of his cousin Lytton Strachey. While being mainly gay, Duncan Grant was seduced on one occasion by Vanessa and the union produced a daughter, Angelica, who was brought up as Clive Bell's daughter. Clive treated her as such and her paternity was not learnt by her until she was an adult.

Leonard Woolf had recently returned on furlough from his job in Ceylon as a colonial administrator, and there was talk of setting up a communal house in Bedford Square where some of them could live. Adrian, Maynard Keynes, Duncan Grant, Virginia and Leonard Woolf were interested. Each person would have their own space but would share the expenses. Food would be cooked by Sophy. Nothing that would raise an eyebrow today, but then considered beyond the boundaries of respectable behaviour.

Outside the frenetic atmosphere of Bloomsbury, Virginia was as involved as her health permitted with the suffrage movement. Concerned that the NUWSS focused on the rights of middle-class women rather than with working-class women, Margaret Llewelyn Davies had tried to bridge the gap between the two and make the suffrage movement more relevant to working-class women. To do this, in 1910 she had formed the People's Suffrage Federation (PSF). Lady Ottoline Morrell, John Maynard Keynes and Mary Sheepshanks were involved, so it was not surprising that Virginia was drawn into the movement.

Virginia offered her services, suggesting she could address envelopes, if nothing else. Her offer of help was taken up, though she was not asked to address envelopes, but was asked to compile a book of 'good extracts on representation', which could be used for reference by speakers and writers.

The formation of the PSF was not well-received by other suffrage groups, who feared their demands were too extreme and would, therefore, damage their chances of success. In response to this, the PSF did not demand that people leave the organisation they were supporting. They could join the PSF as well. Though certainly committed to the cause of women's emancipation, Virginia was sometimes overtaken with the pessimistic feeling that activism such as membership of the PSF was a waste of time, that anything she could do would not alter the course of history one jot.

Having lived for three months in Bedford Square with Virginia close at hand, Leonard Woolf realised he had a decision to make.

Either he could return to Ceylon, where he was doing well and enjoying the work, or he could ask Virginia if she would marry him, and if so, he would have to withdraw from the post and stay in London, with no job or income to tide him over. As the day for returning to Ceylon approached, he made up his mind. In January 1912, he asked her to marry him. Being Virginia, she prevaricated. She fell ill again and briefly entered the nursing home to rest. Taking a risk, 7 on May Leonard resigned from the Colonial Office and at the end of that month, Virginia accepted Leonard's proposal.

Virginia's letter to Violet Dickinson announcing her engagement was typically dramatic. 'I'm going to marry Leonard Woolf. He's a penniless Jew,' she wrote. While Leonard was certainly a Jew and now without a job, he did have intelligence, boundless energy and contacts. He first helped Virginia's cousin Marny with her work among the poor in Hoxton. He was appalled at what he saw of the conditions people were living in. It turned him to Socialism, as being the only way to solve the multiple problems faced by the urban poor, and subsequently earned his living writing left-wing articles, editing journals and writing books.

Virginia also introduced him to Margaret Llewelyn Davies, her friend of many years' standing. Miss Llewelyn Davies immediately recruited him to investigate and write about the Women's Co-operative Guild. He also had a part-time job at Roger Fry's art gallery where one of his tasks was to explain and soothe art connoisseurs as they met Picasso's and Matisse's work for the first time. He was also writing a novel, *The Village in the Jungle* and followed it with *The Wise Virgins,* which was published on the day war broke out – 4August 1914, which rather detracted from its saleability, as people had other things to think about.

The couple were married in the midst of a thunderstorm at St Pancras Registry Office, with the taxi driver so unused to venturing into that area of London that he had to ask his customers for directions. The registrar got muddled up with the names of Virginia and Vanessa, both names he had never met before, and Vanessa interrupted the registration procedure by asking how she could change the name of her younger son. It was as well Leonard's mother did not attend the ceremony. She would not have been pleased at the informality. George and Gerald, dressed for a proper wedding in frock coats, were at the wedding breakfast given by the Bells. They were not impressed by Duncan Grant who wore an assortment of clothes obviously borrowed from a number of different people of different sizes and shapes.

Quentin Bell, Virginia's nephew, considers that Leonard and Virginia were very happy in their marriage, and, compared with their friends, relatively monogamous. He says, 'Their love and admiration for each other, based as it was upon a real understanding of the good qualities in each, was strong enough to withstand the major and minor punishments of fortune, the common vexations of matrimony and, presently, the horrors of madness'. Perhaps because of her previous experience of sexual abuse by her half-brothers, Virginia was not interested in the physical side of their relationship, and Leonard persuaded her very early in their marriage that her sanity would be threatened by pregnancy, so they remained childless, to Virginia's great sorrow.

The Women's Co-operative Guild

March 1913 saw the Woolfs embarking on a tour of the industrial north of England, visiting Co-operative halls and committee meetings and in June they attended the Annual Congress of the Women's Co-operative Guild in Newcastle. Leonard and Virginia were observers, so not entitled to vote. There were delegations from 302 branches, and the Women's Labour League, the National Men's Guild, and the Co-operative Union. On their return to London, Virginia was again ill but much later, in 1930, she wrote about her experience of the congress, which was published as the introduction to the book of reminiscences by Guild women.

The article begins by presenting the day of the congress from a middle class observer's viewpoint and is not kind. She describes 'the woman who was wearing something like a Lord Mayor's chain around her neck' and the proceedings in the hall: 'a bell struck; a figure rose; a woman took her way from among us; she mounted a platform; she spoke for precisely five minutes; she descended.'

The boredom of the whole proceedings is admirably portrayed. The reader feels embarrassed for these worthy ladies, dressed in their Sunday best, who are asking for mundane things like a limit to the hours women have to work, an increase in pay, help with household chores, and baths. All they talked about was 'matters of fact,' wrote Virginia. 'To expect us', (middle class women,) 'whose minds, such as they are, fly free at the end of a short length of capital, to tie ourselves down again to that narrow plot of acquisitiveness and desire is impossible,' she wrote. 'We have baths. We have money'. So any sympathy they might feel was spurious. Ladies, on the other hand, 'desire Mozart and Einstein – that is, they desire things that are ends, not things that are means.' So not only does she mock the working-class women of the Guild but also the middle-class women with intellectual pretensions, people such as herself.

Nor were the things these women wanted ever likely to happen because they did not have the vote, so had no way of persuading politicians that their demands were legitimate.

She then brings us more up to date with a description of a visit she made to the Guild office to collect the manuscript of the book which is envisaged. She gives a cruel picture of the office secretary, Miss Kidd, 'dressed in a peculiar shade of deep purple'. 'She was very short,' she adds, 'but, owing to the weight which sat on her brow and the gloom which seemed to issue from her dress, she was also very heavy. ...When she clicked her typewriter one felt she was making that instrument transmit messages of foreboding'.

Then she read the accounts of these women's lives and expresses her astonishment at what the human spirit can survive. The concept of honour is as alive in these women as on the battlefield. They have a steely determination to educate themselves and to improve life for their children and the Guild has given them hope and the possibility of self-determination. Finally, she reveals that Miss Kidd was raped by her employer when she was seventeen, and was a mother by the age of eighteen.

So at the end we are moved almost to tears by her description of these working-class women and their spirit, and have travelled the same journey from boredom and scorn to understanding and appreciation of the women's strengths, a journey travelled by Virginia Woolf herself in the fifteen years since she attended the congress in 1915.

Virginia's novel, *The Voyage Out,* sent in 1913 to George Duckworth's publishing house and, much to Virginia's surprise, accepted, was not published until March 1915. But immediately it had been sent off, she began to fret about what the impact would be, what people would think about it, whether the writing was good enough, a host of worries that precipitated another bout of madness, culminating in July the following year in another attempt at suicide.

She fell ill again in 1915 and Leonard has described what she was like when she was depressed. 'The most distressing problem was to get Virginia to eat,' he writes.

> If left to herself she would have eaten nothing at all and could have gradually starved to death ... In the early acute, suicidal stage of her depression, she would sit for hours overwhelmed by hopeless melancholia, silent, making no response to anything said to her. When the time for a meal came, she would pay no attention whatsoever to the plate of food put before her and, if the nurses tried to get her to eat something, she became enraged. I could usually induce her to eat a certain amount, but it was a terrible process. Every meal took an hour or two; I had to sit by her side, put a spoon and fork in her hand, and every now and again ask her quietly to eat and at the same time touch her arm or hand. Every five minutes or so she might eat a spoonful.

Leonard learned that it was 'no use arguing with the insane, and that there is a terrible sanity about their insanity.' Virginia, he said, had an extraordinarily clear and logical mind and one of the unusual things about her was that it was combined with a 'soaring intelligence'. Her insanity was in her beliefs. She believed she was not ill and that her symptoms were a result of her faults; she believed she heard voices and that the doctors and nurses were in a conspiracy against her. All her actions and conclusions made sense, if her original beliefs had been based in reality, but they were not.

Meanwhile, while Virginia alternated between manic excitement and deep depression, and Leonard struggled to get her back on an even keel, war was declared. The gay young men who had been part of the Bloomsbury Group registered as conscientious objectors, moving out of London to take up residence with that other member of the group, Lady Ottoline Morrell in her country house near Oxford, where they were ostensibly employed on the land.

Leonard was doing some writing: reviewing for the *New Statesman*, the *New Weekly*, the *Co-operative News* and the *Times Literary Supplement* and began to write a book about the Co-operative movement. He read and reviewed work by Freud, and felt proud that he recognised at once the importance of his thinking.

He was also given exemption from military duties because of the tremor in his hands, which the examining doctor interpreted as St Vitus Dance, but which was an inherited condition. His own doctor also thought that because of his responsibility for Virginia's health, he should not be conscripted.

Leonard remembers those war years as the worst period of his life, worse even than the Second World War, which brought with it Virginia's suicide. The First World War was worse because, he says, nothing seemed to happen except the pitiless slaughter in France. His two younger brothers were in the army in France and one had been killed and the other seriously injured.

Meanwhile at home, the Woolfs had bought a house in Richmond called Hogarth House. Leonard had to do all the organising of their move from rented accommodation because of Virginia's illness. He organised repairs and cleaning, had their furniture moved out of storage and arranged for staff to run the house. He, Virginia, and four nurses moved in, in April 1915. This kind of nursing required no qualifications. The nurses were paid about as much as agricultural labourers, that is, not very much. It was hard, depressing work, which entailed cleaning, bed-making, dressing the patient, serving meals, supervising the patient at all times and restraining them when necessary. Housework was used as a kind of therapy for women patients, an attempt, one supposes, to bring them back to reality. Many women moved from nursing to less distressing domestic work.

By November Virginia gradually returned to normal life. In 1916 she was hosting the Richmond branch of the Women's Co-operative Guild and bringing in speakers, not just from the accepted list of Guild speakers, but also her brother Adrian, who talked about pacifism; and Ray Strachey, who presumably spoke on votes for women. She also persuaded E. M. Forster to talk about literature.

The Woolfs had long toyed with the idea of running a printing press and in 1917, they saw one and bought it. They set it up in the basement of their house in Richmond and produced the books themselves. It saved Virginia from the agony of having her work read by another publisher before it was actually in print and gave both Leonard and Virginia the great pleasure of putting together the physical aspects of their mental effort.

They began by printing and publishing their own work but then included the work of their friends and contacts: Katherine

Mansfield, T.S. Eliot, E.M. Forster, Gorky's *Reminiscences of Tolstoi*, Robert Graves, Clive Bell. By 1920 they took on a part-time employee so were able to expand their publications to almost double their previous output. Eventually, because they wanted to write rather than publish books, the press became a commercial enterprise. The books would no longer be printed in the larder, bound in the dining-room, with printers, binders and authors being interviewed in the sitting room, and Virginia rolling and smoking endless cigarettes.

By the time they took on Richard Kennedy, a sixteen-year-old reject from Marlborough School, in 1928, they were struggling to meet the demand for copies of *Orlando*. Besides Richard, a Miss Belcher and a middle-aged lady whom Richard called Ma Cartwright were the only employees. They worked away in the basement with the occasional rat scurrying across the floor. Richard wrote: 'All hands to the pumps with *Orlando*. Mrs W, Ma Cartwright, Miss Belcher and I all lined up at the packing bench and slashed away with our butcher's knives in order to send out review copies of *Orlando*. I took them to the Post Office in relays. Mrs W. is a pretty fast worker considering she's not a professional like Miss Belcher and myself.'

A Room of One's Own

Orlando made Virginia a rich woman. In the first six months the Hogarth Press sold 8,104 copies and the book sold very well in America when published by Harcourt Brace. In the first six months, 13,031 copies were sold. *Orlando* was followed almost immediately by *A Room of One's Own*. Lady Tweedsmuir confessed that 'although I was conscious of Virginia's mounting reputation as a writer and read her novels, I was ... slightly puzzled and put off by them'. Her other work such as *The Common Reader* however, she read again and again and thought her 'exquisite little essays ... a greater achievement than anything in her novels.' Would she have thought that about *A Room of One's Own*? Perhaps not. The Buchan household was run entirely to accommodate John Buchan, who stuck to a rigid timetable and whose money kept the household going. She would have relished Woolf's description of her visit to an Oxbridge college, though – how she was warned off the grass by the beadle, and her access to the library barred by another college official because she was not a member of the college, which she could not be because she was a woman. She might, however, have been disconcerted with Virginia's stress on the importance for a woman of an independent income, when she herself relied so completely on her husband.

A Room of One's Own is addressed to an audience of young women at a university college – she does not specify which. Virginia contrasts the meal she ate at the men's college with one taken at a women's college. Novelists don't write about what they eat, she says, but she will break the mould and describe what was presented to her on both occasions. At the men's college: 'soles, sunk in a deep dish, over which the college cook had spread a counterpane of the whitest cream'. After that came partridges 'with all their retinue of sauces and salads, the sharp and the sweet, each in its order', potatoes and sprouts 'foliated as rosebuds but more succulent'. And the pudding, 'wreathed in napkins, a confection which rose all sugar from the waves.' And the wine: 'the wineglasses had flushed yellow and flushed crimson; had been emptied; had been filled.'

At the women's college:

Here was the soup. It was a plain gravy soup. ... One could have seen through the transparent liquid any pattern that there might have been on the plate itself. But there was no pattern. The plate was plain. Next came beef with its attendant greens and potatoes – a homely trinity, suggesting the rumps of cattle in a muddy market, and sprouts curled and yellowed at the edge... There was no reason to complain of human nature's daily food, seeing that the supply was sufficient and coal miners were doubtless sitting down to less.

She reserves her most acerbic comments, however, for the pudding: prunes and custard. 'If anyone complains that prunes, even when mitigated by custard, are an uncharitable vegetable (fruit they are not), stringy as a miser's heart and exuding a fluid such as might run in misers' veins who have denied themselves wine and warmth for eighty years and yet not given to the poor, he should reflect that there are people whose charity embraces even the prune.'

This was followed by cheese and biscuits and water to drink, with the water jug passed round a great deal. 'It is in the nature of biscuits to be dry, and these were biscuits to the core'. That was all. The meal was over.

So, she wonders, why the difference? Money, she concludes. Gold and silver piled up in the foundations of the men's college over many centuries. So why did not women do the same? Well, how could they? They had children to bear and bring up. And if they had not had children, any earnings they might have achieved were not in their gift. Everything they earned belonged to the husband.

She takes herself off to the British Museum, then the home of the British Library, and discovers that there are acres of books written about women by men but none written by women about men. And the newspaper she picks up casually in a café while having lunch makes no mention of women. They are invisible.

And so she goes on, making fun of Professor Trevelyan's view of history, inventing a sister for Shakespeare, Judith, who came to an untimely early death so was unable to write as her equally gifted brother did, speculating on the reason women started to write novels in the eighteenth century, comparing Jane Austen to Charlotte Bronte, realising the importance of even a small amount of money to ensure independence, and the freedom from bearing ten or twelve, children and settling for two or three.

So what, she asks her audience, are you waiting for? With exquisite irony she points out that there have been two colleges for women in existence since 1866, married women have been allowed to own property since 1880 and for a full nine years they have had the vote. With all these resources at their command, they can carry on the work never achieved by Judith Shakespeare.

> My belief is that the poet who never wrote a word … still lives. She lives in you and me, and in many women who are not here tonight, for they are washing the dishes and putting the children to bed… My belief is that if we live another century or so – I am talking about the common life which is the real life and not of the little separate lives which we live as individuals – and have five hundred pounds a year … and rooms of our own; … if we have the freedom and courage to write exactly what we think, … then the opportunity will come and the dead poet who was Shakespeare's sister will put on the body which she has so often laid down.

Written in the 1920s, *A Room of Ones Own* is light-hearted in its approach, and fun to read. As the 1930s progressed, however, the international situation became more and more gloomy. Hitler came to power in 1933, and two years later the Woolfs travelled through Germany, a journey they did not enjoy, At each village they came to there were giant notices saying 'Jews not wanted here'. It was the suppression of individuality by Hitler, Stalin and Mussolini, the classing of individuals not as people but as 'pawns or pegs or puppets in the nasty process of silencing their own fears or satisfying their own hates' that Leonard Woolf and his contemporaries found so chillingly depressing. They watched with resignation as the world slid towards war.

The Spanish Civil War intruded into the Woolf family's life when Julian, the son of Vanessa and nephew of Virginia suddenly threw up his job teaching English in China and returned home, aged twenty-nine, saying he could no longer stand on the sidelines. He must go and fight the fascists in Spain. Vanessa and Virginia urged him if he must go, to go as an ambulance driver. He left England at the beginning of June and was killed in July. His mother was distraught and needed a great deal of support, which Virginia gave her, visiting or writing to her every day for many months. She was at the same time finishing off another feminist polemic, *Three Guineas*, which Leonard says she found much more difficult to write than *A Room of One's Own*.

Three Guineas

In *Three Guineas* she returns with the tenacity her father showed about money and how it was spent, to the education of 'the daughters of educated men' and again laments the disparity between what she calls 'Arthur's Education Fund' and the nonexistence of a similar fund for Arthur's sisters. But this time she carries her analysis much further. She explores the link between education and the situation that leads countries to war, and concludes that women have always been outsiders – outside the establishment that has gobbled up the men of her acquaintance and turned them into patriots, in which their individuality has been swamped and undervalued by the organisations, be it church, civil service, armed forces, universities, legal system, to which they belong. These organisations, supporters of a capitalist state, do not value individualism and independent opinion, any more than do Hitler and Mussolini. Patriotism is one of the causes of war, she concludes, so women's education should have nothing to do with the kind of education that turns out men who think war is acceptable. They should not instigate the kinds of rites, rewards and pageantry so beloved of the English establishment. Women, she says, do not own England in the way that men do. 'Her sex and class has very little to thank England for'. The English establishment is now considering fighting to defend itself from fascism, just as women fought in the previous century to establish their right to participate in the society they lived in. 'They were fighting the tyranny of the patriarchal state as you are fighting the tyranny of the Fascist state', she says. One way forward for women would be to refuse to take part in any activity that supports a war. They are already barred from fighting, but they could carry this much farther. They could refuse to manufacture armaments, refuse to encourage men to go to war, refuse to nurse the injured. Women should be internationalists. 'As a woman,' she writes, 'I have no country. As a woman I want no country. As a woman my country is the whole world.' A startling conclusion from a writer who is often hesitant to commit herself to didactic utterances, and a stance she is to back away from when war is actually declared.

Along the way, she explores why women have risen no further than the lowest ranks in the Civil Service and why they earn on average £250 a year, which is adequate but does not compare with the thousands that are paid out to the upper echelons of the Civil Service. The names to which 'Miss' is attached do not seem to enter the four-figure zone. 'The sex distinction,' she says, 'seems ... possessed of a curious leaden quality liable to keep any name to which it is fastened circling in the lower spheres.'

Married women are not allowed to work in the Civil Service. 'In Whitehall, as in heaven, there is neither marrying nor giving in marriage.' Married women should be entitled to a half share of their husband's salary when all expenses have been met, seeing as he is paid more than a woman so he can support his wife and family, but, she comments, 'The fact is that the tastes of the married woman are remarkably virile. She spends vast sums annually upon party funds, upon sport, upon grouse moors.... She lays out thousands and thousands of pounds upon clubs to which her own sex is not admitted; upon racecourses where she may not ride; upon colleges from which her own sex is excluded.' There are only two conclusions to be drawn from this: either she is extremely altruistic or, more likely, that her spiritual right to a share of half her husband's income peters out in practice to an actual right to board, lodging and a small annual allowance for pocket money and dress.'

Much of what she says about women's position in society has been said before, but certainly not with the wit and acute intellectual analysis that Virginia Woolf brings to bear on the subject. And she knows that what she writes will be read across the Western world and that it points the way forward to what still needs to be achieved to bring any meaningful freedom to women. Acquiring the vote was not enough. Writing about the peace movement, Jill Liddington considers that the arguments Virginia Woolf makes were somewhat anachronistic, an argument with her dead nephew Julian. They were certainly based on what people had experienced in the First World War but she was soon to change her mind about the importance of an international outlook

Three Guineas was well received by many feminists but severely criticised by other sections of the community though, for once, she does not seem to have minded the criticism. The Woolfs' minds were on other things. It was not so much a case of if the country went to war, but when. And if Germany won the war, then Leonard, a left-wing Jew, would not have an easy ride. Virginia's brother Adrian, with Harold Nicholson and his wife Vita Sackville West, had all acquired poison so they could commit suicide in the event of a German invasion. The Woolfs kept enough petrol in the car to be able to asphyxiate themselves, although Virginia said she did not want to die in a garage.

At the end of August just before war was finally declared on 3 September 1939, the Woolfs were in the process of moving their London home from Tavistock Square to Mecklenburg Square. The man on the removal van said, 'I shan't be here tomorrow, sir', to Leonard, explaining that he had received his call-up papers. There were sandbags everywhere and men digging trenches. They were at their house in Rodmel, Sussex, on the day war broke out.

From then until Virginia's death they lived mainly in Sussex, with occasional excursions to London. Virginia was asked to join the local Women's Institute, which she was unsure about. She wrote that because she and Leonard were in the Labour Party, they were considered to be rampant left-wingers. She must have found the WI both parochial and conservative, but she joined it anyway, retreating, perhaps, into the Englishness that she had rejected so vehemently in *Three Guineas.* She became treasurer, alongside the president, Mrs Chavasse, thus joining the ranks of the gentry, which at that time ran the WI both at branch, county and national level. An uncomfortable place for her to be. Besides the tuppences she collected from the members, she concerned herself mainly with putting on plays, introducing outside speakers and giving a talk herself on the *Dreadnought* incident.

The text for this talk disappeared but was discovered in 1955 among WI papers. This must have been quite a find but the WI magazine, then called *Home and Country,* made no comment on it. Since the *Dreadnought* hoax made mock of national and imperial institutions, perhaps it is not surprising the editorial board of *Home and Country* offered no account of its discovery or the contents.

A popular feature of WI life at this time was the pageant, which forms the setting for her novel *Between the Acts,* begun in 1938 but not finished until February 1941. It is an elegy for the England she knew as a child and the England that had been reinvented following the First World War, the Englishness threatened by a new war with Germany, with all the horrors that the bombing of the civilian population would bring. The book is a description of one day in the life of a village, a day when the annual pageant celebrating the history of England takes place. The title, though apparently about the play, could be interpreted as the time between the two world wars. In *The Long Road to Greenham* Jill Liddington notes that some women, ardent pacifists during the 1920s and 30s, abandoned their pacifist stance as the realities of Nazi atrocities against the Jews became known – Maude Royden certainly did – so Virginia Woof, was in good company.

As the war progressed Sussex was far from the safe retreat that some may have thought it would be. On Sunday 18 August when they were sitting down to lunch, 'there was a tremendous roar and we were just in time to see two planes fly a few feet above the church spire, over the garden and over our roof, and looking up as they passed above the window we saw the swastika on them', writes Leonard. They also witnessed bombing. Their house in Rodmel was safe, but the London house was wrecked. Fortunately, they had been able to bring their goods and chattels away and store them in barns around Rodmel, apart from the books – which were stacked in every conceivable space in their house.

In spite of being in the midst of a war zone, Leonard believed that Virginia was coping well with the stress. But in 1941 he became more and more anxious about her state of mind, and on Friday, 28 March, while working in the garden, he realised that she was not in the house. She had gone for a walk. He rushed in the direction of the river and found her stick on the bank, but no sign of Virginia. It was three weeks before the police found her body. She had left a letter for Leonard and one for her sister Vanessa, the two most important people in her life. In Leonard's she said, 'I feel certain I am going mad again... So I am doing what seems the best thing to do... You have given me the greatest possible happiness. You have been in every way all that anyone could be.... Everything has gone from me but the certainty of your goodness. I can't go on spoiling your life any longer.'

10

Looking Forward

Miss Llewelyn Davies, Miss Deneke, Dr Emslie Hutton, Miss Lodge, Miss Rathbone, Miss Royden, Miss Wilkinson, Mrs Woolf, what do these women have in common? Well, all bar two are unmarried, and none of them have children. This in itself is a break with what was the accepted career path for women in the nineteenth century. They stood on their own feet and made their mark in the world. They did not have children, except for Maud Royden who adopted two war orphans then passed their care over to her friend and housekeeper Evelyn Gunter, so they were free to join pressure groups, chair committees, speak in public. All except Ellen Wilkinson were middle class women with independent incomes and, although unmarried, they lived away from the family home but did not have to take sole responsibility for running their own household. They paired up with like-minded women who shared the responsibility: Margaret Llewelyn Davies with Lilian Harris, Eleanor Rathbone with Elizabeth Macadam, Maude Royden with Evelyn Gunter, Eleanor Lodge with Janet Spens. Helena Deneke with her sister Margaret. Whether these partnerships had a sexual element to them I very much doubt. When Eleanor Rathbone's niece, who was gay, was attempting to explain the situation to her aunt, she reported that Eleanor completely failed to understand what she was trying to convey.

In spite of not marrying, they were not without family support. The majority were youngest children with a plethora of brothers and sisters, and innumerable nephews and nieces, many of whom they loved and with whom they had meaningful relations. Being the youngest or nearly the youngest of large families, they often lost their mothers at an early age and witnessed the difference in treatment between their brothers and themselves, which they resented, again excluding Ellen Wilkinson.

This burning resentment led to an equally burning determination to tip the balance more in favour of women in society, and obtaining the vote was just one of the important factors in the battle. An important one, though not as important as they expected it to be, since, as Virginia Woolf put it, 'Even when the path is nominally open – when there is nothing to prevent a woman being a doctor, a lawyer, a civil servant – there are many phantoms and obstacles, as I believe, looming in her way.' How right she was, and how hard women have had to work since she wrote that in 1931 to defeat those unacknowledged phantoms and obstacles.

Ellen Wilkinson is a different kettle of fish. It was often the pattern in working-class families for the younger children to be better educated than the older ones because there was more money coming into the family when the older ones were earning. She nevertheless felt the same burning anger at the injustices in society. Her urge to right the wrongs of the world sprang not from envy of her siblings, since she was the most privileged of them, but from the class divisions within society. And having no independent means of support, her actions had, of necessity, to be channelled through jobs that paid a reasonable wage.

I chose to write about these eight women because I thought that each one, in her particular way, battled in a particular field: Margaret Llewelyn Davies giving working class women a voice, Maude Royden in the Church, Dr Emslie Hutton in medicine, Helena Deneke in the Women's Institute, Eleanor Lodge in education, Eleanor Rathbone and Ellen Wilkinson in politics, and Virginia Woolf influencing public opinion via literature and leftwing politics and seeking access for women into the professions.

Their achievements ended in the 1940s because of their old age or death. Their work, however, was carried on by the second wave of feminism, which began in the 1960s in America as a delayed reaction to women's forced return to domesticity after the Second World War. The French philosopher Simone de Beauvoir was a significant influence on this revival. Feminists now focused on sexuality, women's place in the family and the workplace, on their reproductive rights and on domestic violence. Not that different, then, from the first wave of feminists. But carrying on from where the first wave left off, they have been able to make many improvements in women's lives and have opened up opportunities for modern women that could not have been dreamed of in earlier times.

While they all had their particular areas of expertise, the first wave of feminists were working towards certain common goals. They realised that there were three factors that would improve women's lives immeasurably: a limit to the number of children they were expected to bear, enough income to ensure they and their families were well fed and housed, which would in turn result in better health; and the education to improve their job prospects, which would result in a better income.

Health
Contraception
Limiting the number of children women had and spacing them to give the woman's body time to recover from one birth before embarking on another pregnancy were seen as crucial factors in health improvement by both middle – and working-class women. One difficulty Maude Royden identified was the promises women made in the marriage ceremony: to love, cherish and obey. Some women, she realised, thought promising to obey meant they gave up any rights to control over their own bodies. The 'obey' bit needed to change and she preached long and loud on the subject. By 1928 it became possible to omit 'obey' from the wedding ceremony, though it could be retained if the bride wished it. This is still the case.

As early as 1877 Charles Bradlaugh and socialist Annie Besant had been prosecuted for publishing Charles Knowton's book *Fruits of Philosophy*, which explained the various kinds of contraceptive available at the time. The trial had proved a wonderful publicity move which stimulated public interest in the subject and the book sold very well indeed. By the end of the nineteenth century the middle classes had started to use contraception of one kind and another, though many working-class women still thought that what the Church preached was morally right and that sex should only be for the procreation of children, not for pleasure.

Many people, whatever their background, thought sex was a dirty word and not a suitable topic for discussion. Maude Royden thought differently, and her willingness to talk about sex openly and to say that it was an act sent from God therefore could not be dirty and should be enjoyed as an expression of a loving relationship was a really brave thing to do. Her preaching ran alongside Marie Stopes's practical help with her book *Married Love,* and the opening of the first of several Mothers' Clinics in1921. Isabel Emslie Hutton's *The Hygiene of Marriage* in 1925 added to the drive to change public opinion to such an extent that by 1930 Lady Denman, President of the Women's Institute, dared to fund Marie Stopes' Natural Birth Control Council while the Ministry of Health in the same year allowed local authorities to give birth control advice.

Contraception for all women who wanted it became very widely available in the 1960s with the invention of the contraceptive pill, which freed women, married or unmarried, from the burden of unwanted pregnancy. It gave women power over their own reproductive system and because of that, led to a revolution in sexual habits and relationships. Casual sex had no consequences, except perhaps the risk of sexually transmitted diseases such as syphilis, which could now be controlled with antibiotics. The number of people cohabiting increased enormously since there was no incentive for the man to marry for sex and no social pressures to marry a girl he had made pregnant. Out went shotgun weddings. In came weddings where the couple were attended by their small daughter or pageboy son. Out went the horror of illegitimacy. In came pre-nuptial agreements. In, eventually, came same sex marriages and civil partnerships. A revolution indeed!

Everything in the garden should have been rosy, but there remains the problem of some men's aggression towards women: violence in and outside the home, rape being one of the most unpleasant manifestations of this. For many years rape was under-reported by women because they felt they would not be believed and because of the trauma of reliving a very unpleasant experience. One of the aspects which was most intrusive was the defendant's right to question the woman about her previous sexual history. If she had a history of having sex with a number of men, how could she cry rape when another man had attacked her?

This situation was changed in 1999 when Vera Baird QC, for the Labour government of the time, brought in an Act that forbade the use of a woman's previous sexual history in a man's defence in court.

In cases where women have been subjected to violence within the family there have been women's refuges since 1971 when Erin Pizzey founded the first one in Chiswick. The movement grew until it covered the whole of Britain and the charity 'Refuge', which developed from this, now supports 3,000 women and children a day. They are funded not only by charitable donations but by the Home Office and Local Authorities.

Abortion

Allied to the prevention of unwanted pregnancies was the question of abortion. Some members of the Women's Co-operative Guild who contributed to *Maternity* admitted to trying to bring about abortions with the use of drugs. These were usually pills bought at the herbalist with contents such as pennyroyal, rue, vervain, or tansy. The information about these pills and who supplied them was passed from woman to woman, and in my case, from mother to daughter. Alternatives were gin, hot baths and jumping off chairs, as well as back street abortionists, some of whom were competent, some of whom were not, though none of them were regulated.

In the first half of the twentieth century abortion was illegal and the Catholic Church and fundamentalist Christian's position is clear – it is a sin. The vastly more liberal attitude of Harold Wilson's Labour Government, however, brought in an Abortion Act in 1967, which allowed terminations with certain inbuilt safeguards. A pregnancy can be terminated in the early stages, when a foetus cannot survive outside the mother's body, then set at twenty-eight weeks' gestation, but now fixed at twenty-four weeks because of the advances in medical knowledge and practice. Two doctors have to agree that pregnancy would involve a risk, greater than if the pregnancy were terminated, of injury to the physical or mental health of the woman or any existing children of her family; to prevent grave permanent injury to the physical or mental health of the women and if there is a substantial risk that the child would be seriously mentally or physically disabled.

This law does not apply in Northern Ireland where the Catholic and Presbyterian churches are a powerful influence. Here abortion comes within the criminal law even when the girl is very young and the pregnancy is the result of rape or incest. In Northern Ireland there are two possibilities for women needing an abortion. They can either buy pills on the internet, though they can end up in court for illegally procuring an abortion, or travel to England, Wales or Scotland where a pregnancy can be terminated legally. In 2014, 837 women had terminations in this way, though this may be an underestimate since women sometimes give a false address. Substantial amounts of money are needed to take this option: money to travel and pay for accommodation and money to pay for treatment in a private clinic. Obviously, this is not available for the poorest women, though the Abortion Support Network in Northern Ireland can sometimes provide financial assistance.

Female Genital Mutilation (FMG)

This was called 'female circumcision' until the process was given a more accurate name. Circumcision implies a much less invasive operation than it actually is, as it appears to compare it with the circumcision of boys. FGM has no known medical benefits but it has a great many dreadful consequences: recurrent infections, chronic pain, and difficulties in childbirth. As the process is performed by women, many of whom think it is a religious imperative (it isn't), with one knife with which they cut a succession of children, there is the great possibility of infection, and uncontrolled bleeding. Children sometimes die. Fortunately it applies to only a small minority of women in this country, but it is nonetheless important.

The subject has only in the last twenty years or so become an issue in Western Europe because of the number of immigrant children who have been mutilated in this way. I was astonished, therefore, to read that in 1929 Eleanor Rathbone and the Duchess of Atholl raised the matter in Parliament. It was not women in Britain who caused them concern but in the African colonies, notably Kenya. Nothing much was done about it, FGM being about women – and women in Africa at that. The procedure was deemed to be a tribal matter, and tribal culture had to be respected. But as one French doctor said in the 1980s at the second International

Interdisciplinary Congress on Women, which was convened to discuss women's lack of power and how to gain it, it was time that respect for culture gave way to respect for women.

This exhortation was followed up in Britain in 1985 by making FGM an offence but again nothing much was done about it. Nobody was prosecuted. In truth, probably no one knew what to do, so the problem was ignored and the practice carried on within immigrant communities. The situation changed, however, in 2003 with the Female Mutilation Act, later amended by the Serious Crime Act of 2015, which identifies a clear path of action. It is a legal duty for regulated health and social care professionals and teachers to report the matter to the police. This applies not only to the carers of children in this country but also to people travelling abroad with children to submit them to the practice.

Finance

Improving women's access to an income was seen to rest on a woman's access to a good education, financial support for any children she cared for whether it was money she earned herself, or money given to her by the state to support the family. Having her own income would tilt the balance of power within the family, so women would be more respected by the men in their lives and have more self-belief.

What women wanted depended on their situation. Virginia Woolf summed up what working class women wanted in 1913 as 'baths and money', which did not appeal to middle-class ladies, she said. They had baths. They had money. They wanted higher things: Mozart and Einstein. She was actually describing Maslow's hierarchy of needs a good fifteen years before he published his paper analysing people's needs. He demonstrated his theory in the shape of a pyramid. At the base was food and shelter. Once you had food, shelter, and baths, though he didn't actually mention the baths, then you moved on to want love, belonging, esteem and self-actualisation. The middle-class ladies were higher up the pyramid than the members of the Guild and they actually wanted interesting jobs with money that would give them access to the good things that money can buy. They also wanted to be paid on a par with men because that way they felt valued. As Virginia Woolf said, however, there were phantoms and obstacles in the way.

Education

The first thing that needed to be done to help women climb to parity with men was a good education, which had evolved to some extent by the beginning of the twentieth century. Grammar schools and university places were available if you could afford it and if parents thought it worth educating a girl. Ellen Wilkinson was instrumental in setting up the new education system in 1945 that separated out the clever children from the not so clever. A pernicious idea, but at least grammar school places were now free, which enabled clever children from poorer families to acquire a good education or at least the best that was available at the time. They could even progress from school to university! Though Oxbridge places were severely restricted, the universities established at the end of the nineteenth or beginning of the twentieth century, places such as Liverpool, Leeds, Bristol, and Manchester, had plenty of places for women and no inhibitions about recruiting them.

Eventually Oxford and Cambridge caught up. In 1974, five Oxford colleges became co-educational, widening the availability of places to women and all the colleges have taken both men and women since 2008. In addition, Oxford at the present time has ten female heads of house, that is masters or principals of colleges and in 2016 Professor Louise Richardson became the first female vice-chancellor. Helena Deneke and Eleanor Lodge would have thrown their academic caps in the air to hear that! Cambridge has rather lagged behind Oxford in its acceptance of women. They were not admitted fully until 1948. The first college to accept women on equal terms with men was Darwin College in 1964, the year it was founded, and there are still three colleges which admit women only: Newnham, Murray-Edwards and Lucy Cavendish.

The idea that women did not need an education because they were going to get married was still prevalent in the 1940s and 50s, with some justification, as women were often obliged to give up work when they married. The bar against employing married women was beginning to break down in the1930s and by 1934 there were eight (!) married women employed in the civil service throughout the whole of Britain. Before the Second World War women teachers had to resign when they married but during the war things changed. Married women were brought back into teaching, and in 1941 unmarried women aged between twenty and thirty were recruited into the war effort just as men were. They could choose between munitions factories or the armed forces. There were auxiliary forces allied to the army, the navy and the air force: the Auxiliary Territorial Service (ATS) the women's branch of the army. These women served in non-combat roles, though they could man (!) anti-aircraft guns and serve as military police. They were officially recognised as part of the British Armed Forces in 1949 but were excluded from close combat until 2016. The Women's Royal Naval Service (WRENS) had been formed in 1917 but disbanded in 1919. They were re-formed in 1939 and were employed in a variety of jobs: as cooks, radar plotters, electricians, weapons assessors. The Women's Auxiliary Air Force (WAAF) was formed in 1939. Although not allowed to fly combat planes, they were employed in a variety of jobs: parachute packing, code and cypher work, crewing barrage balloons, analysis of reconnaissance photographs, meteorology, and plotters in the operations rooms. They were paid two-thirds the rate for men doing similar work. The force was very much diminished by 1949, when it was renamed the Women's Royal Air Force.

Equal Pay

At the end of the war the government tried to push women back where they thought they belonged: in the home. But the genie was out of the bottle and in spite of the government closing day nurseries and other support services, women, aided by the economic situation, fought back. There was a shortage of labour across the whole of the country and part-time work, including evening shifts, and workplace crèches were introduced. Manufacturers however did not offer equal pay for equal work. Women were still paid substantially less than men doing similar work. This carried on into the 1960s when the women machinists employed by the Ford Motor Company in Dagenham came out on strike for parity with the male employees.

The dispute was finally resolved by Barbara Castle. Mrs Castle, like Ellen Wilkinson, a redheaded, energetic Northerner with no children, has been described as 'one of the most significant Labour Party politicians of the twentieth century'. Because of the changes in public opinion brought about by both the first and second wave of feminists, Barbara Castle could work more effectively in government than Ellen Wilkinson had been able to. Women in the Houses of Parliament were no longer considered freaks. As Minister of Transport Barbara Castle had introduced breathalysers, seat belts and the 70 mph speed limit, and she now intervened in the Dagenham dispute and persuaded the women to return to work and accept a pay rise which would bring them ninety-two per cent of the men's wages. She brought in the Equal Pay Act in 1970 and went on as Minister of Health and Social Services to introduce the Mobility Allowance, and the Invalid Care Allowance. She made many political enemies when she tried to limit the power of the unions, however, and was sacked from the cabinet by James Callaghan, when he took over as Prime Minister when Harold Wilson resigned.

Job Opportunities
Politics

The Houses of Parliament were not receptive to the way many women need to work. They made no provision for childcare, there was no part time or flexible working, voting often took place in the evenings. In spite of these difficulties, women appeared to have reached the top in politics when Margaret Thatcher was made Prime Minister in 1979. But it was not the triumph it might have appeared to be. She had made her way up the Conservative hierarchy by having a rich husband who could support her, so she had no money worries, and there were no issues about childcare for her two children as she could afford to pay people to look after them. It was however a momentous occasion and many women thought that as a woman she would appoint more women to her cabinet. Not so. The cabinet remained resolutely male. Only a small handful of women, Edwina Currie and Angela Rumbold among them, achieved office of any kind. Margaret Thatcher's main achievements were that she went to war with Argentina over the Falklands, got rid of much red tape, introduced the 'right to buy' when council houses were sold off cheaply to their occupants, deregulated and privatised state-run monopolies and broke the power of the unions, all of which was welcomed by many, though by no means all, at the time.

Medicine

While an Oxbridge education for women and politics was difficult for the great majority of women because of the unavailability of college places, women's education in medicine was likewise limited. In the 1960s there was a quota for women taking medicine: twenty-five per cent of the student intake was for women, seventy-five per cent for men. The 1970s saw a change, however. With the invention of the contraceptive pill, women's career aspirations changed. A career in medicine, with the long training that involved, no longer seemed an impossibility and the opening of new universities provided possible ways into the profession. The number of women employed as medical practitioners has gradually increased until in 2016 the number of men on the Specialist register is 54.6% while that of women is 45.4%. The register of general practitioners, however, shows that women now outnumber men, 51.6% to 48. 4%. Women have the same problem in medicine as they have in other professions, however. They are underrepresented in the upper echelons of the discipline.

The Church

We can see therefore that the work of Eleanor Rathbone and Ellen Wilkinson, Eleanor Lodge and Helena Deneke, Margaret Llewelyn Davies, Virginia Woolf and Isobel Emslie Hutton, has paid dividends and laid the way for further improvements in women's life chances. But what of Maude Royden, who took on that most intransigent and conservative of institutions, the Church? She would be very gratified, I think, to know that in the twenty-first century her wishes have been granted, in Great Britain at least. There are three traditional holy orders in the Church of England: bishop, priest and deacon. In England women have been ordained deacons since 1985, the first woman taking up the post in 1987. The same applies to both Wales and Scotland. Women priests have been permitted since 1992 with the first ordained two years later in 1994 in Bristol Cathedral while it was not until 2014 that the first bishop was ordained. This was Libby Lane, who was made Suffragan Bishop of Stockport. Suffragan bishops are subordinate to metropolitan or diocesan bishops. The first diocesan bishop was Rachel Treweek, ordained bishop of Gloucester in 2015. These decisions were not easily come by and the distress caused among some members of the Anglican Community was intense with the result that some left the Church of England and became Roman Catholic. To help others adjust to the situation, the Church created a special post – a provincial Episcopal visitor – a so-called 'flying bishop' to minister to clergy, laity and parishes who do not accept the ministry of women.

So the eight women whose lives we have followed, typical of that first wave of feminists, always knew they were in the struggle for the long term. They would be gratified to know that much of what they worked for has been achieved. However, the price of freedom is eternal vigilance. While society has come a very long way since the nineteenth century, there is no guarantee it will not slip back. Let us hope that in another hundred years women will not have to look back to the beginning of the twenty-first century as a golden time when women had freedoms our descendants can only dream of.

Bibliography

Alcock, John B. and Young, Antonia eds. *Black Lambs and Grey Falcons.* (New York, London: Berghahn Books, 2000)

Bartley, Paula. *Ellen Wilkinson. From Red Suffragist to Government Minister.* (London: Pluto Press, 2014)

Bell, Quentin. *Virginia Woolf. A Biography.* (London: Pimlico Press, 1996)

Brittain, Vera. *The Women at Oxford: A Fragment of History.* (London: Harrap, 1960)

Bruley, Sue. *Women in Britain since 1900.* (Basingstoke :Macmillan,1999)

Davies, Margaret Llewelyn ed. *Maternity. Letters from Working Women.* (London: Virago,1978) Misleadingly there are two versions of this book; the first published in 1915, is called *Maternity. Letters from Working Women* and was reprinted by Virago in 1978; and the second, another reissue by Virago, again in 1978, entitled *No One But a Mother Knows. Stories of Motherhood Before the War,* the First World War, that is. Apart from the cover, they are identical.

Davies, Margaret Llewelyn ed. *Life as We Have Known it.* (London: Virago, 2011)

Deneke, Helena and Norris, Betty. *The Women of Germany.* (The National Council of Social Service, of the Women's Group on Public Welfare, 1947)

Fitzroy, Yvonne and McLaren, Eva Shaw. *Scottish Nurses in the First World War.* (Leonaur, 2013)

Fletcher, Sheila. *Maude Royden: A Life.* (Oxford: Basil Blackwell,1989)

Gaffin, Jean and Thoms, David. *Caring and Sharing. The Centenary History of the Co-operative Women's Guild.* (Manchester: Co-operative Union Ltd, 1983)

Hewitt, Margaret. *Wives and Mothers in Victorian Industry.* (London: Rockcliff,1958)

Hutton, Isabel Emslie. MD. *The Hygiene of Marriage.* (London: Heineman, 1948)

Hutton, Isabel, CBE, MD. *Memories of a Doctor in War and Peace.* (London: Heineman, 1960.)

Kennedy, Richard. *A Boy at the Hogarth Press.* (London: Hesperus Press, 2011)

Liddington, Jill. *The Long Road to Greenham.* (London: Virago. 1989)

Lodge, Eleanor C. *Terms and Vacations.* (Oxford: Oxford University Press, 1938)

Pedersen, Susan. *Eleanor Rathbone and the Politics of Conscience.* (New Haven and London: Yale University Press,2004)

Philips, David. *Investigating Education in Germany: Historical studies from a British Perspective*. (London: Routledge, 2015)

Powell, Anne. *Women in the War Zone. Hospital Service in the First World War*. (Stroud: The History Press, 2009)

Ramelson, Marian. *The Petticoat Rebellion*. (London: Lawrence and Wishart, 1967)

Rice, Margery Spring. *Working Class Wives*. (London: Virago, 1981)

Rowbotham, Sheila. *A Century of Women. The History of Women in Britain and the United States*. (London and New York: Penguin, 1997)

Royden, A, Maude. *Women and the Sovereign State*. (London: Headley Bros., 1917)

The Threefold Cord. (London: Victor Gollancz, 1947)

Scott, Gillian. *Feminism and the Politics of Working Women*. (London: UCL Press. 1998)

Smith, Harold L. *The British Women's Suffrage Campaign 1866–1928*. (London: Routledge, 2010)

Stopes, Marie Carmichael. *Married Love. A New Contribution to the Solution of Sex Difficulties*. (London, 1918)

Strachey, Ray. *The Cause*. (London: Virago, 1978)

Westfield College, University of London. 1882–1932.

Leonard Woolf. *Beginning Again. An Autobiography of the Years 1911 to 1918*. (San Diego, and London: Harcourt Brace Jovanovich, 1975)

Downhill All the Way. An Autobiography of the Years 1919 to 1939. (San Diego and London: Harcourt Brace Jovanovich, 1975)

Woolf, Virginia. *Selected Essays*. (Oxford: Oxford University Press, 2008)

A Room of One's Own and *Three Guineas* (London: Vintage, 2001)

Between the Acts (Oxford: Oxford University Press, 2008)

Websites

www.etheses.dur.ac.uk Tscharnke, Denise Kathrin. *Educating German Women: The Work of the Women's Affairs Section of British Military Government 1946–1951*.

Archives

Oxfordshire History Centre, St Luke's Church, Temple Road, OX4 2HT
03/1/1C/1
03/1/1/C1/2
03/1/1/C1/11
03/1/1/PRI

Weston Library, University of Oxford
Deneke, Helena. Papers.

Lady Margaret Hall archive
Brown Books 1936–7; 1956–7; 1974–5.
Deneke, Helena. *What I Remember* Vols. 1–5

Timeline

1792	*Vindication of the Rights of Women* by Mary Wollstonecraft
1836–1848	Chartist movement
1839	Women given access to their children in the event of divorce or separation
1839	British and Foreign Anti-slavery Convention in London
1840	Establishment of the Penny Post
1840s	Expansion of the railways
1848	Queen's College, Harley Street established
1861	J.S. Mill *The Subjugation of Women*. Birth of Margaret Llewelyn Davies
1864	Schools Enquiry Commission inspects girls' schools as well as boys'.
1867	Lydia Becker forms Manchester Women's Suffrage Society
1868–1871	Kensington Society discusses votes for women
1869	Women speak in public at Architectural Society
1869	Girton College, Cambridge founded Newnham Hall, Cambridge founded Eleanor Lodge born
1870	Women get the right to sit on Boards of Education
1872	Eleanor Rathbone born
1875	Russell Gurney Bill confers on universities the power to admit women to study medicine
1876	London University admits women to all courses Maude Royden born
1878	Helena Deneke born Lady Margaret Hall, Oxford, founded
1879	Somerville Hall, Oxford, founded
1881	Women in the IOM get the right to vote for members of the House of Keys,
1882	Virginia Stephen born
1883	Women's Co-operative Guild founded Margaret Llewelyn Davies joins Women's Co-operative Guild

1886	St Hugh's, Oxford, founded
1887	Isabel Emslie born
1890	Eleanor Lodge enrolls at LMH
1891	Ellen Wilkinson born
1893	Independent Labour Party founded
	Eleanor Rathbone goes up to Somerville Hall, Oxford
1895	Virginia Stephen's mother dies, precipitating a bout of madness for Virginia
1896	Eleanor Rathbone is secretary of the NUWSS
	Eleanor Rathbone works as 'Friendly visitor' for Liverpool Central Relief Society
1897	Liverpool Settlement set up
	NUWSS established
1899	Margaret Llewelyn Davies elected secretary of WCG
	Morley College for working men and women opened in London
1899–1902	Second Boer War in South Africa
1900	Helena Deneke enrolls at St Hugh's in Oxford
	Labour Party formed
1902	Seebohm Rowntree's work on poverty in York published
1903	Women's Social and Political Union founded (know as suffragettes)
	Annie Kenney and Christabel Pankhurst of the WSPU arrested
1904	Death of Virginia Stephen's father, which is followed by another bout of madness in Virginia
1905	School of Social Science and training for social work set up at University of Liverpool
	Isabel Emslie enrolls in Edinburgh Medical School
1906	WSPU turns to violence against property
	Eleanor Lodge made vice-principal of LMH
	Establishment of Bloomsbury Group
	Stephen family visit Greece. Death of Thoby Stephen. Vanessa marries Clive Bell
1907	Mud March organised by suffragists
	Ellen Wilkinson joins ILP
1908	Old Age Pensions given to people over 70
	Anti-suffrage movement formed
1910	Royal Commission on Divorce
1910	People's Suffrage Foundation established
	Virginia Stephen: *Dreadnought* incident
1911	Liberal PM Asquith excludes women from Franchise Bill
	Maternity grant paid to women
	An Adventure published
1912	Suffragettes smash windows in London
	NUWSS meeting at the Albert Hall
	Conciliation Bill extends men's suffrage
	Eleanor Rathbone gives evidence to Royal Commission on poverty
	Liberal government takes up issue of decasualisation of dock labour
	Ellen Wilkinson joins Manchester Society for Women's Suffrage
	Virginia Stephen marries Leonard Woolf

1913	'Cat and Mouse' Act
	Death of Emily Wilding Davison
	Suffrage Pilgrimage
	International Suffrage Congress in Budapest
	Helena Deneke moves to Lady Margaret Hall
	Maude Royden edits suffrage newspaper *The Common Cause*
	Labour Party promises to support votes for women
	Ellen Wilkinson sets up Suffrage and Labour clubs in Manchester
	Virginia Woolf joins People's Suffrage Federation; tours industrial North
1914	August. War declared
	Union of Democratic Control formed
	Eleanor Rathbone assumes leadership of SSAFA
1915	WCG's *Maternity* published
	Mary Sheepshanks writes an open letter to German and Austrian women expressing solidarity
	NUWSS split between supporters of war and pacifism
	Peace Congress in the Hague
	Church League for Women's Suffrage begins to campaign for admittance to priesthood.
	Ellen Wilkinson joins WILPF
	Ellen Wilkinson appointed national organiser for Amalgamated Union of Co-operative Employees
	Isabel Emslie joins Scottish Women's Hospitals; sent to Troyes then Salonika
1916	Virginia Woolf hosts WCG meetings
1917	January. Fall of Asquith. Lloyd George becomes PM.
	NUWSS organizes demonstration of war workers
	February. Women over 30 get the vote.
	Isabel Emslie goes to Serbia with Scottish Women's Hospitals
	Great fire in Salonika
	Married Love by Marie Stopes published
	Maude Royden asked to speak at City Temple
	Two workers funded by suffrage movement set up 'cantines anglaises in France
	WSPU wound up.
	October. Revolution in Russia
	Family Endowment Committee set up
	Syles-Picot Agreement divides Middle East between France and Britain
	Balfour Agreement says Britain is sympathetic to Jewish homeland
1918	Women over 21 can stand for Parliament. 17 women stand as candidates: only one is elected
	Last offensive by Germans in Northern France. Eleanor Lodge caught up in retreat
	Isabel Emslie made head of American Scottish Women's Hospital in Serbia
	Armistice

NUWSS reforms as NUSEC (National Union of Societies for Equal Citizenship)

Starvation in Europe

Maude Royden adopts a war orphan

Restoration of Pre-war Practices act means women lose jobs

1919   Peace treaty signed

National Federation of Women's Institutes founded

Enabling Act gives independence from Parliamentary oversight to Church of England

Nancy Astor elected first woman MP

Government of India Act ensures assessment of situation every ten years

Ellen Wilkinson negotiates 48 hour week for Co-op laundresses

AUCE amalgamates with NUDAW

1920 University of Oxford admits women

Maude Royden sets up the Guildhouse and is elected to National Church Assembly

1920   Scottish Women's Hospitals in Serbia wound up

1921   Establishment of International Co-operative Guild

Women could be called for jury service

Margaret Llewelyn Davies retires from WCG

Eleanor Lodge made Principal of Westfield College

Economic recession in West

Margaret Wintringham elected to Parliament

Ellen Wilkinson attends Congress of Red Trade Union International in Moscow

1922   Eleanor Rathbone fails to get elected to Parliament for Liverpool seat

Mussolini comes to power in Italy

Island of Ireland divided into Irish Free State and Ulster

1923   Matrimonial Act grants divorce for women because of adultery of husband

Maude Royden becomes head of WILPF

Work starts on revision of C of E marriage ceremony

1924   Labour Party refuses to accept members who are Communists

Zinoviev letter

Ellen Wilkinson wins Middlesbrough seat in Parliament

1925   Eleanor Rathbone publishes *The Disinherited* Family

Labour Party puts family allowances on legislative agenda

Ellen Wilkinson introduces Bill to allow women into police force

Isabel Emslie Hutton publishes *The Hygiene of Marriage*

Isabel Emslie Hutton tackles malaria in Albania

1926   General strike May 3

First Women's Peace Pilgrimage

Isabel Emslie Hutton helps women to gain permission to fly commercial planes

Isabel Emslie Hutton develops regime for children at Ellen Terry Home for Blind and Defective children

1927	In Russia Stalin forces Trotsky out of Central Committee, leading to isolationism.
	Trades Disputes Act limits union activities
	Ellen Wilkinson elected onto National Executive of Labour Party
	Labour Party returned to power. 14 women in Parliament, 2 in cabinet
1928	Equal Franchise Act
	Foundation of Townswomen's Guild. Demise of NUSEC
	Ellen Wilkinson persuades Speaker to allow women to eat dinner in Strangers' dining room
	Virginia Woolf publishes *A Room of One's Own*
1929	Labour win most seats in election. Ramsay Macdonald PM in minority government.
	Eleanor Rathbone elected to Parliament as Independent
	Female Genital Mutilation raised in Parliament
	Sarda Act about child marriages in India
	Wall Street crash. Great Depression
1930	Round table talks on India
	Eleanor Rathbone's portrait painted
	Eleanor Rathbone visits Palestine and offends Grand Mufti
1931	Anomalies Act removes married women's entitlement to unemployment pay
	Ramsay Macdonald forms cross-party National government
	October election: Labour majority wiped out. Ellen Wilkinson loses seat and resumes work for NUDAW
1932	Ellen Wikinson helps with German elections
1933	Maude Royden begins broadcasting sermons
	Hitler comes to power
	Mein Kampf published
	Ellen Wilkinson starts contributing to *Time and Tide*
1934	Peace Pledge Union formed
	German Jews denied health insurance
1935	Mussolini invades Abyssinia. Emperor Haile Selassie flees
	Jews not allowed to hold German citizenship
	Ellen Wilkinson elected MP for Jarrow
	The Woolfs travel in Germany
1936	Eleanor Lodge dies
	Hitler remilitarizes Rhineland
	Spanish civil war
	Jarrow march
	Ellen Wilkinson visits Germany clandestinely
	Ellen Wilkinson visits Spain as rep. for Committee for Victims of Fascism
	Ellen Wilkinson helps set up Medical Aid Committee
	Ellen Wilkinson persuades NUDAW to levy members for aid to Spain
1937	Guildhouse closes
	Virginia Woolf's nephew Julian Bell killed in Spanish civil war
	Eleanor Rathbone chairs Committee of Enquiry into breaches of international law

Eleanor Rathbone visit Roumania and Spain
4,000 children rescued from Basque Country
Ellen Wilkinson organizes 'Milk for Spain'

1938   Kristallnacht
Eleanor Rathbone sends medical supplies and food to Spain
Munich Agreement
Isabel Emslie Hutton accompanies husband to India. Sets up clinic for coolies in Simla
Virginia Woolf publishes *Three Guineas*

1939   Eleanor Rathbone establishes Parliamentary Committee for Refugees.
Rescues thousands of refugees from Spain
September 3 War declared
Eleanor Rathbone forms Parliamentary Action Group

1939–45   Women recruited into armed forces.
Married women allowed to remain in posts in teaching and civil service

1940   Maude Royden breaks with peace movement. Visits USA
Eleanor Rathbone attacks Chamberlain
May. Churchill becomes PM
Eleanor Rathbone works to release low risk enemy aliens
Ellen Wilkinson made Parliamentary secretary to Herbert Morrison: responsible for Air Raid shelters and housing the homeless

1940–1941   Blitz

1940   Bombing of Coventry
Isabel Elmslie Hutton thrift shop in Delhi to aid war charities
Isabel Emslie Hutton chairs Ladies' Advisory Committee of Auxiliary Nursing Service in India
Isabel Elsmslie Hutton made director of Red Cross Welfare Services in India

1941   Virginia Woolf commits suicide

1942–1943   Massacre of Polish Jews

1943   Eleanor Rathbone forms National Committee for Rescue from Nazi Terror

1944   Maude Royden marries Hudson Shaw after death of his wife
Hudson Shaw dies
'Save Europe Now' charity formed

1945   Peace declared
Family Allowance Bill gives 5 shillings a week per child to the mother
Ellen Wilkinson made Vice-chair of National Executive Council of Labour Party
Ellen Wilkinson made a Privy Councillor
Ellen Wilkinson helps set up United Nations
Ellen Wilkinson becomes Minister of Education. Sets up three tier secondary education with free grammar school places
Ellen Wilkinson visits Germany and writes secret report for Clement Attlee.

Timeline

1946	Helena Deneke visits British Zone of Germany
	Eleanor Rathbone dies
1947	*The Threefold Cord* published
	Ellen Wilkinson dies from an overdose
1948	WI's Denman College established
1956	Maude Royden dies
1960	Isabel Emslie Hutton dies
1961	Contraceptive pill introduced for married women
1967	Abortion act allows termination of pregnancy in some cases
1968	Barbara Castle MP intervenes in Ford Dagenham pay dispute
1970	Equal Pay Act
1970s–80s	Oxbridge becomes fully available to women
	25% quota for women medical students abolished
1971	Women's refuges established by Erin Pizzey for victims of domestic violence
1973	Helena Deneke dies
1979	Margaret Thatcher becomes first woman Prime Minister
1985	Women ordained as deacons in Church of England
1992	Women admitted to priesthood in Church of England
1999	Use of a woman's previous sexual history not allowed as evidence in court in rape cases
2003	Female Mutilation Act makes it a legal duty to report cases
2004	First woman bishop appointed in Church of England

Acknowledgements

Archivists are the most patient and helpful people in the world. They go to enormous trouble to help people they may never meet with the information they need. In this instance I'd like to thank the archivists at the Bodleian Library, University of Oxford for their unvarying courtesy; Nicola Wood of Queen Mary University, London; Julie Parry, head archivist at the People's History Museum, Manchester for photographs of Ellen Willkinson; Hull History Centre archivists for photographs of the Women's Co-operative Guild and Margaret Llewelyn Davies; archivist Oliver Mahoney for all his help at Lady Margaret Hall and the Principal and Fellows of LMH for permission to publish photographs of Helena Deneke and Eleanor Lodge. My thanks go to Mollie Binns for access to her family archive. I'd also like to thank my editor, Shaun Barrington, for direct and prompt answers to my questions and for help along the way. Finally my family, in particular Stuart and Lucy, who have found time in their busy lives to read and criticise what I have written. Without their comments this book would have been considerably longer.

Index